THE FOOTBALL ENCYCLOPEDIA

Brazil and England contest their 2002 World Cup
quarter-final in Japan's Shizuoka Stadium Ecopa.
The 50,600-capacity arena hosts the bigger
matches of two Japanese J-League sides, Jubilo
Iwata and Shimizu S-Pulse.

THE FOOTBALL ENCYCLOPEDIA

CLIVE GIFFORD

KINGFISHER

Published 2016 by Kingfisher
an imprint of Macmillan Children's Books
20 New Wharf Road, London N1 9RR
Associated companies throughout the world
www.panmacmillan.com

Copyright © Macmillan Publishers International Ltd 2006

Consultant: Anthony Hobbs
Cover design: Matthew Kelly

ISBN 978-0-7534-3966-1

First published in 2006 by Kingfisher
This fully revised and updated edition published
2016 by Kingfisher

9 8 7 6 5 4 3 2
2TR/0816/WKT/UG/128MA

A CIP catalogue record for this book is available from
the British Library.

Printed in China

Note to readers: The website addresses listed in
this book are correct at the time of publishing. However,
due to the ever-changing nature of the internet, website
addresses and content can change. Websites can contain
links that are unsuitable for children. The publisher cannot
be held responsible for changes in website addresses or
content, or for information obtained through third-party
websites. We strongly advise that internet searches
should be supervised by an adult.

CONTENTS

THE BEAUTIFUL GAME

Pelé described football as the 'beautiful game', and the emotion and loyalty football inspires in its fans means that this simple sport has much to live up to. But football delivers with ease – cramming dynamic action, breathtaking skills and heartstopping tension into 90 minutes of play. It is sport as drama, making heroes and villains out of its players, managers and officials. From its recognized beginnings in the 19th century to its global dominance today, football has provided great moments of excitement, celebration and despair; no other game has the same power to unite and divide.

▲ Football is a sport that generates intensely strong bonds between supporters and their teams. This fan, facepainted in the national colours of Portugal, awaits an international match against the Netherlands.

RAPID GROWTH

In little over a century, football has boomed from a casual pursuit carried out by a small group of amateur gentlemen to a highly sophisticated, money-spinning sport that is played and watched by millions of people. As football has grown, dozens of changes have occurred. Some have involved the laws of the game – from the two-handed throw-in, introduced in 1883, to the backpass law for goalkeepers that was adopted 99 years later. Other changes – such as the arrival of promotion and relegation up and down a league – have shaped the competitions of which matches are a part.

Football's adaptability has been one of its strengths. Another great part of its appeal is that people of all ages and skill levels can play the game. At its most basic, football is a simple sport that can be enjoyed without expensive equipment and played almost anywhere – from a sandy beach to an office or hallway with a crumpled ball of paper.

The simplicity of football is a big selling point with new fans. The finer details of rules and tactics may pass them by at first, but the basics of the game and the skills of star players – their pace, ball control, passing, shooting and tackling – can be admired by almost anyone.

▼ Football arouses the emotions of players as well as fans. Here, Bayern Munich's Carsten Jancker (left) and Thomas Helmer are inconsolable after their team was beaten by Manchester United in the last minute of the 1999 Champions League final.

▼ *Argentina and Barcelona star Lionel Messi (front) battles for the ball with Manchester United's Michael Carrick during a Champions League game. Outrageously skilful, Messi was voted the world's best player for four years in a row (2009–12).*

▲ *Football can be played practically anywhere, in almost any conditions. These South African schoolchildren are enjoying a casual game just days before their country hosted the 2010 World Cup.*

THE NUMBERS GAME

In its full version, football is a game in which two teams of 11 people play two halves of 45 minutes. Today, more than 50 million footballers around the world play in official competitions. Many millions more play the game on a regular basis – a survey by world football's governing body, the *Fédération Internationale de Football Association* (FIFA), estimates that figure to be more than 265 million. Top leagues, such as Serie A in Italy, Spain's La Liga and Germany's Bundesliga, attract millions of viewers. In 2015, English Premier League games or highlights were broadcast to more than 190 countries. Each of the 2014 World Cup's 64 matches was watched by an average TV audience of around a million, while the 2014 final attracted almost one billion viewers.

▲ *A Brazilian goalkeeper holds a commemorative football celebrating Brazil's successful bid to host the FIFA World Cup for the first time since 1950. Major tournaments generate huge interest and millions are spent on stadiums and facilities for the huge numbers of visiting fans.*

THEN AND NOW

Going back in time 140 years, a modern football fan would be surprised to find no referees, corners or pitch markings at a game. Players wore coats and even top hats; they handled the ball in the air and wrestled with each other on the ground. Over time, football has evolved into the game that we know today.

▶ The referee's whistle was first blown at a football match in 1878. British firm Acme Whistles, astonishingly, has sold over 200 million Acme Thunderer whistles, which have been heard at World Cups and in top leagues around the globe.

PITCHING UP

Unlike in most sports, the pitch in football can vary in size. Most are around 100m long and 65–70m wide. Back in the 1860s, a pitch could be as long as 180m. The first markings arrived in 1891, including a centre circle and a line running the width of the pitch, 10.98m in front of the goal line. A penalty could be taken from any point along that line. It was another 11 years before the pitch markings we know today were introduced. Since then, only two additions have been made – the penalty arc at the front of the penalty area (in 1937) and the corner quadrants (in 1938).

▶ Referee Ken Aston came up with the idea of red and yellow cards after a stormy World Cup game in 1966. Here, he sends off Italy's Georgio Ferrini in 1962.

▲ At the 2002 World Cup, held in Japan and South Korea, the grass at the Sapporo Dome was grown away from the stadium and then moved as an entire pitch into the arena on a cushion of air.

THE MEN (AND WOMEN) IN BLACK

Referees did not feature in early games of football because the sport's founders believed that gentlemen would never intentionally foul or cheat. Instead, each side had an umpire to whom they could appeal. By 1891, games were controlled by a referee in order to cut down on controversial decisions and long stoppages for debate, and the two umpires became linesmen. (Since 1996, linesmen have been known as assistants.) Despite often being described as the 'men in black', referees have played in all sorts of colours. Early referees tried to keep up with play dressed in the popular fashions of the time – trousers, a blazer and even a bow tie.

GOALS

To score a goal, a team has to propel the whole of the ball over the goal line, between two posts that are set 7.32m apart. On many occasions, controversy has raged over whether the ball crossed the line – from the 1966 World Cup final between England and West Germany to the DFB-Pokal Cup final in 2014 between Borussia Dortmund and Bayern Munich.

Early goals consisted of just two posts. Following arguments over the height of a shot, a white tape was fitted to the posts, 2.44m above the ground. Wooden crossbars began to replace tape in the 1870s. Goal nets came later, invented by an engineer from Liverpool, John Alexander Brodie.

They were first given a trial in January 1891, when Everton's Fred Geary became the first footballer to put the ball in the back of the net. Incidentally, that game was refereed by Sam Widdowson, who had invented shinpads 17 years earlier.

FACTFILE The Belgian referee at the 1930 World Cup final, Jean Langenus, wore a dinner jacket, golfing plus-four trousers and a red striped tie.

BOOTS AND BALLS

No game is complete without the football, 40 million of which are sold every year. It is the referee's job to check the match ball and spare balls for size (68–70cm), weight (410–450 grams) and correct air pressure. Modern footballs are made from leather or synthetic materials, with a waterproof outer coating. Brazilian club Santos pioneered the use of a white ball (instead of the traditional brown leather ball) for greater visibility during evening games. Early footballs were made from the inflated bladder of a pig or sheep, covered in a leather shell that was secured with a set of laces. Contrary to popular myth, footballs of the past were not heavier than today's, at least when they were dry. Without a waterproof covering, however, early balls soaked up moisture and gained weight.

Football boots were certainly heavier in the past. Originally, players used their heavy work boots, tying them up over the ankle. The boots often had reinforced toecaps, and players sometimes nailed metal or leather studs into the soles. Modern boots are lightweight and flexible, allowing a player to 'feel' the ball on his or her foot. Their soles come in a range of stud, dimple and blade patterns. Each design gives the right level of grip for a particular pitch condition.

> **FACTFILE**
> India withdrew from the 1950 World Cup when FIFA refused to allow their footballers to play in bare feet.

▲ Alex James, a star for Arsenal in the 1930s, tries out a muscle-enhancing machine. Today's players undergo carefully planned exercise regimes and eat a diet that is scientifically monitored by their clubs.

KITTED OUT

Today's lightweight football kits are the result of years of research and development. During the first ever international fixture, in 1872, the Scotland and England teams wore knickerbockers (long trousers), long shirts and bobble hats or caps. Gradually, football kit developed to give players more freedom of movement, although shorts remained almost knee length until the 1960s. Numbers appeared on shirts regularly for the first time in the 1930s, but player names did not arrive until the late 1980s. In 1924, the English Football Association (FA) began to insist that teams have a second strip (known as an away strip) that could be worn in the event of a colour clash. Today, kit manufacture is a highly profitable business. Teams often have two or even three away strips; they update their kit design every season and sell many thousands of replica shirts to supporters.

▲ Some modern boots have moulded dimples for playing on hard or artificial pitches; others have screw-in studs to give grip on wet or soft pitches.

▼ Samuel Eto'o wears Cameroon's radical all-in-one kit at the 2004 African Nations Cup. The figure-hugging design gave opponents little material to tug or pull, but broke FIFA's rule that shirts and shorts have to be separate. An earlier Cameroon kit with sleeveless shirts – worn for the 2002 World Cup qualifying games – was also declared illegal.

FOOTBALL'S ORIGINS

An alehouse in Victorian England seems an unlikely place to launch a sport that would become the world's biggest and most popular. Yet that is precisely what occurred in 1863 at the Freemason's Tavern in London, England. There, representatives of 12 clubs met to form the Football Association (FA) and draw up a single set of rules for the game.

HISTORY MYSTERY

No one knows where the first forerunner of football was played. The Ancient Greeks took part in a team ball game known as *episkyros* or *pheninda*, while the Romans played *harpastum*. Paintings dating back more than 2,000 years show men and women enjoying the Ancient Chinese game of *tsu chu*, in which players tried to propel a ball made of stuffed animal skin through bamboo goal posts up to 10m tall. During the Ch'in dynasty (255–206BCE), a form of *tsu chu* was used to help train soldiers.

In medieval Europe, games of mob football were so unruly and violent that the leaders of several countries, including Charles V in France and Oliver Cromwell in England, attempted to ban the sport. In contrast to mob football, the Italian game of *calcio* was first played in the

16th century by aristocrats and religious leaders, including three popes. Each team was made up of 27 players, and goals were scored by kicking or throwing the ball over a certain spot on the edge of the field.

GETTING ORGANIZED

By the late 18th and early 19th centuries, a kicking-and-rushing ball game was played in public schools and universities across Britain, but rules varied from place to place. In 1848, players at Cambridge University drew up football's first set of rules.

This attempt to bring order into the game had only limited success, and so in 1863 representatives of 12 clubs (including the Crusaders, No Names of Kilburn and Crystal Palace) met in London. They formed the FA, developed the laws of the game and, eight years later, set up the world's oldest surviving cup competition, the FA Cup. The first ever international, between England and Scotland, was played in 1872, and in 1888 the first football league was founded in England.

▼ *This illustration shows a friendly international game between England and Scotland in 1878. Between 1873 and 1888, Scotland lost just one out of 31 international matches.*

▼ *The Japanese game of* kemari *is at least 1,500 years old. Players had to stop the ball from touching the ground by juggling and passing it with their feet. This re-enactment was held to celebrate Japan's co-hosting of the 2002 World Cup.*

HIT THE NET

www.11v11.com
The website of the Association of Football Statisticians has historic photos and features on football's early history.

http://uk.women.soccerway.com
This website contains results of all leading women's football clubs and national competitions.

www.soccerballworld.com/History.htm
A thorough guide to the history and evolution of the soccer ball, from its ancient origins to the latest versions.

▼ *Mana Iwabuchi of Japan pursued by Lauren Holiday in the 2015 Women's World Cup final between USA and Japan.*

WHAT'S IN A NAME?

Around the world, many teams have taken their names from European clubs. Here are just a few:

ARSENAL LESOTHO
Lesotho Cup winners 1989, '91, '98

LIVERPOOL
Namibia, league champions 2002

BARCELONA
Ecuador, league champions '95, '97, 2012

EVERTON
Chile, league champions 1950, '52, '76, 2008

JUVENTUS
Belize, league champions 1999, 2005

BEREKUM CHELSEA FC
Ghana, league champions 2011

AJAX CAPE TOWN
S. Africa, league runners-up 2008, 2011

QPR FC
Grenada, league champions 2002

THE WOMEN'S GAME

Women's football struggled from the beginning against male prejudice that it was 'unladylike' for females to play the game. Interest in women's football reached its first peak after World War I thanks to the exploits of the Dick, Kerr Ladies side (see page 81). The women's game was then stifled for almost half a century following the introduction of a ban on women playing at the grounds of FA member clubs. Between 1969 and 1972, bans were lifted in a number of countries and women's football slowly began to expand. The first European Championships for women were held in 1984, while an Olympic competition was launched in 1996. More than 60 nations entered the qualifying competition for the first Women's World Cup in 1991.

FOOTBALL EXPORTS

Football spread rapidly around the globe in the late 19th century. The game was exported first by British players and then by converts from other European nations, particularly to their colonies. Football was introduced to Russia in 1887 by two English mill owners, the Charnock brothers, while resident Englishmen founded Italy's oldest league club, Genoa, six years later.

In 1885, Canada defeated the USA 1-0 in the first international match to be played in the Americas. In Argentina, British and Italian residents encouraged the formation of South America's first club, Buenos Aires, in 1865. The first league in South America was set up 28 years later.

In 1904, FIFA was founded in Paris, with seven members: Belgium, Denmark, France, Holland, Spain (represented by Madrid FC), Sweden and Switzerland. Over time, FIFA became the dominant organization in world football. In 1930, it had 45 member nations; in 1960, that figure stood at 95. In May 2012, FIFA welcomed South Sudan as its 209th member.

▶ *W. R. Moon of Corinthians, an English amateur team, poses for a photograph in his kit. Corinthians helped to spread football by touring the world. Their 1910 trip to South America inspired the formation of the famous Brazilian side Corinthians Paulista.*

THE GLOBAL GAME

FIFA is in control of world football. At continental or regional level, the game is organized by six confederations. The traditional powerhouses of international football have been Europe and South America, home to the world's richest clubs and to the winners of every World Cup. But as other regions begin to exert more influence, the global game is changing.

BALANCE OF POWER

Great advances have been made by the federations and national teams of regions outside Europe and South America. More and more national football teams have become truly competitive, thanks to the emergence of high-quality footballers in Africa, Asia, Oceania and North and Central America. Australia performed well at the 2006 World Cup (its first since 1974), narrowly losing to eventual winners Italy in the second round, and New Zealand was the only team at the 2010 World Cup not to lose a game. African nations have featured in three of the last four Olympic football finals, winning two golds and one silver. By 2015, the continent had 11 teams ranked in FIFA's top 50. There have also been strong showings by Japan, Costa Rica and the USA at recent international tournaments.

As a reflection of this, African and Asian nations have been chosen to host many tournaments, including the World Cups of 2002 (South Korea and Japan), 2010 (South Africa), 2022 (Qatar) and the Women's World Cup of 2007 (China). Additionally, Africa and Asia now enjoy more automatic places at the World Cup than ever before.

▲ Steve Mokone was the first black South African to play professionally in Europe. From the 1950s, he starred for Coventry City, Dutch side Heracles, Spain's Valencia, Marseille in France and Italy's Torino. Mokone later played in Australia and Canada.

> **FACTFILE** A European side has reached the final of all but two World Cups (1930 and 1950).

◄ Argentina line up to play Germany in the 2006 World Cup. At the time, only keeper Roberto Abbondanzieri played club football in Argentina. After the tournament he signed for Spanish club Getafe.

CONCACAF
Confederation of North, Central American and Caribbean Association Football
www.concacaf.com
Founded: 1961
Members: 41

Mexico and the USA – traditionally the strongest CONCACAF nations – have hosted three World Cups, while smaller nations such as Costa Rica have reached the tournament. CONCACAF teams have often been invited to play in South America's Copa America competition, and the federation actually includes two South American nations, Guyana and Suriname.

UEFA
Union of European Football Associations
www.uefa.com
Founded: 1954
Members: 52

As the most powerful confederation, UEFA was awarded 13 of the 32 places at the 2014 World Cup. It runs the two largest competitions after the World Cup – the European Championships and the UEFA Champions League. Thousands of foreign footballers play in Europe, but UEFA clubs may soon be forced to include a minimum number of home-grown players in their squads.

CONMEBOL
Confederación Sudamericana de Fútbol
www.conmebol.com
Founded: 1916
Members: 10

CONMEBOL teams have won nine men's World Cup finals, whilst the Brazilian women's national team were World Cup runners-up in 2007. Argentina won the 2004 and 2008 Olympic men's finals and are rarely out of the top five of FIFA's world rankings. Domestic leagues, however, are suffering with clubs in debt and most of the continent's top players heading for Europe and elsewhere to play.

CAF
Confédération Africaine de Football
www.cafonline.com
Founded: 1957
Members: 56

Africa was not awarded an automatic World Cup place until 1970, but the CAF sent six teams to the 2010 World Cup including the host nation, South Africa. While national sides continue to improve, the domestic game struggles because of a lack of finance and the movement of its best players out of Africa. In 2010, for example, more than 570 African footballers were playing in the top leagues of Europe.

AFC
Asian Football Confederation
www.the-afc.com/english/intro.asp
Founded: 1954
Members: 47

Asian football is booming. The highly successful Asian Champions League was set up in 2002, and national leagues are now well supported. Many foreign footballers play in Asia – more than 29 Brazilians played in Japan's J-League in 2013, for example. Australia joined the AFC in 2006, but all eyes are now turning to China, which has the world's largest pool of potential players and supporters.

OFC
Oceania Football Confederation
www.oceaniafootball.com
Founded: 1966
Members: 11

Football has struggled for support in Oceania. In the larger countries, it has to compete with more popular sports, while smaller nations suffer from a lack of finance, facilities and players. Australia, the OFC's biggest and most successful nation, became frustrated by the lack of an automatic World Cup place for the confederation. In January 2006 it left the OFC to join the Asian Football Confederation.

FACTFILE
Australia was the first OFC side to reach a World Cup, in 1974.

HAVE BOOTS, WILL TRAVEL

Football is flourishing all over the world, but Europe remains the most attractive destination for the world's top players. The globe's 20 richest clubs are all European, and this situation is unlikely to change for some time as a result of the huge sums of money that teams receive from television rights, advertising and qualifying for the Champions League. The revenue enables European clubs to pluck the best talents from around the globe. At the 2014 World Cup, only one of Uruguay, Ghana and Ivory Coast's 23-man squads played club football in their home country. In contrast all of Russia's, 22 of England's and 20 of Italy's footballers played at home.

In the past, South American club football held on to many of its stars. Every member of Brazil's 1970 World Cup-winning side played for a club in his home country. That state of affairs has changed, with hundreds of players moving to Europe in search of higher wages and the chance to play in the most prestigious competitions, from Serie A and La Liga to the Champions League.

◀ Givanildo Vieira de Souza, known as Hulk, stars for Brazil in a 2013 friendly game against Italy. By the age of 25, the powerful striker had played all over the world for clubs in Brazil, Japan and Portugal before being signed by Russian side, Zenit Saint Petersburg in 2012.

HIT THE NET

www.worldsoccer.com
World Soccer magazine's website focuses on global soccer and its best players, teams and competitions.

http://uk.soccerway.com
A comprehensive match website, searchable by continent, to give you the fixtures and results of all leading football competitions.

www.soccerstats.com
Get the latest football news and competition standings from around the world.

Alfredo di Stefano (in white) lashes Real Madrid's second goal past Eintracht Frankfurt keeper Egon Loy. Despite making a number of splendid saves, Loy conceded seven goals.

MADRID'S MAGNIFICENT SEVEN

Football's capacity to surprise, excite and above all entertain has rarely been better showcased than in the final of the fifth European Cup, in 1960. Real Madrid, winners of the first four competitions, met Eintracht Frankfurt in front of a record crowd of more than 130,000 at Scotland's Hampden Park. Eintracht took an early lead. Was Real's reign as the undoubted masters of Europe about to end? The answer was an emphatic no. Led by Hungarian genius Ferenc Puskas and Argentinian all-rounder Alfredo di Stefano, the Spanish side put on a dazzling display of attacking football. In an electrifying 45 minutes, Real went from 1-0 down to 6-1 up, courtesy of goals by both Puskas and di Stefano. But the enterprising German side were just as committed to attack. They fought back, scoring two goals and hitting the woodwork twice, while Real countered with their seventh and di Stefano's third goal to eventually triumph 7-3. No one who witnessed the game would ever forget the spectacle of Europe's finest club side playing at the peak of its skills.

BASIC SKILLS

In the words of former Liverpool manager Bill Shankly, 'Football is a simple game based on the giving and taking of passes, on controlling the ball and on making yourself available to receive a pass.' Shankly's words highlight the most fundamental skills in football.

BALL CONTROL

The world's top players, such as Cristiano Ronaldo and Lionel Messi, appear to control the ball effortlessly. Their easy command and movement of the ball masks thousands of hours of practice and training, often from a very early age. As children, many great footballers spent long hours playing games with a tennis ball, crumpled ball of paper or a battered piece of fruit.

Players can control the ball with any part of their body except for their hands and arms. Cushioning is a technique in which a player uses a part of the body to slow down a moving ball and then bring it under control with his or her feet. High balls can be cushioned using the chest, thigh or a gentle header to kill the ball's speed and bring it down. For a low, incoming ball, the foot is preferred – either the inside of the boot or its instep (where the laces are). A ball that is rolling across the pitch can be stopped with the sole of the foot – a technique known as trapping.

▲ French female footballers practise their close control skills by keeping the ball up using their head and feet. Good ball control only comes with hundreds of hours of practice.

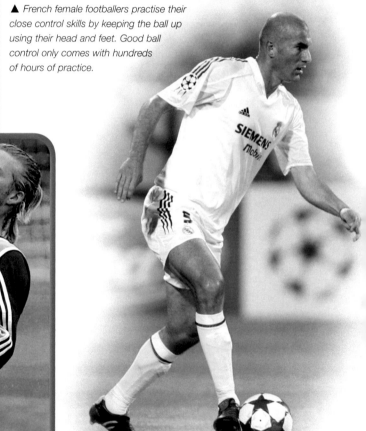

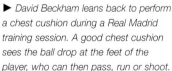

▶ David Beckham leans back to perform a chest cushion during a Real Madrid training session. A good chest cushion sees the ball drop at the feet of the player, who can then pass, run or shoot.

▲ French legend Zinedine Zidane uses the side of his foot to control the ball during a Champions League match against Bayer Leverkusen.

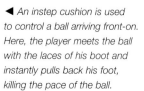

◀ An instep cushion is used to control a ball arriving front-on. Here, the player meets the ball with the laces of his boot and instantly pulls back his foot, killing the pace of the ball.

SHIELDING AND OBSTRUCTION

When footballers have the ball at their feet, they are said to be in possession and have a number of options. These include: running with the ball; dribbling with the ball close to the feet; passing; shooting; and shielding the ball. Shielding or screening involves a player putting his or her body between the ball and an opponent to prevent the other player from gaining possession. This gives the shielding player crucial time to decide on the next move, which may be a pass backwards to a team-mate or a sharp turn and an attempt to play the ball round the opponent. Shielding players have to be careful not to hold, push or back into the other player. They must also keep the ball close by and under control, otherwise the referee may award an indirect free kick for obstruction (in which a player unfairly blocks an opponent's path to the ball). An obstruction usually occurs when a player steps into the path of an opponent when the ball is several metres away.

◀ *Sergiy Nazarenko of Ukrainian side Dnipro Dnipropetrovsk shields the ball from FC Utrecht's Etienne Shew-Atjon during a 2004–05 UEFA Cup match.*

▼ *Australia's Nick Carle challenges Japan's Uchida Atsuto for the ball.*

▶ *Pavel Nedved of Juventus hits a long instep drive pass during a Serie A match against Messina.*

PASS MASTERS

Passes can be made with a thrust of the chest or with a carefully directed header. Usually, however, they are made with one of three parts of the boot – the outside, the instep or the inside. The inside or sidefoot pass is the most common and accurate pass, allowing players to stroke the ball around with a high level of precision. Some players attempt as many as 60 or 70 passes in a game, most of which are sidefoot passes. At the 2014 World Cup Italy's Daniele De Rossi made an average of 106 passes per game.

For longer passes, players tend to use the instep. This allows them to propel the ball with force. The instep can also be used for lofted drives that send the ball into the air as a cross or a clearance, as well as to stab down on the back of the ball. This makes the ball rise up at a steep angle, known as a chip. A pass's weight – the strength with which it is hit – is as important as accuracy for the pass to be successfully completed. At the 2014 World Cup, strong passers such as Germany's Toni Kroos and Argentina's Javier Mascherano completed 85 per cent or more of their passes successfully.

▶ *Brek Shea plays an accurate sidefoot pass for his MLS side, FC Dallas, with his foot striking through the middle of the ball. This picture was taken shortly before his move to the English Premier League to join Stoke City.*

MOVEMENT AND SPACE

Football is a dynamic, fast-moving sport. Throughout a game, pockets of space open and close all over the pitch. A player who has an awareness of where space exists, or where it will shortly open up, is a great asset to a team. Equally valuable is the ability to move into that space to receive a pass. The more space a player is in, the more time he or she usually has to receive the ball, control it and attack with it.

► Mesut Özil picks a pass to play to a Real Madrid team-mate. Top players such as Özil play with their head up, scouring the pitch for team-mates' moves and runs. Özil moved to Arsenal in 2013.

SPOTTING AND CREATING SPACE

The ball can zip around a pitch far more quickly than even the fastest of players. Good footballers make the ball do the work, moving it around with quick, accurate passes. Vision is the priceless ability to spot a pass, space or goalscoring opportunity that other players do not see, or before they do. Players with good vision look to move into space, timing their run to give a team-mate who has the ball a chance of making a pass that cannot be intercepted by an opponent. Once the ball has left the passer's control, he or she often moves into a position to receive a return pass. All players, not just midfielders and attackers, must be capable of passing well and moving into space to receive passes in return.

Players can create space for themselves or for team-mates through quick, agile movement and the use of feints or dummies,

with which they attempt to fool a nearby opponent into thinking they are moving one way, before sprinting off in another direction. World-class players such as Mesut Özil, Lionel Messi and Andrés Iniesta are particularly skilled at outwitting an opponent in this way to find space.

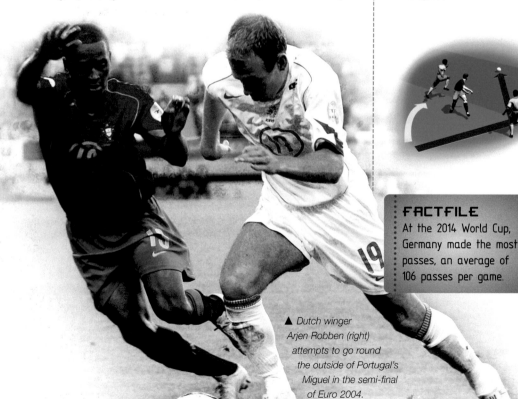

▲ Dutch winger Arjen Robben (right) attempts to go round the outside of Portugal's Miguel in the semi-final of Euro 2004.

◄ A wall pass (also known as a one-two pass) is a classic way to cut out an opposition player. It involves two passes that must be hit quickly and accurately, with the first passer running on to collect the return ball.

FACTFILE
At the 2014 World Cup, Germany made the most passes, an average of 106 passes per game.

▲ Making space can be crucial to winning the ball at a throw-in. Here, one player makes a decoy run towards the thrower, dragging a defender with him and creating space in which a team-mate can collect the ball.

OFFSIDE

Teams have to stay aware of Law 11, the offside law, throughout a match. In 1847, under the rules of Eton College, being offside was known as 'sneaking'. A player was caught sneaking when there were three or fewer opposition players between him and the goal at the moment a team-mate passed the ball forwards. The rule has been tinkered with over the years. The most notable change came in 1925, when the number of players between the attacker and the goal was reduced from three to two. The result was a goal avalanche, as defences struggled to cope with the rule change and attackers took advantage. In the English leagues, for example, 1,673 more goals were scored in the 1925–26 season than under the old law in the previous year.

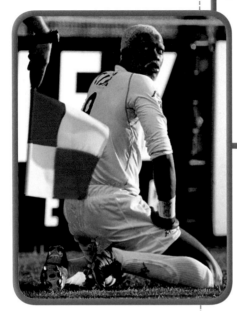

▲ French striker Djibril Cissé looks ruefully at the referee's assistant after being signalled offside in a French league match.

Today, a player is offside if, at the moment the ball is played, he or she is in the opposition half and is nearer the opponent's goal line than both the ball and the second-from-last opponent. That opponent can be an outfield player or the goalkeeper. Players cannot be offside in their own half or if they receive the ball directly from a goal kick, throw-in or corner.

Being in an offside position is not always an offence. Referees must judge whether the player in an offside position is involved in active play, moves towards the ball or does anything to make it harder for an opponent to play the ball. This tests an official's judgement to the limit. Is a player offside but a long way from the ball involved in 'active play'? Perhaps he or she is drawing defenders out as markers. If a referee does stop the game, an indirect free kick is awarded to the opposing team where the player was judged offside.

▲ Here, the player at the top left of the picture is in an offside position when the ball is struck. The referee decides that he is not interfering with play, however, and awards the goal.

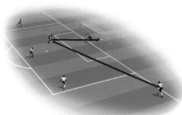

▲ You cannot be offside if you are behind the ball when it is played. This scorer receives the ball from a team-mate who is ahead of him, so he is onside and the goal is given.

HIT THE NET

www.dynamic-thought.com/OffsideClickette.html
Diagrams and animations that fully explain the offside law.

www.fifa.com/development/education-and-technical/referees/laws-of-the-game.html
View the latest laws of the game as approved by FIFA or download them in PDF format.

www.asktheref.com
A site for budding referees – learn more about the laws of the game and the jobs of football officials.

www.futsalplanet.com
A website dedicated to futsal, with tournament news and results as well as links to the laws of the game.

SMALL-SIDED GAMES

In many countries, children under the age of 11 play matches that feature six, seven or eight players per team. These small-sided games give young footballers an invaluable chance to see more of the ball and improve their control, passing and movement. Futsal is FIFA's official five-a-side game. A match lasts for 40 minutes (two halves of 20 minutes) and is played on a pitch the size of a basketball court, without surrounding boards or walls. Futsal was devised by a Uruguayan, Juan Carlos Ceriani, in 1930. The game flourished and developed throughout South America, with the first international competition – the South American Cup – taking place in 1965. The first futsal World Championship took place in the Netherlands in 1989. Held in Thailand, the 2012 Futsal World Cup was won by Brazil, the fifth time they have been crowned champions.

▲ Spain and Brazil battle it out in the final of the 2004 Futsal World Championship, held in Taipei, Taiwan. Spain won the 40-match tournament, beating the Brazilians 5-4 in a penalty shootout after a 2-2 draw.

OFFICIALS

Frequently abused by players, managers and supporters, referees are football's guardians and the enforcers of its laws. Their job is to impose order on a match and prevent intimidation, injury and cheating.

THE REFEREE'S ROLE

Referees perform a surprisingly large number of tasks before and after a match. These include checking the goals, nets and balls and deciding whether the pitch and weather conditions are suitable for the game to go ahead. Afterwards, they write a report containing details of disciplinary actions and other important incidents. On the pitch, the referee runs the game. His or her duties range from adding on time because of injuries, other stoppages and time-wasting, to deciding whether the ball is in or out of play or has crossed the goal line. If a player commits a foul or breaks a law, referees must stop play and order a restart, such as a drop ball or a free kick. They can caution players and team officials, and even abandon a match if weather, crowd trouble or another factor makes the game unplayable. Referees have to follow the laws of the game, but they have a certain amount of freedom to interpret aspects of the rules as they wish. For example, if a player is fouled when his or her side is in a promising position, a referee may let the match continue, playing the advantage rule to keep the game flowing.

ASSISTANTS AND THE FOURTH OFFICIAL

A referee relies on his or her assistants as extra pairs of eyes. Referee's assistants indicate when the ball goes out of play and whether a goal kick, corner or throw-in should be awarded. They also use flag signals to point out that a substitution has been requested, a player is offside or whether an offence has taken place out of the view of the referee. A referee can consult with an assistant if he or she was closer to the action, but it is up to the referee to make the final decision. In some competitions, a fourth official carries out duties before and after a match and also performs touchline tasks. These include helping with substitutions and displaying the amount of time added on at the end of a game for stoppages.

FACTFILE In 1998, English referee Martin Sylvester sent himself off after punching a player during a match in the Andover and District Sunday League.

▲ The fourth official checks the boot studs of Paraguayan substitute Nelson Vera in a World Youth Championship match against Uruguay.

▲ Referee Stephane Lannoy shows Mario Balotelli a yellow card after the Italian striker took his shirt off to celebrate a goal he scored at Euro 2012.

▼ Managers and team officials can be cautioned or sent off if they use abusive language or do not behave responsibly. Here, Martin O'Neill argues with UEFA Cup officials as he is sent off during a match.

◄ Early in a game, a good referee talks to players to calm them down or issues verbal warnings rather than yellow and red cards. Here, Nicole Petignat tries to soothe AIK Solna's Krister Nordin in the first UEFA Cup game to be refereed by a woman, in 2003.

TOP-FLIGHT PRESSURES

Thousands of amateur referees give up their weekends and evenings for free, purely to give something back to the game they adore. In contrast, officials in charge of major championship matches are minor celebrities who are paid significant sums. This is a reflection of the importance of their job. Top referees have their performances assessed, attend training seminars, undergo regular medical checks and are tested for fitness. A referee may run between 9.5 and 11.5km during a match (even further if extra time occurs) and often has to sprint to keep up with play. Referees work in a harsh, unforgiving climate, in which footage from multiple cameras and slow-motion television replays are broadcast over and over again, highlighting each poor decision. However, the very technology that has put referees under the spotlight is now coming to their aid with goal line technology being adopted, for example: the English Premier League used this for the first time in 2013.

▲ *Referee Horacio Elizondo shows the red card to France's Zinedine Zidane during the 2006 World Cup final. The midfielder was sent off for headbutting Italian defender Marco Materazzi in the chest during extra time.*

CAUTION

A player is shown a yellow card if he or she:

- is guilty of unsporting behaviour, such as simulation;
- shows dissent by word or action;
- persistently breaks the rules, by making repeated foul tackles for example;
- delays the restart of play;
- fails to stand at the required distance at a corner kick or free kick;
- enters or leaves the field of play without the referee's permission.

A player is sent off if he or she receives two yellow cards or one red card. Red-card offences include a very dangerous tackle, spitting and stopping a goal with a deliberate handball.

SIMULATION

Looking out for contact in the penalty area during a fast-moving attack is especially difficult for an official. In the modern game, attackers appear to fall to the ground under the slightest pressure from an opponent. Referees have to judge if a foul was committed or whether the attacker was guilty of 'simulation'. Many people think that simulation is only about diving without contact in order to win a free kick or a penalty. It is actually defined as pretending to be fouled in any way to gain an advantage. At the 2002 World Cup, Rivaldo was guilty of a simulation that led to Turkey's Hakan Ünsal being sent off. In a 2009 game in Colombia, Carmelo Valencia simulated a foul to get opposing goalkeeper Agustín Julio sent off. Valencia later received a one-game ban. In 2011, the MLS began to use match video reviews to punish simulating players with fines and bans. Other leagues may now do the same.

▲ *AC Milan midfielder Andrea Pirlo battles for the ball with Deportivo La Coruña's Juan Carlos Valerón. The referee has to decide in a split second if a foul was committed and, if so, whether it is serious enough for a booking or a sending off.*

RED-CARD RECORDS

FASTEST IN A TOP LEAGUE
Ten seconds – Giuseppe Lorenzo, Bologna v Parma, 1990

FASTEST IN THE WORLD CUP
55 seconds – José Batista, Uruguay v Scotland, 1986

MOST IN ONE MATCH
36 – Claypole v Victoriano Arenas (Argentina), 2011

DEFENDING

Compared to strikers or creative midfielders, defenders are rarely praised as match-winners. Yet the foundation of every successful team is a composed, secure defence. Defending consists of a range of individual skills allied to good teamwork and understanding between players so that they defend as a unit. Defenders require strength and excellent heading and tackling skills, along with intense concentration, quick reactions and bravery. But, in truth, all players must defend if their side is to remain competitive in a match.

▼ After tracking Bayern Munich's Arjen Robben (right), Real Madrid's Adriano times his tackle to rob his opponent of the ball. In situations like this, team-mates look to pounce on the ball to gain possession.

▲ Portugal's Nuno Gomes (left) and Russia's Alexei Bugaev challenge for the ball. Forceful tackles that target the ball, not the player, are a key part of defending.

TRACKING AND TACKLING

The two keys to defending well are denying the opposition the chance to score and winning the ball back. As soon as an opponent gets the ball, defenders try to get between the ball and their goal and close down space. Defenders spend much of a game tracking opponents as they make runs and closing down the player with the ball to delay his or her progress. This is called jockeying. The aim is to slow down an attack until the defending side is in a stronger position. The defender tries to shepherd the attacker into a weaker position, such as near the sideline where there is little support. When a defender has cover from nearby team-mates, he or she may make a tackle. The defender should stay on his or her feet in order to gain possession.

► This attacker has spotted a weak pass by an opponent and reacts quickly to make an interception. Sometimes, attackers drop back to help their team defend.

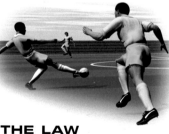

FALLING FOUL OF THE LAW

Many of football's laws, such as obstruction, apply to defenders. A jockeying defender must be careful not to commit a foul, such as pushing, holding or shirt-pulling. A poorly timed tackle may result in a foul. Tackles from behind are especially risky, often leading to a yellow or red card if the defender makes contact with the attacker. A professional foul is a deliberate foul made to deny an attacking side a clear goalscoring chance. Two of the most common types are using the hands or arms to stop a goalbound ball and bringing down an attacker with the ball when he or she has a clear path to goal. Both should result in a sending off.

▲ *A supporting defender can step in to help if his team-mate is beaten. Here, Pablo Zabaleta (right) challenges Chelsea's Fernando Torres for the ball after his Manchester City team-mate, Vincent Kompany, has been brushed aside.*

CLEAN SHEETS

Goalkeepers and defenders are especially proud of a clean sheet – a game in which their side does not concede a goal. Clean sheets are usually credited to goalkeepers, but in truth they depend on a solid defence as well as midfielders and strikers who are willing to chase, harry, track and tackle. Italy has a reputation for producing some of the world's finest defenders. Between 1972 and the 1974 World Cup, the Italian defence helped keeper Dino Zoff to play 1,142 minutes – more than 12 matches – without conceding a goal. The run was finally ended by Haiti. In 2009, Edwin van der Sar set an English record of 1,311 minutes unbeaten in goal for Manchester United. The world record in professional football is held by Brazil's Geraldo Pereira de Matos Filho, better known as Mazaropi. Playing for Vasco da Gamain 1977–78, he did not concede a goal for over 20 games, a total of 1,816 minutes.

> ## FACTFILE
> Juventus went unbeaten in the competitive Serie A league during the 38-game 2011–12 season.

▶ *Tamas Priskin of Gyor makes a defensive header above Ferencvaros' Zolta Gera.*

DEFENSIVE FORTRESS

During periods of open play, defending teams mark opponents man-to-man or with a zonal system (see page 62). At corners and free kicks from a wide position, they tend to mark man-to-man. A team may also try to catch out attackers by playing an offside trap (see page 62). Communication between defenders is crucial to prevent attackers getting free and into space to score. Certain teams equipped with highly skilled defenders who work well together have been able to squeeze the life out of opposition attacks. The AC Milan side of 1992–93, for example, scored 26 goals and conceded only two during their entire nine-game Champions League campaign. In England, Chelsea hold the record for conceding the fewest goals in a season (2004–05) – just 15 goals in 38 matches.

▲ *Real Madrid's Ivan Helguera and David Beckham hurl themselves bravely into the path of the ball to block a fierce shot from Asier del Horno of Athletic Bilbao.*

LONGEST UNBEATEN LEAGUE RUNS (IN GAMES)

108	ASEC Abidjan (Ivory Coast), 1989–94
104	Steaua Bucharest (Romania), 1986–89
85	Esperance (Tunisia), 1997–2001
71	Al-Ahly (Egypt), 2004–07
63	Sheriff Tiraspol (Moldova), 2006–08
62	Celtic (Scotland), 1915–17
61	Levadia Tallinn (Estonia), 2008–09
60	Union Saint-Gilloise (Belgium), 1933–35
59	Boca Juniors (Argentina), 1924–27
	Pyunik Yerevan (Armenia), 2002–04
58	AC Milan (Italy), 1991–93
	Olympiakos (Greece), 1972–74
	Skonto Riga (Latvia), 1993–96
56	Benfica (Portugal), 1976–78
	Peñarol (Uruguay), 1966–69

GOALKEEPING

Goalkeepers are a breed apart. They have a different role to their team-mates and even look a little different, as they must wear a shirt that distinguishes them from other players and officials. The crucial last line of defence, keepers can be forgotten when things are going well, but singled out for abuse when they make a mistake that leads to a goal. Goalkeepers can also be match-winners thanks to their saves and decisions, their agility and bravery.

▲ *Goalkeeper Shay Given stretches to make a diving save. The veteran has made 125 international appearances for the Republic of Ireland.*

KEEPING CONTROL

Goalkeepers are allowed to control the ball with their hands and arms, but otherwise they must obey most of the same rules as outfield players. Until 1912, keepers could handle the ball anywhere in their own half, but now handling is restricted to their penalty area, with several key exceptions. Goalkeepers cannot handle the ball:

- after releasing it and without it touching another player;
- after receiving it directly from a throw-in;
- if it has been deliberately kicked to them by a team-mate.

If a goalkeeper handles the ball in any of these situations or if the referee judges that the keeper is time-wasting with the ball in hand (known as the six-second rule), an indirect free kick is awarded. This can be dangerously close to the goal. In the 1990s, a law was passed to reduce time-wasting and speed up play. It banned keepers from controlling a ball from a throw-in or backpass with their arms or hands.

In the past, goalkeepers could be barged into heavily, but today they are well protected by referees. Even so, they have to be brave to dive at an opponent's feet, risking injury. If keepers foul or bring down an attacker, they may give away a penalty and even be sent off if the referee decides that a professional foul has been committed.

▲ *Chelsea's Czech goalkeeper Petr Cech gathers the ball cleanly at the feet of Manchester City defender Aleksandar Kolarov.*

◄ *At the 2003 Women's World Cup, Norway's Bente Nordby clears a dangerous ball by punching it firmly away from goal.*

A KEEPER'S SKILLS

To achieve a clean sheet, goalkeepers need more than supreme agility and the talent to make diving saves. Top keepers train hard to improve their handling skills, learning to take the ball at different heights and from different angles. They must be able to stay alert for the entire game. Many minutes can go by before, suddenly, they are called into action. Keepers need good decision-making skills, too, as a cross or shot may call for them to choose whether to try to hold the ball in a save, punch it away or tip it over the bar or round a post. Goalkeepers are in a unique position to see opposition attacks developing, and they must communicate instructions to their team-mates. They line up walls at free kicks and command their goal area, urging defenders to pick up unmarked opponents. A defence and keeper that communicate well can be a formidable unit.

▶ *Italian keeper Gianluigi Buffon instructs his defenders. Clear, decisive communication between a keeper and his or her outfield team-mates can snuff out many opposition attacks.*

DEFENCE INTO ATTACK

With the ball in hand, keepers have several ways in which they can move the ball to a team-mate or up the pitch (known as distribution). They can roll it out on the floor, looking for options to kick the ball; they can kick it straight from their hand; or they can throw the ball. Keepers launch the ball from their hand into the opposition half by using their boot instep to strike it on the volley or half volley. Sometimes, keepers aim their kick for a tall winger or wide midfielder who is close to the sideline. This move is often rehearsed on the training ground. Keepers can bowl the ball out underarm, usually to a nearby team-mate, or they can use a more powerful sidearm or overarm motion for maximum distance. A third option, the javelin throw, is often the quickest way to get the ball moving. Fast, accurate distribution from the keeper can be vital in turning defence into a rapid breakaway attack.

HIT THE NET

www.goalkeepersaredifferent.com
A fabulous website that is dedicated solely to keepers and is packed with quirky facts.

http://finesoccer.com/category/goalkeeping
This newsletter contains advice, drills and tips from the world of goalkeeping.

www.jbgoalkeeping.com
An impressive coaching website, with short online videos, covering all aspects of the keeper's game.

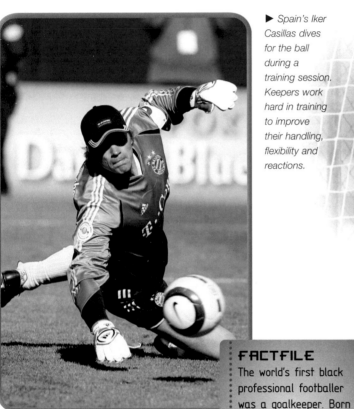

▲ Germany's Oliver Kahn goes to make a save. In 2002, Kahn was FIFA's Goalkeeper of the World Cup. During the following league season with Bayern Munich, he set a Bundesliga record of 737 minutes without conceding a goal.

▶ Spain's Iker Casillas dives for the ball during a training session. Keepers work hard in training to improve their handling, flexibility and reactions.

FACTFILE
The world's first black professional footballer was a goalkeeper. Born in the Gold Coast (now Ghana), Arthur Wharton turned out in 1889 for Rotherham United in the English league.

▶ In a one-on-one situation, many keepers come off their line to narrow the angle – reducing how much of the goal the attacker can see. They stay upright for as long as possible to increase the chance of the shot striking them.

GOALSCORING KEEPERS

In 1882, goalkeeper James McAulay was pressed into service as a centre-forward and scored in Scotland's 5-0 defeat of Wales. Since then, many keepers have scored goals for their club or country. Some goals have been scored from long goal kicks that have caught out a defence or by goalkeepers running into the opposition's penalty area in the dying seconds of a game. Others have come from spot kicks in a penalty shootout (see page 31). A well-taken penalty by Portuguese keeper Ricardo knocked England out of Euro 2004, for example. A few keepers have become legends for their goalscoring feats from regular penalties and free kicks. The German Hans-Jörg Butt scored 28 goals, while Paraguay's José Luis Chilavert struck 62 times. This staggering tally was passed in August 2006 by Brazilian goalkeeper Rogério Ceni, playing for São Paulo. In 2011, Ceni struck his 100th goal with a free kick from outside the opposition team's penalty area.

ATTACKING

As soon as a team gains possession of the ball, with time and in space, its players' thoughts turn to attack. There are many ways in which a team can launch an attack, from a fast drive into space by a player who is sprinting forwards and pushing the ball ahead, to a slow, probing attack in which many players keep the ball securely in possession and look for an opening.

BEATING OFFSIDE TRAPS

Some teams play an offside trap (see page 62), in which defenders move up in a straight line to catch opponents offside. Beating an offside trap takes cunning, skill and awareness. A perfectly weighted through pass can unlock the trap if the ball is collected by a player who stays onside until the moment the ball moves ahead of him or her. A long diagonal pass that switches play forwards and across the pitch may also work. The receiver makes a run from a deep position, staying onside until the ball moves ahead, then collects the ball behind the defence. Individual brilliance – such as dribbling or playing a short 'push and go' pass – can also beat some offside traps.

▲ Ludovic Giuly of Barcelona threads an accurate through pass between Shakhtar Donetsk defenders Anatoliy Tymoschuk and Mariusz Lewandowski in a 2004 Champions League game.

◄ France's Franck Ribéry dribbles between Dutch defender Khalid Boulahrouz and forward Robin van Persie during a Euro 2008 group match. Great teamwork and accurate counter-attacking saw the Dutch side win 4-1.

▲ A push and go pass can beat a lone defender or an offside trap. The attacker pushes the ball past the defender and then sprints to collect it.

TEAM ATTACKS

Many attacks rely on two or more team-mates working together to create a promising position. The wall pass (see page 18), for example, is a good way of propelling the ball past a defender with two quick movements. Attacking players also make decoy runs that draw defenders in one direction, creating space for another attacker to run into. Using the full width of the pitch can be vital to the success of an attack. Full-backs, wing-backs or wingers who are in space near the sideline may join an attack and make an overlapping run down the line. Receiving the ball, they may be able to head further forwards to put in a cross or cut infield and move towards goal. An overload is a situation in which the attacking side has more players in the attacking third of the pitch than the defending team. Classic ways of creating an overload are through a counter attack – in which one side's attack breaks down and the opposition launches a rapid, direct attack – and an accurate long pass that is received by an attacker who is supported by team-mates, with only an isolated defender to beat.

SET PIECES

Set pieces are often planned in training. They are attacking moves made from a restart such as a free kick, corner or throw-in. If a team has a player who can throw the ball a long way, it may treat a throw-in that is level with the penalty area as if it were a corner. Often, a target player just inside the penalty area will attempt to flick the throw into the goal area. Mostly, set pieces are planned from corners and attacking free kicks (see page 30). At a corner, a team's tallest players or its best headers of the ball move up, usually from defence, to join strikers and attacking midfielders in the penalty area. Corners are sometimes played short to catch the defending team off guard, but usually they are whipped into the goal area. The attacking side looks for a header or shot on goal or a flick-on to a team-mate.

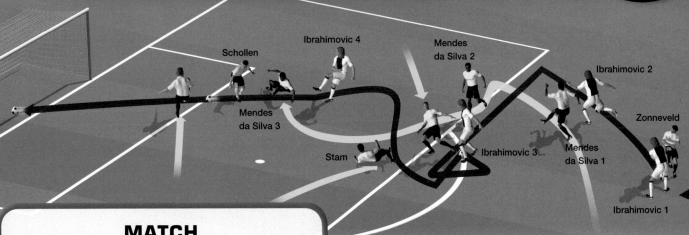

Schollen
Ibrahimovic 4
Mendes da Silva 2
Ibrahimovic 2
Mendes da Silva 3
Zonneveld
Stam
Ibrahimovic 3
Mendes da Silva 1
Ibrahimovic 1

MATCH ACTION

Swedish international Zlatan Ibrahimovic moved from Ajax to Juventus for £10.81 million in late August 2004, but a week earlier he had given the Ajax fans a solo goal to savour. In a Dutch league game against NAC Breda, Ibrahimovic received a pass with his back to goal, defender David Mendes da Silva on his back and another Breda player, Mike Zonneveld, close by. Winning a tackle with Zonneveld, Ibrahimovic twisted past da Silva and headed goalwards. Weaving his way to the edge of the penalty area, Ibrahimovic's options looked limited with four defenders around him. Yet with supreme balance and a series of feints and turns, he avoided the lunging tackle of Ronnie Stam. At the very last moment, when a shot with his right foot looked likely, Ibrahimovic switched the ball to his left foot to slide a shot past goalkeeper Davy Schollen. Ajax won the game 6-2.

MATCH MAGICIANS

Some attacks are inspired by a piece of individual skill, trickery and brilliance. A player may be able to break free from a defence with a sudden change of pace and direction or a trick move such as the Cruyff turn or a dragback. Some players can simply outpace a defence, bursting through to score. Dribbling – jinking and moving with the ball under close control to beat defenders – is one of the most exciting sights on a football pitch. Stanley Matthews, Maradona and Garrincha were all electrifying dribblers, while today's dribbling superstars include Gareth Bale, Cristiano Ronaldo, Lionel Messi and Franck Ribéry. Weaving, high-speed dribblers can sometimes open up a game by themselves. They strike fear into defenders who know that one false move or a poorly timed challenge will allow the dribbler to go past or perhaps give away a free kick or penalty.

▼ *Ghana's Stephen Appiah (left) attempts to twist and turn sharply past Zimbabwean defender Cephas Chimedza in the African Cup of Nations. Dummy movements, stepovers and sharp turns are all ways of wrong-footing a defender.*

▲ *An unexpected piece of brilliance can open up a defence or result in a goal. Here, whilst playing for Sevilla, Jesus Navas unleashes an overhead kick against Barcelona. In 2013, he moved to Manchester City for £14.9 million.*

GOALSCORING

Players who score goals regularly are the most valuable of all footballers. But scoring is not just reserved for the strikers in a side. A successful team needs its midfielders to contribute a number of goals each season, while tall defenders who are experts at heading often score five or six goals per season from set pieces. For out-and-out strikers, goals are what they play for and are judged on. As Argentinian striker Gabriel Batistuta once said, 'Goals are like bread. I need them to live.'

THE GOALSCORER'S ART

Pace, power, accuracy, confidence and a deadly eye for a chance are just some of the qualities required to be a top goalscorer. Some skills can be honed in training – close ball control or swerving a shot, for example. Other qualities, such as confidence and vision, are harder to master. Football has got quicker at the highest level and most strikers need great pace to break past increasingly mobile defenders or into space to receive the ball before anyone else. Strength to hold off a challenge can be an asset, too. Some strikers, however, rely more on wits, fast reactions and ball skills to dribble through a crowded penalty area. Others are taller, stronger players who can score with towering headers or blasted shots. Most crucially of all, strikers have to be able to spot a goal chance and take it well. They need to react instinctively, using their vision to time runs into a scoring position. Once on the ball, they rarely have long to shoot. In an instant, strikers have to weigh up their options, know where the goal, defenders and keeper are, and hit a shot with enough pace, bend or accuracy to beat the goalkeeper.

FACTFILE In 1998, Atlético Mineiro's Edmilson Ferreira celebrated a goal by eating a carrot in front of the fans of rival Brazilian team America MG. His actions caused crowd trouble and incensed America's players, one of whom was later sent off for a scything foul on Ferreira.

OWN GOALS

An own goal is technically any goal in which the last person to touch the ball before it crossed the line was a player on the defending team. In practice, however, an own goal is awarded not only when the ball has been deflected, but also when a defending player has made a genuine error or caused a major change in the course of the ball. The history of professional football is littered with outrageous own goals. Among the most common are goalkeeping errors, skewed defensive clearances that are sliced into the net, and misdirected headers. A handful of players have scored two own goals in the same game, such as Georgia's Kakhaber 'Kakha' Kaladze in a 2010 World Cup match versus Italy, and Stoke City's Jon Walters in a 2013 Premier League game against Chelsea.

◄ Manchester United's Wayne Rooney hits a volley to score against Liverpool in an English Premier League match. His thunderous shot is ideal for striking at goal from outside the penalty area.

FACTFILE
The world record for own goals in one game is a staggering 149! In the last match of the 2002 Madagascan league season, against champions AS Adema, Stade Olympique l'Emryne repeatedly scored own goals from the kick-off in protest at a refereeing decision in their previous game.

► Germany's Miroslav Klose bears down on goal during the semi-final of the 2006 World Cup against Italy. Klose's five goals made him the top scorer of the tournament and helped take Germany to third place.

▲ When a goalscoring chance comes, strikers need poise and accuracy to put it away. Here, Fernando Torres scores the winning goal of the Euro 2008 final, placing the ball past the German goalkeeper, Jens Lehmann.

▶ Fabian Espindola (left) roars with joy after scoring for Real Salt Lake against LA Galaxy in 2011. The Argentinean scored more than 30 goals for Real Salt Lake before moving in 2013 to New York Red Bulls.

FACTFILE Nigerian international Celestine Babayaro scored on his debut for Chelsea in a 1997 pre-season match against Stevenage Borough. By celebrating with a somersault, however, Babayaro broke his leg.

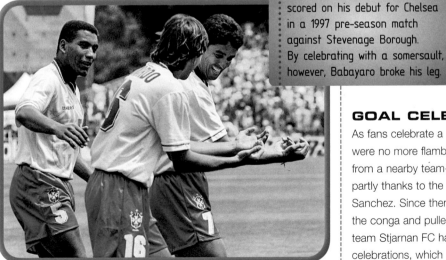

▲ Brazil's Mauro Silva (left), Leonardo (centre) and Bebeto pretend to rock babies at the 1994 World Cup. The celebration – during a 3-0 victory against Cameroon – was in honour of striker Bebeto's newborn son.

GOALSCORING RECORDS

ALL-TIME LEADING GOALSCORERS
Artur Friedenreich (Brazil)
1,329 goals (1909-39)

Pelé (Brazil)
1,281 goals (1956-77)

Franz Binder (Germany)
1,006 goals (1930-50)

MOST INTERNATIONAL GOALS
109 – Ali Daei (Iran), 1993–2006

MOST GOALS IN ONE INTERNATIONAL MATCH
13 – Archie Thompson (Australia), 2001

FASTEST INTERNATIONAL GOAL
8 seconds – Davide Gualtieri (San Marino) against England, 1993

FASTEST INTERNATIONAL HAT-TRICK
Inside 3½ minutes – Willie Hall (England), 1938

MOST HAT-TRICKS IN CONSECUTIVE MATCHES
4 – Masahi Nakayama (Japan) for Jubilo Iwata, 1998

FASTEST GOAL
2 seconds – Vuk Bakic (Serbia) for GSP Polet, 2012

FASTEST OWN GOAL
8 seconds – Pat Kruse (England), playing for Torquay United, 1977

GOAL CELEBRATIONS

As fans celebrate a goal, so do players. For many years, celebrations were no more flamboyant than a simple punch of the air and a hug from a nearby team-mate. That all changed in the 1980s and 1990s, partly thanks to the acrobatic backflips of Mexican striker Hugo Sanchez. Since then, players have rocked imaginary babies, danced the conga and pulled off spectacular gymnastic moves. Icelandic team Stjarnan FC have gained fame for their elaborate team celebrations, which include all the team members pretending to row a boat and reel in a player acting as a fish. This performance clocked up over a million views on YouTube in 2011. Referees can penalize teams for time-wasting or removing shirts during such celebrations.

FREE KICKS AND PENALTIES

Referees award a free kick when a player breaks one of the laws of the game. Common free-kick offences are mistimed tackles, shirt-pulling, obstruction and offside. There are two types of free kick – indirect, which cannot be scored from without a second player touching the ball, and direct, which can be scored from directly and is awarded for more serious fouls. If a direct free-kick offence is committed by the defending team inside its penalty area, the referee may award a penalty.

FREE KICKS

Both types of free kick are taken from where the foul or offence was committed, although a rule change means that in some competitions the referee can move a kick 9m closer to goal if the other team wastes time or shows dissent. Opposition players must move at least 9m away from the ball, giving the team taking the kick valuable possession in space and with time. Some free kicks are taken quickly to get the ball moving in the middle of the field. Wide free kicks are often crossed with pace towards the goal area.

Attacking free kicks engage the two teams in a battle of wits. Players on the defending side mark attackers in the penalty area and form a defensive wall to block a direct shot. The kick taker may pass to a team-mate in space or try to hit a cross or shot past the wall. Some free kick specialists rely on powerful and direct strikes, while others – such as David Beckham, Cristiano Ronaldo and Oleksandr Aliyev – are famous for the extreme bend they put on the ball.

FACTFILE
The first ever penalty was given by mistake to Scottish club Airdrieonians in March 1891. The new law did not actually take effect until the following season.

THE KICK OF DEATH

Originally nicknamed the 'kick of death', the penalty kick was introduced in 1891. It has created more controversy than any other aspect of the game. The reason is simple. A penalty is an outstanding opportunity to score, as the taker is one-on-one with the goalkeeper and all the other players are outside the penalty area. In certain situations, the referee can order the kick to be retaken – for example, if the taker misses but a defender entered the area before the kick. Penalty takers must hit the ball forwards and cannot make contact with the ball again until it has touched another player. Some penalty takers favour accuracy over power, aiming the ball low into the corner of the goal; others blast the ball. For the keeper, trying to figure out where the ball will go is a guessing game.

◀ Manchester United's Wayne Rooney curls a free kick towards the penalty area.

▲ Juventus keeper Gianluigi Buffon shows excellent reactions to save a penalty from AC Milan's Christian Brocchi during an Italian Super Cup match.

▼ *Lionel Messi takes a free kick during a 2013 Champions League match between Barcelona and AC Milan. He strikes across the back of the ball to make it swerve round the defensive wall and into the corner of the goal.*

PENALTY SHOOTOUTS

Tense and nailbiting, a penalty shootout is guaranteed to bring fans to the edge of their seats. Professional football's first shootout took place in England in 1970. In the semi-final of the Watney Mann Invitational Cup, lowly Hull City held a full-strength Manchester United team to a 1-1 draw. In the shootout that followed, Manchester United's Denis Law became the first player to miss a shootout spot kick, but his side ended up 4-3 winners. The first shootout in a major tournament was in the 1972 Asian Nations Cup, when South Korea beat Thailand in the semi-final. Germany lost the first European Championships shootout to Czechoslovakia in 1976, but defeated France in the first World Cup shootout six years later.

▲ *AC Milan's Giampaolo Pazzini scores on a penalty kick during the Serie A match between AC Milan and Cesena, February 2015.*

In a shootout, five players per side are chosen to take one penalty each, all at one end of the pitch. A shootout is not considered to be part of the actual match, meaning that a goal is not added to a player's season or career tally. Neither penalty takers nor team-mates are allowed to score from a rebound – each player has just one shot at glory. The keeper knows this and often does his or her best to intimidate a penalty taker. If the scores are level after each team has taken five penalties, the competition goes into sudden death. Teams take one penalty each until one side misses and the other scores. On the rare occasion that all the players on the pitch, including the goalkeeper, have taken a penalty and the scores are level, the cycle begins again in the same order. Does this ever happen? Occasionally and spectacularly. In 2007, England and Holland played in the semi-final of the European Under-21 championships. It took 32 penalties before the Dutch won.

FACTFILE Tied games at the knockout stage of a competition used to be settled by tossing a coin or drawing lots. In 1954, Spain and Turkey drew 2-2 in a play-off to decide who would qualify for the World Cup. A blindfolded Italian boy, Luigi Franco Gemma, drew lots to decide the winner. Spain were knocked out.

▲ *Oliver Neuville of Germany keeps his nerve to place a penalty past Argentina's Leonardo Franco. Germany won the shootout 4-2 to book a place in the last four of the 2006 World Cup.*

MOST PENALTIES IN A SHOOTOUT

PENS	SHOOTOUT SCORE	COMPETITION
48	KK Palace 17 Civics 16	Namibian Cup, 2005
44	Argentinos Juniors 20 Racing Club 19	Argentinian league, 1988
40	Obernai 15 ASCA Wittelsheim 15	French Cup, 1996
40	Tunbridge Wells 16 Littlehampton Town 15	English FA Cup, 2005

SNAPSHOT

BAGGIO'S PENALTY MISS

'The difference between heaven and hell is one minute,' said Spanish international Josep Guardiola after an epic 4-3 win over Yugoslavia at Euro 2000. For Italy's Roberto Baggio, six years earlier, it took mere seconds. In the final of the 1994 World Cup, Italy and Brazil were locked in a 0-0 stalemate. Extra time ended and a nerve-shredding penalty shootout began. With Italy 3-2 down, Baggio stepped up to take his side's pressure-laden fifth penalty. He decided to drive the ball down the middle, as he knew that Taffarel, the Brazilian keeper, tended to dive to one side.

Taffarel did dive, but Baggio sent the ball sailing high over the bar to hand the World Cup to Brazil. Baggio later wrote, 'It was the worst moment of my career. I still dream about it. If I could erase a moment from my career, it would be that one.' What is often forgotten is that two Italians before Baggio, Daniele Massaro and the highly experienced Franco Baresi, missed their penalties. Even if Baggio had scored, Brazil would have had the chance to win with their fifth spot kick. That said, the photograph of a crushed Baggio remains the iconic image of the 1994 World Cup.

Roberto Baggio hangs his head in disbelief as Brazilian players celebrate victory in the final of the 1994 World Cup.

FOOTBALL LEGENDS

From France's Zinedine Zidane to Argentina's Lionel Messi, football has been lit up by the talents of thousands of highly committed and skilful players, all of whom have enthralled spectators and inspired their teams to great achievements. Packed into this section are profiles of more than 75 of the finest players to have graced the game.

> **KEY**
> Country = international side
> Caps = international games
> Goals = international goals
>   (to June 2015)

GOALKEEPERS

PETER SCHMEICHEL
Denmark, born 1963
Caps: 129   Goals: 1

After playing for Hvidøvre and then Brøndby, Schmeichel became one of the best keepers of the 1990s after Alex Ferguson took him to Manchester United in 1991 for the modest fee of £550,000. The high point of his international career came with winning the 1992 European Championships, while the silverware poured in at club level. The hugely committed Dane redefined one-on-one goalkeeping, standing menacingly tall and large or bravely sprawling at an attacker's feet. After winning a treble (English Premiership, FA Cup and Champions League) with Manchester United in 1999, he moved to Sporting Lisbon and helped the Portuguese side win its first league title in 17 years.

He made a surprise return to the English Premiership in 2001, with Aston Villa and then Manchester City, before injury forced him to retire.

▶ *Iker Casillas focuses up the pitch during a 2013 La Liga match between Real Madrid and Valencia.*

IKER CASILLAS
Spain, born 1981
Caps: 162   Goals: 0

Spain's number one keeper for more than a decade, Casillas has, so far, played for just one club, Real Madrid, for whom he has made over 650 appearances and won five La Liga titles. In 2000, he became the youngest goalkeeper to play in a Champions League final, which Real won 3-0. With his razor-sharp reflexes and superb positioning, Casillas has been voted keeper of the year five times and has captained Spain to two European Championship titles and the 2010 World Cup.

GAO HONG
China, born 1967
Caps: over 100   Goals: 0

An instinctive shot-stopper, Gao Hong began playing football for her factory team before moving to the Guangdong club in southeast China. She became a member of the Chinese national side in 1989 and played in both the 1995 and 1999 World Cups. Gao was in goal for China's two Asian Games successes, in 1994 and 1998, and she also won a silver medal at the 1996 Olympics. At the end of her international career, she appeared in the WUSA league for the New York Power.

◀ *Peter Schmeichel makes a typically brave save for Manchester City in 2002.*

> **FACTFILE** Peter Schmeichel showed great striker skills in the 1995-96 UEFA Cup when he came up for an attack and scored with a header against Russian side Rotor Volgograd.

BEST GOALKEEPER AT THE WORLD CUP

Since 1994, FIFA has given an award to the best keeper of the tournament.

YEAR	WINNER
1994	Michel Preud'homme (Belgium)
1998	Fabien Barthez (France)
2002	Oliver Kahn (Germany)
2006	Gianluigi Buffon (Italy)
2010	Iker Casillas (Spain)
2014	Manuel Neuer (Germany)

LEV YASHIN
Soviet Union, 1929–90
Caps: 75 Goals: 0

In South America, Yashin was called the Black Spider. In Europe he was the Black Panther; but everywhere he was regarded as the finest goalkeeper of his era and, possibly, of all time. Blessed with extraordinary anticipation and agility, Yashin made countless, seemingly impossible saves and stopped as many as 150 penalties during his career, which was spent entirely at Moscow Dynamo. In 1954, he made his debut for the national team. Yashin's bravery, vision and shot-stopping skills helped the Soviets to an Olympic title in 1956, the European Championships crown in 1960 and a semi-final place at the 1966 World Cup. With Moscow Dynamo, Yashin won six league titles and two Soviet Cups. In 1963, he became the first – and still the only – goalkeeper to win the coveted European Player of the Year award.

▲ *Lev Yashin makes a great save at the 1966 World Cup.*

GORDON BANKS
England, born 1937
Caps: 73 Goals: 0

'Banks of England' was as secure a keeper as any nation could call upon in the 1960s. During his ten-year international career, he kept 35 clean sheets and was on the losing side just nine times. His professional career began at Chesterfield, before a £7,000 move took him to Leicester City. In 1962, Banks made his debut for England, with whom he won the 1966 World Cup. The following year, he moved to Stoke City, but a car crash in 1972 caused Banks to lose the sight in his right eye. The accident ended his career in Britain, although he did play in the USA for the Fort Lauderdale Strikers in 1977–78.

FACTFILE
Gordon Banks won FIFA's Goalkeeper of the Year award a record six times.

▲ *Gordon Banks in action for Stoke City in 1972. Throughout his career, Banks trained tirelessly on angles and repeat drills to improve his strength and agility.*

MATCH ACTION

Brazil and England played a tense yet thrilling match in the group stages of the 1970 World Cup, with Brazil winning 1-0. In the tenth minute, Jairzinho slipped a high cross into the English penalty area. Rising high, Pelé headed the ball down fiercely towards the far post, with Gordon Banks seemingly stranded. The ball bounced just short of the line and a goal seemed certain. Yet Banks showed electrifying reactions, scrambling across his line and clawing the ball almost vertically upwards and over the crossbar. Pelé was stunned and later called it 'the greatest save I ever saw'. Few who witnessed it would disagree.

Tommy Wright

Pelé

Alan Mullery

Tostao

Banks 2

Banks 1

PAT JENNINGS
Northern Ireland, born 1945
Caps: 119 Goals: 0

Calm, gentle and seemingly unflappable, Northern Ireland's Pat Jennings famously received no formal coaching before joining his local team, Newry Town. A short spell with Watford followed, before he moved to Tottenham Hotspur in 1964. There he won the FA Cup, two League Cups and the UEFA Cup. In the 1967 Charity Shield match against Manchester United, a kick from Jennings sailed over the head of the opposing keeper, Alex Stepney, to score a memorable goal. Jennings was sold to Tottenham's north London rivals Arsenal in 1977, where he played for eight seasons. He came out of retirement to play his 119th game for his country at the 1986 World Cup.

▲ Pat Jennings tips the ball over the bar during a World Cup qualifying game against England in 1985.

> **FACTFILE** Between 1966 and 1977, Sepp Maier played an astonishing 422 consecutive games for Bayern Munich.

▶ Dino Zoff organizes Italy's defence during the 1982 World Cup. Voted Italian goalkeeper of the century, Zoff once remained unbeaten in goal for Juventus for ten games.

▲ Manuel Neuer was voted German footballer of the year for the 2014–15 season, a rare accolade for a goalkeeper.

MANUEL NEUER
Germany, born 1986
Caps: 58 Goals: 0

A dynamic sweeper-keeper, comfortable on the ball and brilliant in one-on-one situations, Neuer joined Schalke 04 in 1991 and didn't leave until 2011 where he moved for a record fee of 22 million euros to Bayern Munich. He made an instant impact, notching up over 1,000 minutes without conceding a goal in a string of games in his first season, winning three Bundesliga titles and the 2012–13 Champions League. Debuting internationally in 2009, he only conceded one goal in Germany's Euro 2012 campaign. More was to come in 2014 where he became a World Cup winner and was voted goalkeeper of the tournament.

DINO ZOFF
Italy, born 1942
Caps: 112 Goals: 0

A true goalkeeping legend, Dino Zoff was rejected as a 14-year-old by both Juventus and Internazionale for being too small. He finally signed for Udinese before moving to Mantova and then Napoli. In 1972, Zoff was bought by Juventus, where he won six Italian league titles, two Italian Cups and a UEFA Cup. Zoff's first international call-up came during the 1968 European Championships. He debuted in the quarter-finals and was part of the side that won the final. A model athlete with intense concentration, Zoff broke many goalkeeping records (see page 23) and in 1982, at the age of 40, he captained Italy to their first World Cup success in the modern era. The oldest player to win a World Cup, Zoff retired shortly afterwards and went on to coach Italy's Olympic team, Juventus and Lazio. He coached Italy to the final of Euro 2000, where they lost narrowly to France.

HOPE SOLO
USA, born 1981
Caps: 176 Goals: 0

The USA number one keeper since 2005, Solo started her professional career with Philadelphia Charge in 2003 before having spells in Sweden and France and returning to the US with a succession of WUSA and WPS teams. In 2013, she joined the Seattle Reign in the newly formed National Women's Soccer League. She has won Olympic gold twice (2008, 2012) and was a member of the USA team that were runners-up at the 2011 World Cup. Solo was voted keeper of the World Cup, a feat she repeated four years later as five clean sheets helped her side become 2015 champions.

DEFENDERS

MARCEL DESAILLY
France, born 1968
Caps: 116 Goals: 3

Marcel Desailly is world-famous as one of the French players who won the World Cup and European Championship crowns in 1998 and 2000. He was born in the African nation of Ghana and came to France as a young child. A skilful and commanding central defender, Desailly began his career with FC Nantes and then Olympique Marseille. In 1993, he won the Champions League with Marseille, before moving to AC Milan and winning the Champions League again the following year. After a series of outstanding performances at the 1998 World Cup, Desailly moved to Chelsea, where he proved a popular leader. In 2004, Desailly retired from international football and left Chelsea to join Qatar's Al-Ittihad club.

▲ Marcel Desailly hits a long pass during France's 1998 World Cup game against Denmark.

FACTFILE World Cup winner Marcel Desailly became the third player to be sent off in a World Cup final when he was dismissed against Brazil in 1998 after receiving two yellow cards.

▲ In 1978, Daniel Passarella captained Argentina to the World Cup trophy on home soil.

DANIEL PASSARELLA
Argentina, born 1953
Caps: 70 Goals: 22

Passarella was a gifted central defender who made surging runs into midfield to build attacks. He was exceptionally good in the air despite being of average height, and struck devastating free kicks. In 298 Argentinian league matches, he scored an astonishing 99 goals. Passarella had success with River Plate before a move to Europe in 1982, first to Fiorentina and then to Internazionale. In 1985–86, he scored 11 goals for Fiorentina, a record for a defender that lasted for 15 years. He won the 1978 World Cup, played in the 1982 tournament and was picked for 1986, but was sidelined through injury. After retiring, Passarella became a coach, managing Argentina at the 1998 World Cup.

ELIAS FIGUEROA
Chile, born 1946
Caps: 47 Goals: 2

This elegant and skilled defender played almost all of his football in the left-back position. Figueroa appeared in three World Cups – 1966, 1974 and 1982 – and in 1974 he was voted the best defender of the tournament. He won the South American Footballer of the Year award an unprecedented three times in a row (1974–76). At club level, Figueroa won league titles in three different countries – the Chilean league with Colo Colo twice, the Brazilian league with Internacional on three occasions and the Uruguayan league with Peñarol five times. He ended his career in the USA, playing for the Fort Lauderdale Strikers alongside Gerd Müller and Teofilio Cubillas, the great Peruvian striker.

RUNE BRATSETH
Norway, born 1961
Caps: 60 Goals: 4

Rune Bratseth began his football career with Rosenborg Trondheim, but did not turn professional until the age of 23. In 1986, he moved to Germany's Werder Bremen for just £65,000. Bremen had bought a bargain, as Bratseth became their defensive linchpin, using his great pace and skill to operate as a centre-back or a sweeper. Bratseth won two Bundesliga titles and a European Cup-Winners' Cup with Bremen, and was twice voted Germany's best foreign import. One of his proudest moments came in 1994, when he captained Norway to their first World Cup finals since 1938. After the tournament, he retired and went on to became director of coaching at Rosenborg.

◄ Rune Bratseth powers away from the Republic of Ireland's John Aldridge at the 1994 World Cup.

FACTFILE In 1976, Bobby Moore played for Team America against England, in a game to mark the USA's bicentenary. One of Moore's team-mates was Pelé.

BOBBY MOORE
England, 1941-93
Caps: 108 Goals: 2

England's finest ever defender, Moore appeared to lack the pace and the commanding physique to be a great central defender. However, he was blessed with a wonderful eye for the game and always appeared to be one step ahead of opposition attackers. His tackling was clean and surgical, and he was very rarely cautioned. One of football's truly outstanding captains, Moore led England in 90 games – a record shared with Billy Wright – including the 1966 World Cup triumph. He spent most of his career at West Ham, only joining Fulham (alongside George Best) at the age of 32, before finally moving to the USA to play for Seattle Sounders and San Antonio Thunder. His friendship with Pelé was cemented in 1970, when the two men played out an epic struggle for supremacy in England's World Cup game against Brazil. Pelé called Moore the greatest defender he had played against.

◀ Bobby Moore, England's captain, celebrates with the 1966 World Cup.

▲ Matthias Sammer (left) was the first defender to win the European Player of the Year award since Franz Beckenbauer in 1976.

MATTHIAS SAMMER
East Germany / Germany,
born 1967 Caps: 74 Goals: 14

Matthias Sammer followed in the footsteps of his father, who played in midfield for East Germany and Dresden. As a midfielder, Sammer led East Germany to victory at the 1986 European Youth Championships. After Germany reunified in 1990, he moved into defence and was a commanding sweeper in the 1994 World Cup and two European Championships. A move to the Italian club Internazionale was short-lived and he returned to Germany to join Borussia Dortmund, with whom he won two Bundesliga titles and the 1997 Champions League. In 1996, he became the first player from the former East Germany to win the European Footballer of the Year award.

PAOLO MALDINI
Italy, born 1968
Caps: 126 Goals: 7

One of the best defenders in world football, Paolo Maldini was a one-club player. He made his first-team debut for AC Milan in 1985 and played over 900 games for the Italian club, mostly at left-back, although he would also play as a central defender or as a sweeper. Maldini was able to read the game extremely well, tackle cleanly and move the ball forwards accurately. He debuted for Italy in 1988 and soon became a regular in the national side. He played in four World Cups and four European Championships, retiring from international football after the 2002 World Cup. Winning seven Serie A titles, Maldini also lifted the Champions League trophy in 2003 and 2007. He eventually retired just short of his 41st birthday.

◀ Paolo Maldini, Italy's longest-serving defender, clears the ball out of his penalty area during the 1994 World Cup final against Brazil.

FACTFILE Paolo Maldini's father, Cesare, also played as a sweeper for AC Milan, lifting the European Cup at Wembley in 1963. His son repeated that feat for the same club exactly 40 years later. Cesare Maldini also managed his son and the Italian team at the 1998 World Cup.

THIAGO SILVA
Brazil, born 1984
Caps: 54   Goals: 4

Tough and skilful, Silva can play in any position across the defence and actually started out as a midfielder in Brazil but moved to Europe in 2004. After spells at Porto and Dynamo Moscow, where he contracted tuberculosis and nearly quit football, Silva joined Fluminense and helped them to win their first ever Copa do Brazil in 2007. AC Milan paid around 10 million euros to bring him back to Europe in 2009 where he won the 2010–11 Serie A before becoming the world's most expensive defender with a move to Paris Saint-Germain. Silva captained Brazil when they won the 2013 FIFA Confederations Cup and has played at two Olympic Games, winning a bronze medal in 2008 and a silver in 2012.

▲ Holland's Ruud Krol at the 1980 European Championships, which were held in Italy.

FACTFILE
Ruud Krol held the record as the most-capped Dutch player for 21 years. His total was finally overtaken in 2000.

▶ Franz Beckenbauer at the 1974 World Cup. Sixteen years later, he became the second man – after Brazil's Mario Zagalo – to have won the World Cup as both a player and a manager.

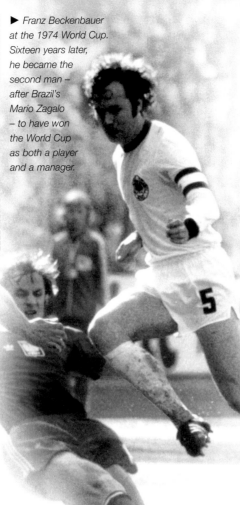

RUUD KROL
Holland, born 1949
Caps: 83
Goals: 4

Krol was a vital part of the great Ajax and Holland 'total football' sides of the late 1960s and 1970s, comfortable playing in almost any defensive position. With Ajax he won six league titles and two European Cups (1972 and 1973). Krol was the last of the Ajax greats to move away, when in 1980 he played for Vancouver Whitecaps in Canada. He returned to Europe the following year to play for Napoli and later for Cannes in the French second division, where injury forced him to retire in 1987. He has since managed in a variety of countries, including Switzerland, Egypt and Belgium.

FRANZ BECKENBAUER
West Germany, born 1945
Caps: 103   Goals: 14

Der Kaiser made his debut for Bayern Munich in 1964 as an attacking inside-left. Just 27 games later, he was in the national side. At the 1966 World Cup, Beckenbauer played in midfield and scored four goals on the way to the final. By the 1970 tournament, he had moved into defence, where he revolutionized the ultra-defensive role of sweeper with his astonishing vision and silky skills on the ball. Time and again he would turn defence into attack, striding up the pitch to release team-mates or take a chance himself. With his stylish attacking play, it is sometimes forgotten that he was a masterful defender, always cool under pressure. In 1972, Beckenbauer won the European Championships with West Germany and was European Footballer of the Year. Two years later, he won the first of three consecutive European Cups with Bayern Munich and also captained his country to World Cup glory. In 1977, he made a surprise move to the USA, playing in a star-studded New York Cosmos team before returning to Germany in 1980 with Hamburg. He became West Germany's coach in 1984, leading the team to two World Cup finals and winning one.

HIT THE NET

www.planetworldcup.com/LEGENDS/wcstars.html
A selection of profiles of many great footballers, including Austria's Hans Krankl, Belgium's Jan Ceulemans and West Germany's Karl-Heinz Rummenigge.

www.rsssf.com/miscellaneous/century.html
A regularly updated list of footballers with 100 or more international caps. Clicking on a player's name reveals a list of all their international matches.

http://www.theguardian.com/football/series/world-cup-s-top-100-footballers
Profiles of 100 great players from past World Cups.

▲ *Franco Baresi won three European Cups with AC Milan, including this triumph in 1989.*

FRANCO BARESI
Italy, born 1960
Caps: 81 Goals: 1

A tough, intelligent defender, Baresi made his first-team debut for AC Milan in 1978. He played 716 games for the club, winning six Serie A titles. Baresi had to wait until 1990 to break fully into the Italian national team, however. Although part of the 1982 World Cup squad, he was not picked to play and refused to appear for Italy while Enzo Bearzot remained manager. He played in both the 1990 and 1994 World Cups and superbly cancelled out the threat of Brazil's Romario and Bebeto in the 1994 final, which Italy lost only on penalties. Milan paid him the ultimate tribute on his retirement in 1997, dropping the number six shirt from their line-up.

HONG MYUNG-BO
South Korea, born 1969
Caps: 136 Goals: 10

An excellent passer of the ball, Hong played for Pohang Steelers in South Korea and for Bellmare Hiratsuke (now Shonan Bellmare) and Kashiwa Reysol in Japan. He is South Korea's most-capped player and a veteran of four World Cups. At the 2002 tournament, where South Korea reached the semi-finals on home soil, Hong was voted the third best player of the World Cup behind Oliver Kahn and Ronaldo. In November 2002, he became the first Korean to play in the American MLS when he signed for Los Angeles Galaxy.

LINDA MEDALEN
Norway, born 1965
Caps: 152 Goals: 64

Medalen started her career as a striker, making her debut for Norway in 1987 and going on to win the 1988 unofficial Women's World Cup and the 1993 European Championships. At the 1991 World Cup she was her side's top scorer, with six goals, as Norway finished runners-up. As Medalen's career progressed, she moved into defence, where her skill in the air and strong tackling helped Norway to win the 1995 World Cup, conceding just one goal in six games. Medalen played in the 1999 tournament, but a knee injury kept her out of the 2000 Olympics, which Norway won. At club level, she won five league championships and three cup competitions for the Norwegian side Asker SKK.

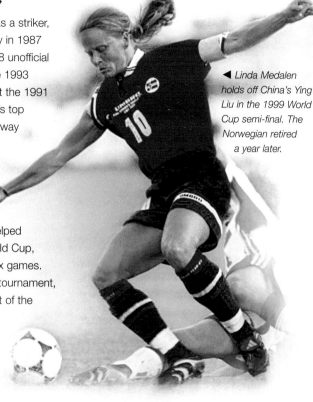

◄ *Linda Medalen holds off China's Ying Liu in the 1999 World Cup semi-final. The Norwegian retired a year later.*

JOHN CHARLES
Wales, 1931-2004
Caps: 38 Goals: 21

The gloriously talented Charles was equally skilled as a bustling, powerful centre-forward or as a hugely commanding central defender. In both positions, he was world class. Appearing in attack for Leeds United, he scored a record 42 goals in one season, while playing internationally as a central defender. In the Welsh side, Charles was joined by his brother, Mel, and team-mates Ivor and Len Allchurch – the first time that any national side had included two pairs of brothers. In 1957, the British transfer record was smashed as he moved to Juventus for £67,000. Charles became a genuine legend in Italy for his towering performances, generous behaviour towards fans and his sportsmanship. In a highly defence-minded league, he scored an astonishing 93 goals in 155 matches, helping Juve win three Serie A titles and two Italian Cups. He later moved back to Leeds, then on to Parma, Cardiff City and Hereford United, before retiring.

◄ *John Charles (right) battles for the ball at the 1958 World Cup. Charles' name is still revered by Juventus fans, who nicknamed him Il Buon Gigante – the Gentle Giant.*

MIDFIELDERS AND WINGERS

LANDON DONOVAN
USA, born 1982
Caps: 157 Goals: 57

Donovan came to prominence early when he was voted the best player of the 1999 FIFA Under-17 World Championship and was signed the same year by Bayer Leverkusen. Returning to the USA on loan with the San Jose Earthquakes, Donovan would later have short loan spells with Bayern Munich and Everton, but in 2005 he joined the LA Galaxy.

He has won five MLS Cups, three with LA Galaxy and two with the San Jose Earthquakes, as well as winning the CONCACAF Gold Cup three times with the US team. Two-footed and capable of devastating attacking bursts from midfield, Donovan's eye for a goal has seen him score more than 150 times in the MLS and other US club competitions. His 56 goals make him, far and away, the US national team's most prolific goalscorer.

◀ *Landon Donovan goes to turn with the ball during an MLS game between LA Galaxy and the Portland Timbers.*

STANLEY MATTHEWS
England, 1915-2000
Caps: 54 Goals: 11

The 'Wizard of the Dribble' made his first-team debut for Stoke City in 1932 and went on to amaze crowds with his sensational wing play, supreme control and ability to dribble through a defence at will. Matthews' dedication to fitness, years ahead of his time, ensured that his career was one of the longest in British football. He joined Blackpool in 1947 and inspired them to an incredible FA Cup triumph in 1953, in what is remembered as the 'Matthews final'. His England career ran from 1937 to 1954, although he only played in 54 of the 119 internationals the team contested, to the outrage of his many fans. He became the first winner of the European Footballer of the Year award in 1956, and in 1961 he returned to Stoke, for whom he played his last game in 1965, aged 50 years and five days. In the same year, he became the first ever serving footballer to be knighted.

▲ *Stanley Matthews (left) exhibits supreme poise, balance and skill on the ball as he takes on Scotland's George Young in 1948.*

FACTFILE Stanley Matthews was praised as one of the most modest and sporting players to ever grace the game. In his 33-year-long career, he never received a booking.

CARLOS VALDERRAMA
Colombia, born 1961
Caps: 110 Goals: 10

Famous for his flamboyant play and hairstyle, Carlos Valderrama was an exquisite passer of the ball in midfield, who would often link with the attack to devastating effect. He played for three Colombian teams – Union Magdalena, Millionarios and Deportiva Cali – before moving to France in 1988, where he won the league title with Montpellier. In 1996, he moved to the USA to play for Tampa Bay Mutiny and then Miami Fusion. Valderrama captained Colombia to three World Cup tournaments in a row (1990–98) and retired from international football after the 1998 tournament. Yet, even past his 40th birthday, Valderrama was still one of the biggest stars in the MLS.

▶ *Carlos Valderrama on the ball during Colombia's 1998 World Cup game against England.*

ALAIN GIRESSE
France, born 1952
Caps: 47 Goals: 6

At 1.63m tall and weighing around 60kg, Giresse was small for competitive football, but his tireless work in midfield caught the eye both at club level, for Bordeaux and Olympique Marseille, and with the French national team. Giresse appeared at two World Cups (1982 and 1986) and also won the 1984 European Championships. He played more than 500 matches for Bordeaux and scored the winning goal in the 1986 French Cup final against Marseille, whom he joined a few weeks later. Giresse went on to manage Paris Saint-Germain and Toulouse. After coaching for the national teams of Georgia, Gabon and Mali, in 2013 he took over as head coach for Senegal.

HRISTO STOICHKOV
Bulgaria, born 1966
Caps: 83 Goals: 37

As an attacking midfielder or a striker, the strong, stocky Stoichkov was surprisingly quick over a short distance and possessed unstoppable power, particularly in his left foot. He emerged as a skilful youngster at CSKA Sofia before moving to Barcelona. Unpredictable and prone to tempers, Stoichkov fell out with Barcelona manager Johan Cruyff when he was asked to play out wide. He later moved to Parma, Japanese side Kashiwa Reysol and the Chicago Fire in the MLS. He arrived at the 1994 World Cup as the star player in an underrated Bulgarian side that sensationally knocked out Germany before losing the semi-final to Italy. Stoichkov finished the tournament as joint top scorer. It was his finest hour as a player.

FACTFILE Stoichkov was banned for the 1985-86 season for his part in a riot involving players and supporters at the 1985 Bulgarian Cup final.

▲ *Stoichkov during the Euro 96 match against Romania. The midfielder's goal won the game.*

DAVID BECKHAM
England, born 1975
Caps: 115 Goals: 17

David Beckham is one of the most recognizable footballers on the planet. He began his career as a youth-team player at Manchester United, then had a loan spell with Preston North End, before announcing his arrival in English football with a Premiership goal from inside his own half against Wimbledon. At the 1998 World Cup he was heavily criticized for kicking out at Argentina's Diego Simeone and receiving a red card. But Beckham's excellence for club and country, particularly his trademark swerving free kicks, won back public support – notably when he ensured England's qualification for the 2002 World Cup with a last-gasp goal against Greece. He also won 'the treble' of Champions League, Premiership and FA Cup with Manchester United in 1999. When David Beckham joined Paris Saint-Germain, in 2013, he donated his entire salary to a local children's charity. He became the first English player to win the league in four different countries (England, Spain, the USA and France).

▶ *In 2006, David Beckham became the first English player to score in three World Cups. He resigned as captain straight after the tournament.*

ANDRÉS INIESTA
Spain, born 1984
Caps: 104 Goals: 12

Quick feet and an even quicker footballing brain has enabled this slight midfielder to become one of the most celebrated players in world football. Joining Barcelona as a youth teamer, Iniesta later formed a formidable central midfield partnership with Xavi Hernández for both club and country. With Barcelona, he has won seven Spanish league championships, four Champions Leagues and five Spanish Super Cups. Internationally, he has been a crucial part of Spain's success, and scored the winning goal in the 2010 World Cup Final.

▲ *Spanish midfield legend Xavi Hernández.*

XAVI HERNÁNDEZ
Spain, born 1980
Caps: 133 Goals: 12

Rising through the ranks of youth and reserve teams at Barcelona, Xavi made his debut for the full Barcelona side in 1998 and has now played more than 670 games for the Spanish club. He has won eight La Liga titles, four Champions Leagues and two FIFA World Cups and enjoyed Euro 2008 and 2012 and 2010 World Cup glory with Spain. Brilliant at finding space even in the most crowded parts of the pitch, Xavi is known as a passing maestro – enabling his side to keep possession and probe for attacks.

MICHEL PLATINI

France, born 1955
Caps: 72 Goals: 41

A truly great attacking midfielder, Platini was the glittering jewel in a French side that suffered semi-final heartbreak at the 1982 World Cup. Two years later, he was top scorer at the European Championships (nine goals) as France won the title. In partnership with Alan Giresse and Jean Tigana, Platini exhibited immense skill and vision. At club level, Platini played for AS Joeuf, Nancy and Saint-Étienne before turning down a transfer to Arsenal in favour of Italian giants Juventus in 1982. He was Serie A's leading marksman three times and was crowned European Footballer of the Year three times in a row (1983–85) – a unique achievement. Retiring in 1987, he went on to manage France and then led his country's bid to host the 1998 World Cup. In 2007, he became president of UEFA.

▲ *Dragan Dzajic (left) and Willie Morgan wave to the crowd after Yugoslavia's 1-1 draw with Scotland at the 1974 World Cup.*

GARRINCHA

Brazil,
1933-83
Caps: 50
Goals: 12

Manuel Francisco dos Santos was nicknamed Garrincha – meaning 'little bird' – at a young age. A small player at only 1.69m tall, a childhood illness had left his legs distorted, with one bent inwards and the other 6cm shorter. Yet those who saw Garrincha play remember him as the greatest dribbler in the history of football. He also perfected the bending banana kick, which he used to great effect for his club side, Botafogo, scoring 232 goals in 581 matches. He also played in Colombia, Italy, and in France for Red Star Paris, but it was on the international stage that Garrincha became famous. He starred in the 1958

DRAGAN DZAJIC

Yugoslavia, born 1946
Caps: 85 Goals: 23

A left-winger for his entire career, Dragan Dzajic boasted lightning-fast acceleration and an eye for a delicate pass. He made over 580 appearances for Red Star Belgrade, scoring 287 goals, winning five Yugoslav league titles and four Yugoslav Cups. Dzalic also spent two seasons in France, where he scored 31 goals for Bastia. He was part of the Yugoslav side that entered the 1964 Olympics and reached the final of the 1968 European Championships, knocking out World Cup holders England along the way. Dzajic finished the tournament as top scorer. After retiring from football in 1979, he went on to become sports director of Red Star.

▼ *England defender Ray Wilson fails to stop the mesmeric Garrincha as he surges down the wing in the 1962 World Cup quarter-final. Brazil won 3-1.*

World Cup, which Brazil won, but went on to eclipse those performances at the 1962 competition. Voted player of the tournament, he was joint leading scorer as he struck two goals to knock out England in the quarter-final, and then two more to beat Chile in the semi-final. Sadly, his life away from football was troubled, and he died of alcohol poisoning at the age of 49.

▲ *Platini skips a challenge during France's 4-1 win over Northern Ireland at the 1982 World Cup.*

CRISTIANO RONALDO
Portugal, born 1985
Caps: 120 Goals: 55

A winger who can play in central
midfield or as a striker, Cristiano
Ronaldo began playing
football on the Portuguese
island of Madeira before
joining Sporting Clube de
Portugal. After impressing
Sir Alex Ferguson in
a pre-season friendly, Ronaldo joined
Manchester United in 2003, where he
blossomed into one of the world's greatest
attackers, bewildering defenders with tricks
and pace, outstanding ball control and
masterful free kicks. He helped Portugal
to reach the final of Euro 2004, only to be
beaten by Greece. His club performances
helped to propel Manchester United to three
successive Premier League titles as well
as the Champions League crown in 2008,
the same year that he won FIFA's World
Footballer of the Year. Ronaldo left United
in July 2009, joining Real Madrid for a
world-record fee of £80 million. He wasted
no time in making an impact, scoring a
staggering 312 goals in his first 300 games
for the famous Spanish club.

FACTFILE Cristiano Ronaldo has
scored 50 or more goals a season for five
seasons in a row and has scored a record
31 hat-tricks for Real Madrid.

▲ Portugal's Cristiano Ronaldo races forwards
with the ball at his feet. After Euro 2008, he
was appointed captain of the national side.

WORLD-RECORD TRANSFERS

PLAYER	FROM	TO	FEE	YEAR
Gareth Bale (Wales)	Tottenham	Real Madrid	£85.3m	2013
Cristiano Ronaldo (Portugal)	Manchester Utd	Real Madrid	£80m	2009
Luis Suarez (Uruguay)	Liverpool	Barcelona	£65m	2014
James Rodriguez (Colombia)	AS Monaco	Real Madrid	£63m	2014
Angel di Maria (Argentina)	Real Madrid	Manchester United	£59.7m	2014
Zlatan Ibrahimovic (Sweden)	Internazionale	Barcelona	£56.9m	2009
Kaka (Brazil)	AC Milan	Real Madrid	£56.1m	2009
Edinson Cavani (Uruguay)	Napoli	Paris Saint-Germain	£55.6m	2013
Radamel Falcao (Colombia)	Atlético Madrid	Monaco	£51m	2013
Fernando Torres (Spain)	Liverpool	Chelsea	£50m	2011
David Luiz (Brazil)	Chelsea	Paris Saint-Germain	£50m	2014

ZINEDINE ZIDANE
France, born 1972
Caps: 108 Goals: 31

The son of Algerian immigrants, Zidane
grew up in Marseille with posters of his idol,
Enzo Francescoli of Uruguay, on his wall. His
first club was Cannes, followed by
Bordeaux, where he won France's
Young Player of the Year award in
1992. In his international debut in
1994, he scored both of France's
goals in a 2-2 draw with the Czech
Republic. In 1995–96, Zidane played 57
matches – more than any other French
player – and he appeared jaded as he
underperformed at Euro 96. But a move to
Juventus in the same year saw him regain his
best form, as he helped the Serie A giants
win two league titles. Zidane was
a key part of the French side that captured
a double of World Cup (1998) and European
Championships (2000). As the best midfielder
in the world, he won World Player of the Year
titles in 1998, 2000 and 2003. Zidane's last
tournament, the 2006 World Cup,
was memorable as he led France
to the final, scoring three goals on
the way and being voted FIFA's
player of the tournament. He
was sent off in the final, however,
for a headbutt to the chest of
Italy's Marco Materazzi.

ENZO SCIFO
Belgium, born 1966
Caps: 84 Goals: 18

One of only a handful of players to have
taken part in four World Cups, Vicenzo
'Enzo' Scifo (see page 87) was born to
Italian parents and became a Belgian citizen
at the age of 18. He was a footballing prodigy,
scoring a staggering 432 goals in just four
seasons as a junior. After joining Anderlecht
in 1980, his silky midfield skills helped the
club to three Belgian league titles in a row
(1985–87), while with the national side he
reached the semi-finals of the 1986 World
Cup. Scifo's moves to Internazionale and
then Bordeaux were both failures, but his
career was reignited at Auxerre. He went
on to enjoy spells in Italy, before rejoining
Anderlecht towards the end of his career.

LUIS FIGO
Portugal, born 1972
Caps: 127 Goals: 32

A darting wide midfielder, Luis Figo won the European Cup-Winners' Cup in 1997 and back-to-back Spanish league titles in 1998 and 1999 with Spanish giants Barcelona. He moved for a world-record fee to Barcelona's fiercest rivals, Real Madrid, winning two league titles and the Champions League in 2002. Figo played at three European Championships, reaching the semi-finals in 2000 and the final four years later. In 2005, he came out of international retirement to help Portugal qualify for the 2006 World Cup, where they reached the semi-final.

▲ *Hagi pushes forwards at the 1994 World Cup.*

GHEORGHE HAGI
Romania, born 1965
Caps: 125 Goals: 34

Moody, unpredictable and outstandingly skilful, Hagi played for Steaua Bucharest from 1987, either in midfield or in a free role in attack. His superb ball skills and vision helped his club to three league titles in a row, as well as to the 1989 European Cup final. Hagi then played for Real Madrid, Brescia, Barcelona and Galatasaray, with whom he won the 2000 UEFA Cup. A linchpin of the Romanian team, Hagi scored a sublime goal from 35 metres out against Colombia at the 1994 World Cup, but he was sent off in his final international match, at Euro 2000.

▲ *Boniek scored all three goals in this 3-0 victory for Poland over Belgium at the 1982 World Cup.*

ZBIGNIEW BONIEK
Poland, born 1956
Caps: 80 Goals: 24

A hard-running attacking midfielder, Boniek won two league titles with Widzew Lodz and starred when the Polish side knocked Juventus out of the 1980 UEFA Cup. He joined the Italian club two years later and formed a deadly midfield partnership with Michel Platini. At Juventus, he won Italian league and cup titles, the European Cup-Winners' Cup and the 1985 European Cup (scoring the two winning goals). A member of three World Cup squads, Boniek scored four goals in 1982 as Poland came third. After joining Roma in 1985, he operated deeper and deeper in midfield and he played as a sweeper in the 1986 World Cup.

FACTFILE Michael Laudrup is the only player to have appeared for Real Madrid in a 5-0 win over Barcelona and also for Barcelona when they have beaten Real 5-0.

▶ *Michael Laudrup challenges for the ball during Denmark's Euro 96 match with Portugal.*

SOCRATES
Brazil, 1954–2014
Caps: 60 Goals: 22

Named after the Ancient Greek scholar, Brazil's Socrates played as an amateur for Botafogo while studying to become a doctor. He turned professional with Corinthians in 1977. The tall, elegant midfielder became a firm favourite with the fans, scoring spectacular goals and threading superb passes around the pitch. He captained two hugely talented Brazilian World Cup sides in 1982 and 1986, but neither team did its talent justice.

FACTFILE
In November 2004, at the age of 50, Socrates played for English non-league side Garforth Town in the Northern Counties League.

MICHAEL LAUDRUP
Denmark, born 1964
Caps: 104 Goals: 37

The peak of Michael Laudrup's international career came in the quarter-finals of the 1998 World Cup, where Denmark lost narrowly to Brazil 3-2 – despite his younger brother, Brian, scoring a goal. Laudrup was much in demand as an attacking midfielder, playing for Lazio and Juventus in Italy and winning five league titles in Spain with Barcelona and Real Madrid. Sadly, he missed out on Denmark's finest hour – their Euro 92 championship triumph, when he argued about tactics with the coach and was dropped.

▲ *Lothar Matthäus appeared at five World Cups.*

LOTHAR MATTHÄUS
West Germany / Germany, born 1961 Caps: 150 Goals: 23

Matthäus began his career at Borussia Mönchengladbach before moving to Bayern Munich in 1984. A powerful midfielder with great stamina, Matthäus could play as a midfield anchor or be more creative, using his passing and vision to bring others into the game. He won six Bundesliga titles at Bayern Munich, plus the Serie A title with Internazionale. A veteran of five World Cups, Matthäus played a record 25 tournament games. He led West Germany to World Cup glory in 1990 and in the same year he was voted World Footballer of the Year. He retired from international football after Euro 2000.

MARIO COLUNA
**Portugal, 1935–2014
Caps: 57 Goals: 8**

Like Eusebio, Mario Coluna was born in Mozambique and played for Portugal. Coluna was often overshadowed by the great striker, but he was a superb footballer in his own right. His 17-year career with Benfica began in 1954. He captained the side in the early 1960s and appeared in five European Cup finals (1961–63, 1965 and 1968). He also led Portugal to third place in the 1966 World Cup. Coluna moved to Olympique Lyonnais towards the end of his career and later became Mozambique's minister of sport.

SUN WEN
**China, born 1973
Caps: 152 Goals: 106**

A legend in women's football, Sun Wen won seven regional championships with Chinese side Shanghai TV, before moving to the USA in 2000 to play for Atlanta Beat. Playing in midfield or attack, she has become one of the world's leading international goalscorers, thanks to her strong shooting, vision and eye for a goal. Sun Wen won both the Golden Boot (top scorer) and the Golden Ball (top player) awards at the 1999 Women's World Cup, where China were narrowly beaten on penalties in the final by the USA. In 2000, she was named FIFA World Player of the Century alongside the USA's Michelle Akers. After China's surprise World Cup exit at the hands of Canada in 2003, she retired.

▲ *Sun Wen goes past Ghana's Mavis Danso at the 2003 World Cup. China won the game 1-0, courtesy of a goal from Sun.*

JAIRZINHO
**Brazil, born 1944
Caps: 82 Goals: 34**

Jair Ventura Filho, better known as Jairzinho, was an electrifying right-winger in a similar mould to his childhood hero, Garrincha. First capped for Brazil in 1964, he was moved to the left wing to accommodate Garrincha in the 1966 World Cup. At the 1970 tournament Jairzinho was moved back to his favoured right side, where he shone, scoring in each of the six rounds of the competition – a record to this day. At club level, Jairzinho spent most of his career at Brazil's Botafogo, also having short spells with Marseille in France, Portuguesa in Venezuela and the Brazilian side Cruzeiro, with whom he won the Copa America in 1976.

◄ *Jairzinho surges forwards during the third-place play-off at the 1974 World Cup. Brazil were defeated 1-0 by Poland.*

STRIKERS

JOHAN CRUYFF
Holland, born 1947
Caps: 48 Goals: 33

Cruyff was one of the game's finest ever players and a pivotal part of the Dutch 'total football' revolution. Blessed with great vision and remarkable ball skills, he is the only player to have a move named after him – the Cruyff turn. He won three European Cups in a row at Ajax, before following his old boss, Rinus Michels, to Barcelona in 1973 and helping them to win Spanish league and cup titles. Cruyff played as a centre-forward, but would drift around the pitch, creating confusion among defenders. His total of 33 goals for Holland would have been higher were it not for his refusal to play in the 1978 World Cup (see page 112). Cruyff later managed both Ajax and Barcelona to success in Europe.

▶ *Johan Cruyff was European Footballer of the Year three times.*

PAOLO ROSSI
Italy, born 1956
Caps: 48 Goals: 20

As a teenager, Paolo Rossi was released by Juventus due to a knee injury, but he went on to star for Italy at the 1978 World Cup. Juve tried to buy him back from Vicenza, but were outbid by Perugia, who paid a world-record fee of £3.5 million. A two-year ban for alleged match-fixing ended just before the 1982 World Cup, by which time Rossi was back at Juventus. After failing to score in the first four games of the tournament, the pressure was mounting. He responded with a fine hat-trick against Brazil, followed by two goals in the semi-final and one in the final to emerge as a World Cup winner and the tournament's leading scorer. Sadly, he was overcome by injuries and he retired in 1987, aged 30.

▼ *Puskas (left) fires in a shot in the 1954 World Cup final against West Germany. His goalscoring ratio at international level – almost one goal per game – was extraordinary.*

FACTFILE In his distinguished career, Puskas won five Spanish league titles, four Hungarian league titles, an Olympic gold medal (1952) and three European Cups.

FERENC PUSKAS
Hungary, 1927–2006
Caps: 84 (4 for Spain)
Goals: 83

A star for his club, Kispest (which became Honved), and his country, Puskas was short, stocky and an average header of the ball. But his sublime skills, vision and thunderbolt of a left-foot shot made him a devastating striker. After the Hungarian revolution in 1956, Puskas searched for a club in western Europe for more than a year. In his thirties and overweight, he was eventually signed by Real Madrid in 1958. He repaid Real's faith by heading the Spanish goalscoring table four times, netting four goals in the 1960 European Cup final and a hat-trick in the 1962 final. In 1966, he began a coaching career, which saw him take Greek side Panathinaikos to the 1971 European Cup final. In 1993, an emotional Puskas was welcomed home to act as caretaker manager of the national team.

FACTFILE George Best made 466 appearances for Manchester United between 1963 and 1974, scoring 178 goals. He was a substitute only once.

GEORGE BEST
Northern Ireland, 1946–2005
Caps: 37 Goals: 9

Best was just 17 when he made his first-team debut for Manchester United. He was the most gifted player to emerge from the British Isles, and its first superstar. A free spirit both on and off the pitch, Best's goalscoring exploits and his eye for an outrageous pass or move quickly made him a legend. He was also a fearless tackler and great dribbler, and was Manchester United's leading scorer five seasons in a row. Sadly, he was denied the biggest stage of all as Northern Ireland failed to qualify for the World Cup during his playing career. In 1974, Best sensationally retired from the game. He made a series of comebacks in England, the USA and, finally, Australia, where he appeared for the Brisbane Lions in 1983.

◀ *George Best was first capped for his country, Northern Ireland, at the tender age of 17.*

LIONEL MESSI
Argentina, born 1987
Caps: 103   Goals: 46

Locals in the Argentinean city of Rosario knew they were seeing a special talent when Messi, not yet in his teens, powered his local children's football team to lose just one game in four years. Moving from Argentina to Spain at the age of 13, Messi was schooled in Barcelona's youth sides before making his official debut for the first team at the age of 17. He has already won seven Spanish league and four UEFA Champions League titles with Barcelona, as well as nine Spanish cup competitions and a 2008 Olympic gold medal with Argentina. His close control, vision and flair is almost unparalleled in the modern game. The 2009–10 season saw Messi score 47 goals, including all four goals in Barcelona's Champions League mauling of Arsenal, and the following season he upped this to a staggering 73 goals in all competitions. Messi did not let up in the 2012–13 season, scoring in 19 Spanish League games in a row against every other team in La Liga.

▶ *Lionel Messi controls the ball during the 2012–13 season, in which he scored 60 goals.*

FACTFILE Dennis Bergkamp's fear of flying has caused the striker to miss many international matches and European games for Arsenal.

DENNIS BERGKAMP
Holland, born 1969
Caps: 79   Goals: 37

Named after the Scottish striker Denis Law, Bergkamp was a product of the famous Ajax youth academy. He played in the Dutch league for the first time in 1986. The most technically gifted Dutch footballer since Johan Cruyff, Bergkamp often played in the space between midfield and attack, where he used his eye for an unexpected pass, plus world-class technique, to create as many goals as he scored. After an unsuccessful spell at Internazionale, Bergkamp moved to Arsenal for £7.5 million in 1995. In his 11 years at the club, he won three Premier League titles and scored or set up more than 280 goals. He retired in May 2006 after the final of the Champions League against Barcelona.

▲ *Dennis Bergkamp brings the ball down moments before his sublime goal against Argentina at the 1998 World Cup.*

MATCH ACTION

Dennis Bergkamp broke the deadlock in a tense 1998 World Cup quarter-final against Argentina with a sensational goal. On the stroke of 90 minutes, Frank de Boer hit a 50-metre pass into the penalty area. Controlling the ball with one delicate touch of his right boot, Bergkamp took a second touch to turn Argentinian defender Roberto Ayala, before shooting powerfully past keeper Carlos Roa. The goal saw Bergkamp become Holland's leading international scorer.

Roa

Ayala 2

Bergkamp 1   Bergkamp 2

Ayala 1

JUST FONTAINE
France, born 1933
Caps: 21 Goals: 30

Fontaine was born and brought up in Morocco before coming to France in 1953 to play for Nice. A relatively slight centre-forward with a real eye for goal, he scored 45 times in three seasons at Nice before moving to Stade de Reims, where he bagged 116 goals in just four years. Yet, going into the 1958 World Cup finals, Fontaine was third-choice striker behind Raymond Kopa and René Bliard. An injury to Bliard allowed Fontaine to start the first game, against Paraguay, in which he scored a hat-trick. He followed this up with a further ten goals in five games. His record of 13 goals at a single World Cup is unlikely to be beaten. In 1962, Fontaine retired after suffering the second double fracture of his right leg. The following year, he became the first president of the French footballers' union.

ROBERTO BAGGIO
Italy, born 1967
Caps: 57 Goals: 27

Blessed with great skill and vision, Roberto Baggio made his professional debut with Vicenza, in the Italian third division, at just 15 years of age. He broke into Italy's Serie A with Fiorentina in 1985, and when Baggio was transferred to Juventus in 1990 three days of rioting by Fiorentina fans ensued. The fee of £7.7 million made him the world's most expensive player at that time. Crowned World Footballer of the Year in 1993, Baggio scored spectacular goals for his country and his clubs, AC Milan, Bologna, Inter Milan and Brescia. In 2004, while playing for Brescia, he scored his 200th Serie A goal. He appeared in three World Cups and scored five out of Italy's eight goals in the 1994 competition. However, Baggio will always be remembered for his costly penalty miss in the final of the tournament (see page 32). The striker was given an emotional send-off in 2004 when he played for Italy for the first time in five years, in a friendly against Spain.

RAÚL
Spain, born 1977
Caps: 102 Goals: 44

Raúl González Blanco made his debut for the Real Madrid first team at 17 – their youngest ever player – and went on to score six times in his first 11 games. In the years that followed, Raúl became the biggest star in Spanish football and the country's all-time leading goalscorer. At club level, he has won two Spanish league championships and three Champions League titles with Real Madrid. Top scorer in the Spanish league twice, Raúl's goals in the 2003–04 Champions League campaign saw him become the first player to net more than 40 times in the competition.

GERD MÜLLER
West Germany, born 1945
Caps: 62 Goals: 68

The Bomber, as Gerd Müller was nicknamed, holds a series of goalscoring records. From 1963, he scored a club record 365 goals in 427 league matches for Bayern Munich. During 16 years with Bayern, he won four Bundesliga titles, four German Cups and three European Cups. For his country, Müller held one of the greatest international striking records, scoring more than a goal every game. His two strikes against the Soviet Union helped West Germany win the 1972 European Championships. Müller's tally of 14 World Cup goals remained a record until 2006, while his final international goal won West Germany the 1974 World Cup on home soil.

▲ Spain's Raúl was the top scorer during the qualifying rounds for Euro 2000, with ten goals from eight games. Here, he chases down the ball during Euro 2004.

▼ Gerd Müller shoots during West Germany's win over Morocco in the 1970 World Cup.

ZICO
Brazil, born 1953
Caps: 72 Goals: 52

The youngest and smallest of three football-mad brothers, Artur Antunes Coimbra (known as Zico) was given a special diet and training regime to build him up when he first arrived at the Brazilian club Flamengo. Sharp, quick-witted and with the ability to hit an explosive shot or take a deadly, curling free kick, Zico won four Brazilian league titles with Flamengo, as well as the Copa Libertadores and the World Club Cup (both in 1981). He scored a staggering 591 goals in his first 11 seasons with Flamengo and returned to the club in 1985 after a spell at the Italian Serie A side Udinese. Zico retired from international football after the 1986 World Cup finals, but went on to play in Japan for Kashima Antlers. In 2002, he became manager of the Japanese national team.

BOBBY CHARLTON
England, born 1937
Caps: 106 Goals: 49

Apart from a final season with Preston
North End, Charlton was a one-club player
with Manchester United, for whom he
made his debut in 1956. Known around
the globe for his trophy-winning exploits
in both the World Cup and the European
Cup, Charlton was one of the few survivors
of the devastating Munich air crash, which
claimed the lives of many of his Manchester
United team-mates. As a player he showed
great sportsmanship and dedication – in
training, he even wore a slipper on his right
foot to encourage him to pass and shoot
with his weaker left foot. Operating as a
deep-lying centre-forward with a phenomenal
shot from either foot, Charlton remains the
record goalscorer for both England and
Manchester United, scoring 245 times
and making 751 appearances in total
for the club. He was knighted in 1994.

▼ *Bobby Charlton's 1970
World Cup campaign was
his fourth in a row as part
of the England squad.*

◄ *Roger Milla
challenges for the ball
during Cameroon's
second-round victory
over Colombia at the
1990 World Cup.*

FACTFILE In 1990,
Andriy Shevchenko played
for the Kiev under-14 team
in a youth tournament in
Wales. Welsh striker Ian
Rush was so impressed, he
gave the young Ukrainian his
football boots.

ROGER MILLA
Cameroon, born c.1952
Caps: 81 Goals: 42

Roger Milla's celebratory corner-flag
dance remains the most memorable image
of the 1990 World Cup, as his four goals
helped Cameroon to become the first
African side to reach the quarter-finals. In the
same year, the veteran striker was voted the
African Footballer of the Year. He had won
the award before, way back in 1976, the
year he moved from Cameroon's Tonnerre
Yaoundé to play for Valenciennes in France.
Milla went on to play for Monaco, Bastia and
Saint-Etienne, and won the African Nations
Cup twice with Cameroon (1984 and 1988).
At the age of 42, he came out of retirement
for the 1994 World Cup to become the oldest
ever player and scorer in the competition.

ANDRIY SHEVCHENKO
Ukraine, born 1976
Caps: 111 Goals: 48

Shevchenko scored just one goal in 16 games
in his first season at Dynamo Kiev, but his
perfect blend of pace and power propelled
Kiev to five Ukrainian league titles and strong
showings in the Champions League. A multi-
million-pound transfer to AC Milan followed
in 1999. On three occasions Shevchenko
scored 24 goals per season in the ultra-
tough Italian league. In 2004, Shevchenko
was voted European Footballer of the Year.
Two years later he moved to Chelsea for
more than £30 million, but returned to Milan
on loan for the 2008–09 season. He then
returned to Kiev, where he made more than
80 appearances before retiring in 2012.

▲ *Andriy Shevchenko shoots for Ukraine against
England during a friendly international in 2000.*

CAROLINA MORACE
Italy, born 1964
Caps: 153 Goals: 105

Italy's finest female player, Morace made
her international and Women's Serie A
debut at the age of just 14. She went on to
win 12 league titles with eight different clubs,
and scored more than 500 goals. A lethal
finisher, Morace was twice a runner-up with
Italy in the European Championships. After
retiring in 1999, she became the first female
coach of an Italian men's professional team,
Viterbese in Serie C. She later became
coach of the Italian women's national side.

▲ *Ruud Gullit shoots against England at Euro 88.*

RUUD GULLIT
Holland, born 1962
Caps: 66 Goals: 17

In 1978, the dreadlocked Gullit started out as a sweeper for Dutch side Haarlem. He possessed great attacking flair, stamina, a tough tackle and a sweet pass. He was the subject of feverish transfer activity, moving to Feyenoord, PSV Eindhoven and AC Milan, with whom he won European Cups in 1989 and 1990. After a season at Sampdoria he moved to Chelsea, and in 1996 he was appointed player-manager of the London club. By winning the 1997 FA Cup he became the first non-British manager to lift a major domestic trophy in England.

KENNY DALGLISH
Scotland, born 1951
Caps: 102 Goals: 30

The only player to have scored over 100 goals for both English and Scottish top-division clubs, Dalglish gave defenders nightmares. He became a legend at Celtic – where he won four league titles and four Scottish Cups – thanks to a quicksilver turn and an icy coolness in front of goal. In 1977, Liverpool signed Dalglish as a replacement for Kevin Keegan. He became Liverpool's player-manager in 1985, winning three league titles. He won a fourth in 1995 with Blackburn Rovers to become one of the few managers to win the English league with different clubs.

DIEGO MARADONA
Argentina, born 1960
Caps: 91 Goals: 34

Diego Armando Maradona was a phenomenal footballer. Stocky and with a low centre of gravity, he conjured mesmeric, weaving runs through the tightest defences, lightning turns that left opposition players kicking at thin air and sublime shots, chips and flicks. Maradona debuted aged 15 for Argentinos Juniors. Calls for his inclusion in the 1978 World Cup squad were ignored by Argentina's coach, Cesar Luis Menotti, but he would appear at the next four tournaments. His finest hour came in 1986, when Maradona was the player of the tournament as he skippered an unremarkable side to World Cup victory (see pages 56–57). Maradona captained Argentina at the 1990 World Cup, where he reached the final, but the following year he failed a drugs test and was banned for 15 months. A further failed test during the 1994 World Cup saw him sent home after playing the first two games. His international career was over. Since then Maradona has battled with drug addiction, but in 2000 he was the joint winner of FIFA's Footballer of the Century award with Pelé.

FACTFILE Diego Maradona's moves to Barcelona in 1982 (for £4.2 million) and then to Napoli in 1984 (for £6.9 million) were both world-record transfers. After nine years at Napoli and a spell at Sevilla, he returned to Argentina with Newell's Old Boys and Boca Juniors.

▼ *The magical Maradona brings the ball under control at the 1986 World Cup.*

ALFREDO DI STEFANO
Spain, 1926-2014
Caps: 31 Goals: 23

To many people, di Stefano was the complete player, years ahead of his time. His astonishing energy helped him play all over the pitch – defending, tackling, unselfishly distributing the ball and creating chances for others as well as for himself. Born in a poor suburb of Buenos Aires, he played for his father's old club, River Plate, in a relentless forward line known as *La Maquina* (the Machine). A move to Europe in 1953 saw him become part of the legendary Real Madrid side that dominated Europe in the 1950s and early 1960s. Di Stefano formed a deadly partnership with Ferenc Puskas, scoring in five European Cup finals in a row. Real Madrid player and coach Miguel Munoz explained: 'The greatness of di Stefano was that with him in your side, you had two players in every position.'

▲ *As well as appearing for Real Madrid (pictured) and Spain, di Stefano also played seven unofficial games for Argentina and four for Colombia.*

JÜRGEN KLINSMANN
**West Germany / Germany,
born 1964 Caps: 108 Goals: 47**

Sharp and athletic around the penalty area and an outstanding goal poacher, Klinsmann was German Footballer of the Year in his first spell at VfB Stuttgart. He then moved to Internazionale, where he won the 1989 Serie A title. He was part of West Germany's 1990 World Cup-winning side, scored five goals in the 1994 competition and captained the team at the 1998 tournament. Klinsmann enjoyed spells with Monaco and, in 1994, the first of two stints with Tottenham Hotspur. The British media and some supporters were suspicious of a player who had a reputation for diving to win free kicks and penalties. But in his first Premiership season, Klinsmann's performances and 29 goals won the support of many fans, and in 1995 he was voted England's Footballer of the Year. The striker moved to Bayern Munich, Sampdoria and Tottenham once more, before retiring in 1998. In 2004, he was appointed Germany's manager and coached an exciting side to third place at the 2006 World Cup.

▲ Jürgen Klinsmann surges forwards with the ball during Germany's Euro 96 qualifying campaign.

EUSEBIO
**Portugal, 1942–2014
Caps: 64 Goals: 41**

Eusebio da Silva Ferreira was the first African footballing superstar. Lethal in the air and equipped with a power-packed right-foot shot, he scored an incredible 727 goals in 715 professional games. Eusebio played his early football for Sporting Lourenço Marques in his home country of Mozambique – a Portuguese colony at the time. The striker was at the centre of one of the fiercest transfer disputes when he arrived in Portugal. He was virtually kidnapped by Benfica to keep him away from rivals Sporting Lisbon. Benfica's £7,500 purchase proved to be one of the buys of the century. Over a 15-year career with Benfica, Eusebio scored at an awe-inspiring ratio of more than a goal a game. He was the Portuguese league's top goalscorer seven times, twice the leading goalscorer in the whole of Europe and the 1966 World Cup's top scorer, with nine goals for Portugal.

LUIGI RIVA
**Italy, born 1944
Caps: 42 Goals: 35**

Luigi Riva started his career with Italy's Legnano, before moving in 1963 to second-division side Cagliari, where he spent the rest of his career. He helped the Sardinian team gain promotion to Serie A and then to win the 1970 league title. Riva was Serie A's leading scorer three times (1967, 1969 and 1970). He was part of the Italian side that won Euro 68 and was the national team's leading goalscorer at the 1970 World Cup. Riva then suffered a broken leg that kept him out of action for six months, but he returned in 1971 to score his 170th league goal. Two years later, he turned down what would have been the world's biggest transfer – for £1.5 million to Juventus. After playing in the 1974 World Cup, Riva announced his retirement.

FACTFILE Luigi Riva had such a fearsome shot that he once broke the arm of a spectator.

▲ Benfica's Eusebio (right) competes for the ball with Cesare Maldini of AC Milan during the 1963 European Cup final.

GEORGE WEAH
**Liberia, born 1966
Caps: 61 Goals: 22**

In 1988, the Monaco manager Arsène Wenger (now at Arsenal), shrewdly plucked the young, raw Weah from Cameroon side Tonnerre Yaoundé. Weah exploded onto the European scene, winning the French league with Monaco in 1991 and Paris Saint Germain in 1994, before moving to AC Milan. A truly devastating finisher, Weah scored many spectacular goals to help AC Milan win two Serie A titles. He was voted African Footballer of the Year four times, and also won European and World Player of the Year awards in 1995 and FIFA's Fair Play Award the following year. He had short spells at Chelsea, Manchester City and in the United Arab Emirates late in his career, before retiring in 2002. A UNICEF ambassador since 1997, Weah has invested much time and money helping to build schools and clinics in his war-torn home country, Liberia.

FACTFILE In 1996, George Weah paid for his team-mates' kit and expenses so that Liberia could enter the African Nations Cup.

RONALDO
Brazil, born 1976
Caps: 98 Goals: 62

Ronaldo Luis Nazario de Lima became hot property as an 18-year-old by scoring 58 goals in just 60 games for Brazil's Cruzeiro. Ronaldo moved to PSV Eindhoven and then Barcelona, where his close control and devastating bursts of pace helped him become Europe's top scorer in 1996–97, with 34 goals. Sold to Internazionale, he was their top scorer in his first season. He then endured four injury-ravaged years. After a poor World Cup final in 1998, many doubted his ability, but he bounced back in 2002 as the tournament's top scorer. A month later, Real Madrid paid £28.49 million for the Brazilian, and in 2006 Ronaldo became the highest scorer in World Cup history, with 15 goals. In 2007, he moved to Italian giants AC Milan, and in 2009 to Brazilian team Corinthians.

FACTFILE
Ronaldo's ex-wife, Milene Domingues, broke the world record for keeping a football off the ground in 1995. She kept the ball in the air for nine hours and six minutes, making 55,187 touches in the process.

▼ Ronaldo shows his pace against Italy. In 2002, he won his third FIFA World Player of the Year award.

MIA HAMM
USA,
born 1972
Caps: 276
Goals: 158

Born with a partial club foot that had to be corrected by plaster casts, Mia Hamm went on to become the world's most famous female footballer. She was the youngest ever player for the US women's team when she debuted against China at the age of 15, and the youngest member of the US side that won the 1991 World Cup. Hamm played in three more World Cups, as well as winning two Olympic gold medals and one silver. A phenomenal all-round player with an icy-cool finish, she was the leading scorer in the history of women's international football for a decade. Hamm was also a founding member of WUSA, playing for Washington Freedom when the league began in 2001.

HENRIK LARSSON
Sweden, born 1971
Caps: 104 Goals: 37

A goalscoring predator, Larsson played in Sweden before being signed by Feyenoord manager Wim Jansen in 1993. Four years later Jansen, by then the manager of Celtic, signed him again. Larsson became the Scottish Premier League's most feared striker, with 28 or more goals in five of his seven seasons. He retired from internationals in 2002, but changed his mind to help Sweden qualify for Euro 2004. Larsson then moved to Barcelona. In his final match for the Spanish side, the 2006 Champions League final, he came on as a substitute to play a key role in Barcelona's win. The striker returned to his former side, Helsingborg, before moving to Manchester United on loan in 2007.

◄ The legendary Mia Hamm playing for the USA at the Women's Gold Cup in 2002. In the final against Canada, her golden goal in extra time secured the trophy.

MARTA VIEIRA DA SILVA
Brazil, born 1986
Caps: 95 Goals: 92

Short for a striker, at under 1.6m tall, Marta is a goal-scoring dynamo who was voted the world's best female player five years in a row (2006–10). She played her early football for several Brazilian clubs before two spells in Sweden, either side of three seasons in the USA, where she won the Women's Professional Soccer (WPS) championship twice with two different clubs – FC Gold Pride and Western New York Flash. A truly prolific finisher, who averages more than a goal per game in club football, Marta has also won four Swedish league titles with Umeå IK, one with Tyresö FF and the 2014 title with FC Rosengård.

◄ Barcelona's Henrik Larsson battles for the ball in a friendly against Japan's Kashima Antlers.

PELÉ
Brazil, born 1940
Caps: 92 Goals: 77

Edson Arantes do Nascimento simply had it all. Considered the finest footballer of all time, Pelé was a masterful attacker with seemingly limitless skills, creativity and vision. He was magnificent in the air, lethal on the ground, could dribble, pass and take swerving free kicks, and saw passes and opportunities that other players could not. His father had been a striker for Fluminense, and at 11 years of age Pelé was spotted by a former Brazil player, Waldemar de Brito, who took him to Clube Atletico Bauru. Four years later, Pelé trialled at Santos, for whom he made his debut aged 15. He would play for the São Paulo side for the next 18 years. Pelé was only 17 when he appeared at the 1958 World Cup, scoring a hat-trick in the semi-final and two superb goals in the final as Brazil won their first World Cup. A pulled muscle cut short Pelé's involvement in the 1962 competition and he had to be content with winning the World Club Cup for Santos. Injured by brutal tackling in the 1966 World Cup, Pelé was outstanding at the 1970 tournament. He retired from international football in 1971 – in front of around 180,000 fans at the Maracana Stadium – and from

club football in 1974. In tribute, Santos removed the number ten shirt from their team line-up.

Pelé later came out of retirement to play in a star-studded line-up at New York Cosmos. He went on to become Brazil's minister of sport and a UN and UNICEF ambassador. He remains one of the most respected figures in world football and, in 1999, he was voted Athlete of the Century by the International Olympic Committee.

▶ *Pelé battles for the ball with an Italian defender at the 1970 World Cup.*

FACTFILE Pelé's father once scored five headed goals in one game, a feat Pelé never managed. However, his header in the 1970 World Cup final was Brazil's 100th World Cup goal.

MATCH ACTION

Against Uruguay in the 1970 World Cup semi-final, Pelé came close to scoring what would have been one of the greatest goals ever seen. A through pass from Gerson saw Pelé and the Uruguayan keeper, Ladislao Mazurkiewicz, racing for the ball just outside the penalty area. Pelé made an outrageous dummy to the left, letting the ball run to the other side of the bewildered keeper. The striker sprinted to collect the ball and hit a first-time shot from a tight angle. The ball sped past Uruguayan defender Atilio Ancheta, only to flash mere centimetres wide of the left post.

▲ *Germany's Birgit Prinz is challenged by Norway's Anneli Giske during the UEFA Women's Euro 2009.*

BIRGIT PRINZ
Germany, born 1977
Caps: 214 Goals: 128

Apart from a spell in the United States in 2002, where her 12 goals in 15 games helped Carolina Courage to win the WUSA championship, Prinz played all her club football for FFC Frankfurt. Here, she won six German league titles, eight German cups and scored over 250 goals (at a rate better than a goal a game). With Germany, she won two World Cups (2003, 2007), five European Championships and three Olympic bronze medals – a staggering haul. She was also awarded the FIFA World Women's Footballer of the Year on three occasions and finished second a further four times, the last in 2010, a year before she announced her retirement.

Pelé 2

Ancheta

Mazurkiewicz

Pelé 1

GABRIEL BATISTUTA
Argentina, born 1969
Caps: 77 Goals: 56

Batistuta played one season for each of his home country's three biggest clubs – Newell's Old Boys, River Plate and Boca Juniors – before moving to Italy in 1991, the year of his international debut. In nine seasons and 269 games at Fiorentina, the striker was rarely off-form, netting 168 goals. He even stayed with the club after relegation, helping them win promotion back into Serie A. In 2000, he joined Roma for the huge fee of £22 million. There Batistuta finally won the Serie A title in 2001. A winner of two Copa Americas, Batistuta scored five goals at the 1998 World Cup as Argentina made the quarter-finals. The 2003–04 season saw him make a lucrative move to Qatar, where he played for Al-Arabi.

MARCO VAN BASTEN
Holland, born 1964
Caps: 58 Goals: 24

One of the coolest finishers in world football van Basten was just 29 when an ankle injury in the 1993 European Cup final effectively ended his playing career – although he struggled on until 1995. Renowned for spectacular goals in crucial contests, van Basten was European Footballer of the Year three times (1988, 1989 and 1992) and in 1988 he hit the headlines as Holland won the European Championships. He scored a hat-trick against England in the quarter-final, the semi-final winner versus Germany and a breathtaking volley from the tightest of angles in the final against the Soviet Union. With Ajax he won three league titles, scoring 128 goals. He then moved to AC Milan, hitting 90 goals in 147 games and winning three Serie A titles and two European Cups.

▶ *Marco van Basten on the rampage in Holland's 3-1 win over England at Euro 88.*

LEADING INTERNATIONAL GOALSCORERS (TO JUNE 2015)

PLAYER	COUNTRY	CAPS	GOALS
Ali Daei	Iran	149	109
Ferenc Puskas	Hungary	84	83
Pelé	Brazil	92	77
Godfrey Chitalu	Zambia	108	76
Bashar Abdullah	Kuwait	134	75
Sandor Kocsis	Hungary	68	75
Majed Abdullah	Saudi Arabia	139	71
Miroslav Klose	Germany	113	71
Stern John	Trinidad & Tobago	115	70
Kiatisuk Senamuang	Thailand	130	70
Hossam Hassan	Egypt	170	69
Gerd Müller	West Germany	62	68

▲ *Argentina's all-time top scorer, Batistuta began the 1994–95 season by netting in each of Fiorentina's first 11 games, a Serie A record.*

HUGO SANCHEZ
Mexico, born 1958
Caps: 57 Goals: 26

Mexico's most famous player, Sanchez spent the peak of his playing career in Spain, scoring over 230 goals for Atlético Madrid and Real Madrid. He formed a lethal partnership with Emilio Butragueno at Real as they won five league titles in a row. Sanchez was La Liga's top scorer in five different seasons and in 1990 he won the European Golden Boot for a record 38 goals in one season. Sadly, his commitments to European football and frequent bust-ups with Mexican football officials meant that he appeared in only a fraction of the international games played by his home country. He had a disappointing tournament at the 1986 World Cup on home soil, scoring just one goal.

> **FACTFILE** Playing for Manchester City in 1974, Denis Law scored a cheeky backheeled goal but did not celebrate – because the goal relegated his former club, Manchester United.

▲ *Denis Law unleashes a shot during a 1974 World Cup game against Zaire.*

DENIS LAW
Scotland, born 1940
Caps: 55 Goals: 30

In 1962, Manchester United paid £115,000 – a world record at the time – to bring the former Huddersfield Town, Manchester City and Torino striker Denis Law to Old Trafford. The money was well spent, as the quick-witted Scot formed a magnificent forward line with Bobby Charlton and George Best, scoring 160 goals in 222 games for the club. Fast over the ground and brave in the air, Law won the 1964 European Footballer of the Year award, as well as league titles and the European Cup with Manchester United, before moving to Manchester City and then retiring in 1974.

SNAPSHOT
MARADONA'S WORLD CUP

Diego Maradona, the Argentinian striker with magical balance and touch, ended the 1986 World Cup with his hands on the trophy and a highly impressive five goals and five assists. Yet these statistics do not tell the story of his true impact, for Mexico 86 was Maradona's tournament. He roused a relatively ordinary Argentinian side into recapturing football's biggest prize (the South Americans had won the trophy on home soil in 1978) and wiped out the memory of a disappointing tournament in 1982.

In a tense quarter-final against England, controversy raged over Maradona's infamous 'Hand of God' goal (see right), but his second and winning goal was pure genius. The Argentinian collected the ball in his own half, then dribbled, twisted and turned through the English defence to score what was later voted the goal of the century. He would score a goal of similar brilliance in the semi-final versus Belgium. At this point, at the age of just 25, Maradona was without doubt the greatest footballer on the planet.

Diego Maradona, clutching the World Cup after his team's epic 3-2 victory over West Germany in the 1986 final, is carried around the Azteca Stadium on the shoulders of ecstatic Argentinian supporters.

▶ Maradona uses his hand to get the ball past England goalkeeper Peter Shilton to score Argentina's first goal in a 2-1 victory.

THE BRAIN GAME

Football is a sport that calls for pace, power, stamina and skill, but it also demands mental agility. Footballers with the ability to think one step ahead of the opposition are highly prized, and such skills can win a match for their team. The same applies to managers and coaches. In the run-up to a match, they have several key decisions to make. They must decide who to select, which formation to play, and choose the tactics they will use in their bid to outwit the opposition.

TEAM SELECTION

To a casual spectator, team selection appears simple – just pick the team's best 11 footballers and tell them to play. With large squads of players, the truth is far more complex. Teams need flair, skill, composure, aggression, sound defensive skills and goalscoring abilities – all in the right quantities. Some players, despite being footballing superstars, may not play well with each other or work with the rest of the team, while other, less heralded players may actually perform a more effective job in a particular game. The way the opposition plays can dictate which players are selected, as can the fitness and performances of individuals. Star players, who would normally be first on the team sheet, may not be picked if they are recovering from injury or suffering from a lack of confidence or form. Both young, talented players emerging from the reserve team and experienced veterans at the end of their careers will have strong cases for a place in the side. It all adds up

▲ In the past, club squads were much smaller. In 1983–84, Liverpool's league- and European Cup-winning team (above) played 66 games with a squad of just 16. Bruce Grobbelaar, Alan Kennedy, Sammy Lee and Alan Hansen played in every game.

▼ West Germany manager Josef 'Sepp' Herberger (right) is chaired off the field as his team wins the 1954 World Cup. Early in the competition, he sent out a weakened side that lost to favourites Hungary. Having already beaten Turkey, Herberger's gamble meant that his side got an easier draw, meeting Turkey again in a play-off that the Germans won 7-2.

to a complex puzzle that managers must solve. As the legendary Ajax and Holland coach Rinus Michels said, 'It is an art in itself to compose a starting team, finding the balance between creative players and those with destructive powers, and between defence, construction and attack – never forgetting the quality of the opposition and the specific pressures of each match.'

PICKING AND PLAYING

Picking the right players for the game ahead can be a tricky task. Managers are often criticized by fans for dropping a favourite player or not playing them in their favoured position. But they have to hold their nerve and go with what they feel is their best team for a particular match. Cesar Luis Menotti was criticized by the Argentinian public and media for refusing to include the teenage prodigy Maradona in his 1978 World Cup squad, fielding veteran striker Mario Kempes instead. But Menotti proved himself to be a strong-willed and clever coach, who surprised opponents with an exciting, attacking approach, and his team went on to beat Holland in the final.

With large squads, coaches at the top sides often rotate and rest key players. In games against supposedly weaker opposition, they might field an understrength side. While resting your best players and giving youngsters first-team experience can bring benefits, it is a risky tactic. Chelsea manager Rafael Benitez discovered this in 2013, when his understrength side was surprisingly beaten in the Premier League by bottom club Queens Park Rangers.

FACTFILE FIFA changed its rules on substitutions in international friendlies in 2004, limiting a side to six subs. The move was prompted, in part, by the mass substitutions of England coach Sven-Goran Eriksson. In 2003, he made 11 substitutions during a game that Australia won 3-1.

SUBSTITUTIONS

Although they were allowed in some friendly matches, substitutes were not a feature of competitive games until the 1960s. Before this time, the lack of subs resulted in all sorts of heroics, from outfield players going in goal to footballers playing on in spite of a serious injury. One of the most famous examples is that of Manchester City's German goalkeeper

Bert Trautmann, who continued playing in the 1956 FA Cup final even though he had broken his neck. Today's managers have the chance to alter their team selection and tactics by making up to three substitutions in most competitions (more in friendly games). The timing and choice of substitutes can be crucial. They can bolster a winning side's momentum, help a defence to hold on to a lead or turn a losing team's fortunes around. In the 2006 World Cup, for example, Australia were losing 1-0 to Japan. Coach Guus Hiddink brought on two substitutes, Tim Cahill and John Aloisi, who scored three goals between them in the last six minutes of the game to secure a 3-1 victory.

◄ *Substitutes can make an immediate impact in some games. Kamil Kopunek celebrates after coming on as substitute and scoring with his very first touch for Slovakia, in their shock win over Italy at the 2010 World Cup.*

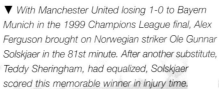

▼ *With Manchester United losing 1-0 to Bayern Munich in the 1999 Champions League final, Alex Ferguson brought on Norwegian striker Ole Gunnar Solskjaer in the 81st minute. After another substitute, Teddy Sheringham, had equalized, Solskjaer scored this memorable winner in injury time.*

▲ *After leading South Korea to the semi-finals of the 2002 World Cup, Dutchman Guus Hiddink – a firm believer in attacking tactics – was made an honorary citizen of South Korea.*

FORMATIONS

The way in which a team lines up on the pitch is known as its formation. The first football international, in 1872, saw two sides field heavily attacking formations. Scotland began playing in a 2-2-6 formation, with two backs, two half-backs (similar to midfielders) and six attackers. England went even further, playing 1-1-8 (eight forwards), but crowded goalmouths saw the game end 0-0.

EVOLVING TACTICS

Although England's eight forwards quickly became a thing of the past, attacker-heavy formations such as 2-3-5 persisted for over half a century. A change to the offside law in 1925 (see page 19) reduced the number of players needed between an attacker and the goal from three to two. It gave attackers more scoring chances and forced a rapid rethink for managers. None was quicker than Arsenal's Herbert Chapman, who, two days after a 7-0 loss to Newcastle, debuted his W-M formation (so named for the shapes the two groups of five players made). The change resulted in a 4-0 win over West Ham. The W-M formation was effectively

3-2-2-3 and was adopted by many sides. Other teams played the *metodo* formation, devised by World Cup-winning Italian coach Vittorio Pozzo. It was also based on 2-3-5, but was effectively 2-3-2-3, with two of the forwards pulled back to link between midfield and attack and to defend against breaks by the opposition.

FOUR AT THE BACK

The arrival of four defenders at the back sounds like a negative formation, but it was first unveiled by the marvellous attacking Brazil side that won the 1958 World Cup. The Brazilian formation was actually 4-2-4, with two wingers up front feeding two central strikers. By the next World Cup, Brazil and many other sides were opting for a slightly less attacking 4-3-3 with an extra player to stop the midfield from being overrun. This formation can work with a single winger who switches flanks at will or with two genuine wingers feeding a single striker. England won the 1966 World Cup playing 4-4-2 with no out-and-out wingers, but they had midfielders with the energy and stamina to add width to an attack, as well as tucking in

◀ Playing as a wing-back, Germany's Philipp Lahm holds off Portugal's Cristiano Ronaldo. Wing-backs play on the flanks. They act like full-backs in defence, but also make attacking runs upfield.

to defend when necessary. This formation is still widely used today. Ahead of the four-man defence, a coach has plenty of options. He may opt for three attackers upfront (4-3-3) or split strikers (4-4-1-1) or no strikers at all. At the final of Euro 2012, Spain did away with out-and-out strikers, starting the game with three attacking midfielders – David Silva, Cesc Fabregas and Andrés Iniesta – instead of a regular centre-forward. They beat Italy convincingly, 4-0.

◀ Josep Guardiola directs one of his Barcelona players from the touchline. In 2013, he became head coach at Bayern Munich.

▲ The Serbia and Montenegro international Sinisa Mihajlovic (left) enjoyed six glorious seasons at Lazio as a powerful sweeper, strong in defence but with an eye for goal, especially from set pieces.

SWEEPING UP

At many clubs around the world, and in Italian football especially, a different system is used at the back, with a sweeper (also known as a 'libero' or 'free man') in the centre of defence. Sweepers tend to play behind the main line of defenders, literally sweeping up loose balls and acting as a last line of defence if an opposition attack breaks through. In some formations, a sweeper can be ultra-negative. This was seen as the case with the *catenaccio* system, invented by Padova coach Nereo Rocco in the early 1950s and popularized by Helenio Herrera's Internazionale side of the 1960s. Effectively

▲ Celebrated coach José Mourinho has won league titles in four countries: Portugal, Italy, England and Spain. He has won three times with Chelsea, the latest being in 2014–15.

a 1-4-3-2 or 1-4-4-1 system, *catenaccio* aimed to stifle attacks with large numbers of defenders, relying on counter attacks by a few forwards. Italy has produced a long line of world-class sweepers including Giovanni Facchetti, Gaetano Scirea and Franco Baresi. But it took a German, Franz Beckenbauer, to show a different side to

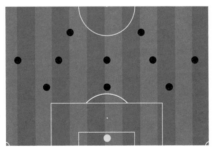

▲ A team often alters its formation after a sending-off. This side has lost its left midfielder (shown by the red arrow) and switches from a 3-2-3-2 system with wing-backs to a 4-3-1-1 formation with a flat back four, three in midfield and split strikers up front.

the sweeper's art. Beckenbauer linked play going forward and would often surge ahead of his defence, creating an extra player in

FACTFILE Ronald Koeman is one of the highest-scoring defenders of all time. Playing mostly as a sweeper, he enjoyed great success with AC Milan, Barcelona and Holland, scoring an incredible 193 goals in 533 games.

attack and opening up the game.

Today, the sweeper is often replaced by one or more deep-sitting midfielders, one of whom can drop back into defence if a defender pushes forwards. These 'anchor' or defensive midfielders – such as Spain's Sergio Busquets or Serbia's Nemanja Matic – are highly prized.

TOTAL FOOTBALL

'Total football' was never quite formation-free football, but it did involve players switching positions and roles within the team with amazing frequency. Under Rinus Michels, defenders would crop up in attack, strikers in midfield and midfielders just about everywhere. It proved a hard system to defend against, but few sides could boast the quality of player to make it work, as it relied on excellent ball skills and very high energy levels. Today, players switch positions with remarkable ease and regularity, so much so that one might wonder why total football caused such a stir. Formations in the past were more rigid, however, with full-backs staying in their half and strikers staying upfield throughout the game. While this gave a team a shape and structure, it could also make it easier for opponents to mark dangerous players and defend.

FORMATIONS

A formation is the way in which a team lines up for a match. This is usually shown in terms of the numbers of outfield players from the defence forwards. In reality, football is a dynamic game and players move around the pitch. Sometimes, they are drawn out of position by an opposition attack. At other times, players choose to move out of position. For example, a central striker may drift out wide or drop back to find space.

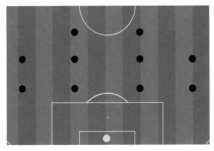

3-2-2-3 formation

3-5-2 formation

4-4-2 formation

4-4-1-1 formation

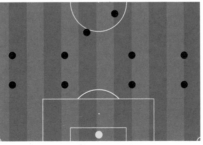

TACTICS

Teams may kick off a game in one of several common formations, but there can be great variation in how they play within that formation and in the tactics they use. For example, a team that lines up as a 4-4-2 side may choose to play defensively, with midfielders tucking in, or aggressively, with one or more midfielders joining the strikers in attack.

TAILORING TACTICS

Managers start a game with what they feel are the best tactics for the players available and the opposition they face. They watch how a match unfolds closely, knowing they can change tactics at any time to exploit an opponent's weakness or to fix problems in their own team's play. Most top footballers can play in several positions. A manager may switch formations using the same players or bring on a substitute with different attributes and skills. In the 2014 World Cup, Netherlands coach Louis van Gaal brought on substitute goalkeeper Tim Krul purely for the penalty shootout with Costa Rica. Krul saved two penalties as the Netherlands won. A year later, at the 2015 Women's World Cup semi-final versus Germany, US coach Jill Ellis changed her usual 4-2-2 formation, switching to a 4-2-3-1 which helped her side triumph 2-0.

TACTICS IN DEFENCE

Teams have several choices about how they defend. Some managers prefer defenders to patrol areas of space that overlap, a system known as zonal marking. This tactic is

often used by Argentinian clubs and many national sides. It requires good communication between defenders. Alternatively, each defender marks an individual player, tracking their opponent's attacking runs throughout the game. Manchester United's Phil Jones, for example, man-marked Real Madrid's Cristiano Ronaldo during their 2013 Champions League game, restricting his chances on the ball in a 1-1 draw. When an opposing team features a dangerous playmaker positioned behind the strikers, a side may nominate an extra central defender to man-mark him or her.

▲ Clint Dempsey heads the ball during the 2011 CONCACAF Gold Cup final between the USA and Mexico. Versatile players such as Dempsey, who can play up front or in several positions in midfield, give a coach more options to change formations and tactics during a game.

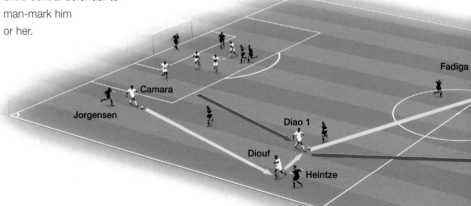

▶ The offside trap is a defensive tactic in which the back three or four players move upfield in a straight line to catch an opponent offside. It can be very effective, but may be beaten by a player dribbling through the line or by a well-timed through pass combined with an attacking run.

MATCH ACTION

A goal down and under pressure from a Danish attack down their right wing, Senegal scored a superb counter-attacking goal at the 2002 World Cup. Senegal's Henri Camara made a firm tackle on Martin Jorgensen and played a quick pass down the wing to El Hadji Diouf. Diouf, closely marked by Jan Heintze, spotted Salif Diao's run and backheeled the ball into his path. Diao hit a perfect pass to Khalilou Fadiga, who was sprinting into the centre circle. As Diao continued his run, Fadiga took the ball into the Danish half before playing a perfectly timed through pass. Racing between two defenders, Diao latched onto the ball and coolly dispatched it into the corner of the goal.

LONG OR SHORT

All teams seek to pass and move the ball into the attacking third of the pitch, where goalscoring chances can be fashioned. The way in which they get the ball there can vary greatly. For many decades, British managers believed that hitting long balls towards tall target strikers in the opponent's penalty area created more goal chances, often through a defensive mistake. In continental Europe and elsewhere, a shorter passing-and-moving game was often preferred, with sides keeping possession for relatively long periods as they looked for an opening in the opposition defence. Another tactic is to rely on pinpoint passing and skilful dribbling to get into the opposition penalty area. Some teams play a counter-attacking game, defending in large numbers and soaking up pressure. When they retrieve the ball, they move it rapidly out of defence with a long pass or by running with the ball. Fast, accurate counter-attacking can catch the opposition off guard and outnumbered, but requires players with good pace and awareness. Many coaches mix up their passing and movement tactics – if their team is behind with only minutes to go, they may switch to a direct style, pushing extra players up into the opposition penalty area to look for headers and knock-downs.

◀ *Cristiano Ronaldo practises free kicks at a Portuguese training camp. Attacking set pieces are often planned and worked on hard in training as they offer a good chance of scoring.*

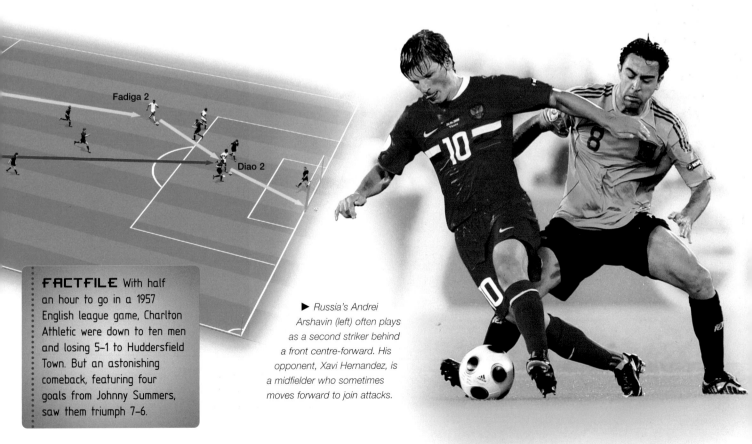

Fadiga 2

Diao 2

FACTFILE With half an hour to go in a 1957 English league game, Charlton Athletic were down to ten men and losing 5–1 to Huddersfield Town. But an astonishing comeback, featuring four goals from Johnny Summers, saw them triumph 7–6.

▶ *Russia's Andrei Arshavin (left) often plays as a second striker behind a front centre-forward. His opponent, Xavi Hernandez, is a midfielder who sometimes moves forward to join attacks.*

THE MANAGER'S ROLE

A successful team needs more than great tactics. It needs to be prepared, instructed and inspired to produce a great performance. Motivating players, directing them and giving them the confidence to perform is all part of a manager's job. Crucially, managers can determine the tone, style and attitude of their side through the players they buy and send out onto the pitch, as well as through their work on the training ground.

THE TEAM BEHIND THE TEAM

Behind the footballers at a major club or national side is a large team of staff. At the helm is the manager and his assistant coaches, some of whom may specialize in training goalkeepers or strikers, or may specifically work with younger players and youth teams. A top club will also include a fitness coach, a dietician and one or more physiotherapists and medical staff to help with players' preparation and injury

▲ José Mourinho oversees a training session before Real Madrid's 2013 Champions League quarter-final against Galatasaray. Head coaches like Mourinho are in charge of an array of coaches and physios, as well as fitness and diet experts.

recovery. Videos of games that interest the management are studied in detail, while scouts are employed to check out and report on forthcoming opposition sides and to watch potential transfer targets in action. Many clubs and national teams also arrange visits from temporary personnel such as sports psychologists, balance and co-ordination specialists, as well as inspirational figures from other sports.

INS AND OUTS

With football clubs becoming increasingly big businesses, a manager's ability to deal profitably and successfully in the transfer market is essential. Some managers are highly prized for their ability to buy players cheaply and sell them for profit or to put together a team on a limited budget that can seriously challenge for honours. European Cup-winning manager Brian Clough was famous for working wonders with bargain buys such as Scottish legend Archie Gemmill who cost Clough's Derby side £66,000. Many modern managers and clubs also have an eye for a bargain. Porto, for example, sold Brazilian striker Hulk to Russia's Zenit St Petersburg in 2012 for a fee believed to be more than £35 million. They had paid less than £15 million to acquire the player from Japanese side Tokyo Verdy. Another Portuguese club, Benfica, bought David Luiz from Vitória in Brazil for 500,000 euros in 2007, and sold him to Chelsea in 2011 for

FACTFILE Irishman Tony Cascarino was sold in 1982 by Crockenhill FC to Gillingham for a new club strip and some corrugated iron to patch up the ground. The total cost was said to be £180.

▶ In 2011, Porto bought Radamel Falcao from Argentinean club River Plate for less than £4 million. After three seasons, in which he scored 72 goals in 87 games, they sold him on to Atletico Madrid for approximately ten times what they had originally paid.

approximately 29 million euros – a truly staggering profit. Other managers are rated for their ability to bring promising youngsters through from their youth set-ups or training academies, and to attract good players on loan from other clubs to help strengthen their side at key stages of the season.

UNDER PRESSURE

Few people in sport are under as much pressure as the manager of a major club or national side. Managers stand or fall by their results. In the past, some managers stayed at clubs for season after season. Miguel Munoz, for example, managed Real Madrid for 417 games during the 1960s. At the top level today, few coaches stay in charge of the best teams for more than a handful of seasons. Between May 2014 and May 2015, a staggering 19 head coaches lost their jobs

in the 20-team Spanish La Liga. In 2007, Leroy Rosenior became manager of Torquay United but new owners arrived at the same time. As a result, he was sacked after just ten minutes in charge. Even recent success does not guarantee a long stay. Real Madrid's Vicente del Bosque had delivered two Spanish league titles, two Champions League trophies and other cups to the Spanish giants in just four years, but was dismissed in June 2003. In 2008, Roberto Mancini was sacked as head coach of Internazionale straight after delivering the club its third Serie A title in a row. In such an unforgiving climate, Alex Ferguson's record of over 1,500 games in charge of Manchester United is quite remarkable.

▲ *Vicente del Bosque holds the World Cup after guiding Spain to victory in 2010. A former Real Madrid player and manager, he was voted World Coach of the Year in 2012.*

◄ *Bora Milutinovic led five different countries to successive World Cups – a unique feat in football management. In 2009, he was appointed coach of Iraq.*

MANAGERIAL MIGRATIONS

Like modern players, top managers often move abroad to further their coaching careers. Whilst teams such as Germany and Italy have never had a foreign coach, more and more have, including England with Sven-Goran Eriksson and Fabio Capello. In the past, British coaches were influential abroad. Willy Garbutt helped shape Genoa into a powerful side, while Fred Pentland coached Athletic Bilbao to Spanish league success in 1930 and 1931. Jimmy Hogan, who used pass-and-move tactics years ahead of his time, worked with Austrian coaching legend Hugo Miesl to set up the Vienna School of attractive football. This created the Austrian *Wunderteam* that remained unbeaten in 14

internationals and narrowly missed out on glory at the 1934 World Cup and 1936 Olympics. Today, managers and coaches swap countries and continents frequently. Dutch coach Guus Hiddink managed many European clubs as well as the national teams of the Netherlands, South Korea, Australia, Russia and Turkey, whilst Italian manager Fabio Capello has coached England and, from 2012, the Russian national team. Globetrotting Luis Felipe Scolari has managed 21 clubs all over the world from China and Qatar to England and Uzbekistan. He has also coached Portugal, Kuwait and Brazil twice.

▼ *Jürgen Klinsmann was appointed head coach of the US men's team in 2011 and led them to nine wins in 2012, including a victory over Italy. The former German striker had only one season as a club manager (Bayern Munich, 2008–09).*

▲ *Globetrotting Frenchman Philippe Troussier has successfully coached and managed Nigeria, South Africa, Japan, China and clubs in Europe.*

GREAT MANAGERS

There have been dozens of truly great managers and coaches in football. Some have been masters at discovering new talents and putting together successful teams on tight budgets; others are football visionaries who have helped to improve the skills and play of the world's biggest stars. Below are profiles of eight of the finest managers in the history of football.

HERBERT CHAPMAN
1878-1934

Only four teams have won the English league three seasons in a row, and Chapman created two of them. After arriving at Huddersfield Town in 1921, he won the league in 1924 and 1925. By the time Huddersfield made it three in a row, Chapman had left for Arsenal. They were in 20th place when he took over, but finished the season second, behind his former side. Arsenal went on to win a hat-trick of league titles, the first two under Chapman. The Englishman took tactics very seriously, and his W-M formation (see page 60) was taken up by many sides. He pioneered large-scale youth coaching, undersoil heating, top-class medical facilities and professional training regimes. Some of his proposals, such as numbered shirts and playing regular evening games under floodlights, were adopted only long after his death.

◀ Herbert Chapman (right) watches an Arsenal match in 1932 alongside trainer Tom Whittaker (left) and star player Alex James.

GIOVANNI TRAPATTONI
Born 1939

Trapattoni's managerial career got off to a flying start, winning the 1973 European Cup-Winners' Cup as caretaker manager of AC Milan, for whom he had played as a fearsome centre-back. After moving to Milan's great rivals Juventus, he enjoyed an unmatched run of success, winning six Serie A league titles, two UEFA Cups and, in 1985, a European Cup. Trapattoni won a further Serie A title with Internazionale in 1989 before moving to Bayern Munich in the 1990s, where he became the first foreign manager to win the Bundesliga. His teams were based on strong defences, usually with three central defenders and exciting attackers who were often bought from abroad. He was finally given a chance to coach the Italian national side at 63 years of age, but the team fell short at the 2002 World Cup and Euro 2004, after which Trapattoni had spells at Benfica, Stuttgart and Salzburg. In 2008, he became coach of the Republic of Ireland national team.

▲ Trapattoni argues with the officials during Italy's match against Bulgaria at Euro 2004.

BELA GUTTMANN
1900-81

The only manager to have won the top club trophy in both South America and Europe, Guttmann is a coaching legend. He was a gifted amateur player for MTK Budapest and appeared at the 1924 Olympics for Hungary. After retiring in 1935, he embarked on a 40-year-long coaching career that took him to Switzerland, Uruguay, Greece, Portugal, Brazil, Romania, Italy and Austria. He won national league titles in five different countries, including the 1955 Serie A title with AC Milan; he won the European Cup twice as coach of Benfica and also lifted the Copa Libertadores with Peñarol. He was a great influence on Gusztav Sebes, the coach of the magical Hungarian sides of the 1950s, and his forward-thinking 4-2-4 formation and styles of play are believed to have inspired Brazil to become the great attacking force of the late 1950s onwards.

JOCK STEIN
1922-85

Jock Stein began his coaching career as assistant manager at Celtic. In 1960, he moved to Dunfermline and beat his old club in the following season to win the Scottish Cup. In 1962, Dunfermline caused a major upset, knocking out top Spanish side Valencia from the Inter-Cities Fairs Cup. Stein moved on to Hibernian for a season before being appointed as the boss of Celtic. He quickly built one of British soccer's finest and most entertaining sides. Under Stein, Celtic won 11 Scottish league titles and, in 1967, overturned the mighty Internazionale to become the first British team to lift the European Cup. The 'Big Man' left Celtic in 1977 for an ill-fated spell at Leeds United, but later became Scotland's coach, guiding them to the 1982 and 1986 World Cup tournaments.

FACTFILE In the 1970s, two managerial legends, Jock Stein and Brian Clough, both had spells at Leeds United that lasted just 44 days.

SIR ALEX FERGUSON
Born 1941

As European football's longest-serving top-flight manager, Sir Alex Ferguson has taken Manchester United to a record 13 Premier League titles and the 1999 and 2008 Champions League crowns. A ruthless and highly driven player, Ferguson carried those attributes into his managerial career, first with East Stirling and then at St Mirren and Aberdeen. He broke the monopoly of Celtic and Rangers to win three Scottish league titles; in 1983, his team defeated Real Madrid to lift the European Cup-Winners' Cup. Ferguson also served as assistant Scotland manager under Jock Stein, taking over in 1985. At Manchester United, Ferguson developed young talents such as David Beckham and Ryan Giggs, and proved to be a masterful player of mind games with rival managers. Knighted in 1999, for his services to the game, 'Sir' Alex announced his retirement from club management at the end of the 2012–13 season, after 26 years with Manchester United.

> **FACTFILE** Alex Ferguson was sacked only once, in 1978, when Scottish club St Mirren fired him for a range of offences that included 'unpardonable swearing at a lady'.

RINUS MICHELS
1928-2005

The man behind 'total football', which revolutionized both Ajax and the Dutch national team, Marinus 'Rinus' Michels had been a centre-forward as a player, winning five caps for Holland in the 1950s. As coach of Ajax in the mid-1960s, he gave 17-year-old Johan Cruyff his debut. Michels later managed Cruyff at Spanish giants Barcelona and in the Dutch team that finished runners-up at the 1974 World Cup. Michels returned to Ajax in 1975 and became coach of German side Cologne five years later. He rejoined the Dutch national side in 1984 and, with a star-studded team, won the 1988 European Championships – Holland's first major trophy. Michels' achievements were acknowledged in 1989, when he was named FIFA's Coach of the Century.

VALERY LOBANOVSKY
1939-2002

A gifted mathematician, Valery Lobanovsky viewed football as a science, and was one of the first managers to analyse the performances of teams and players. His management style was strict, yet it enabled creative talents such as Oleg Blokhin and Andriy Shevchenko to flourish. After four years in charge of Dnipro Dnipropetrovsk, he was appointed coach of Dynamo Kiev, guiding them to five Soviet league titles between 1974 and 1981 and two European Cup-Winners' Cup victories (1975 and 1986). He also coached the Soviet Union in three spells, reaching the 1988 European Championships final, only to be defeated by Rinus Michels' Dutch team. After spells with the United Arab Emirates and Kuwait, he returned to Kiev in 1996, taking them to five Ukrainian league titles in a row (1997–2001) and reaching the semi-finals of the Champions League in 1999.

▶ Rinus Michels with Johan Cruyff during their time at Barcelona.

HELENIO HERRERA
1917-97

The well-travelled Argentinian Helenio Herrera was a tough manager who liked to control almost every aspect of a club. At Spain's Atlético Madrid, he won back-to-back league titles. After spells with Malaga, Valladolid and Sevilla, he joined Barcelona. Under his management, they won two Spanish titles and two Inter-Cities Fairs Cups. Internazionale liked what they saw and headhunted him in 1960. Herrera's reign and his use of *catenaccio* tactics (see page 60) coincided with Inter's most glorious era, in which they won three Serie A titles, two European Cups and two World Club Cups. Herrera was also in charge of the Italian national team during qualification for the 1962 World Cup, but by the time the tournament began, he was manager of Spain.

◀ In November 2004, Alex Ferguson celebrated his 1,000th game in charge of Manchester United by beating Lyon in the Champions League.

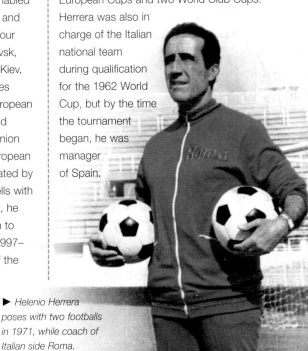

▶ Helenio Herrera poses with two footballs in 1971, while coach of Italian side Roma.

Lothar Emmerich of West Germany fires a shot past England's George Cohen (far left) and Martin Peters during the epic 1966 World Cup final at Wembley.

THE WINGLESS WONDERS

The tactics of England manager Alf Ramsey caused much debate at the 1966 World Cup. His midfield had no wingers, but did include a striker, Bobby Charlton, and the tough-tackling defender Nobby Stiles. The English defence was in top form and the Wingless Wonders, as Ramsey's team was nicknamed, cruised to the final against West Germany. It was, therefore, a shock when England fell behind to a Helmut Haller strike in the 12th minute. Stirred into action, England went 2-1 up with goals from Geoff Hurst and Martin Peters, only for Wolfgang Weber to equalize in the dying seconds of the game. In a World Cup first, the final went into extra time and two events passed into football folklore. First was the controversial goal awarded to Geoff Hurst in the 101st minute – even today, it is unclear if the ball crossed the line. Then came Hurst's third goal, which left no one in any doubt. His thumping shot into the roof of the net secured England an historic 4-2 win and made him the only player to score a hat-trick in the final of the World Cup.

GREAT SIDES

What makes a great team? Great footballers, managed brilliantly, playing with spirit and supported by passionate crowds, often triumph. Yet, assembling a team of superstars does not guarantee success. Sometimes, unheralded players gel together to win against the odds. Over the last 15 years, Japan, Chile, Burkina Faso and Iraq have lit up world football by triumphing over more powerful nations. Similar upsets occur at club level – provincial side Toluca's rise to win the Mexican league, for example. This chapter looks at some of the world's great national and club sides over the years. The key word is 'some'; there are dozens of other successful teams, from Argentina's Independiente – the most frequent winner of the Copa Libertadores – to Olympiakos, who in 2015 won their 17th Greek league title in 19 years. The focus in this section is on sides that at one point in their history were especially exciting, revolutionary or dominant in the football competitions in which they played.

NATIONAL SIDES

▶ Hungarian goalkeeper Gyula Grosics gathers the ball under pressure from England's Stan Mortensen. Hungary's 6-3 win condemned England to their first home defeat to a team from the continent.

HUNGARY
Founded: 1901

The Hungarian national team of the 1950s was quite exceptional and one of the few sides at club or international level to change the way football is played. Organized at the back by the dependable Jozsef Bozsik, Hungary brimmed with attacking talent thanks to Zoltan Czibor, Sandor Kocsis, Nandor Hidegkuti and Ferenc Puskas. At a time when almost every side played the W-M formation (see page 60), coach Gusztav Sebes devised a simple but devastating alternative. Hidegkuti was the team's centre-forward, but he played very deep, allowing Puskas, Kocsis and other team-mates to raid forwards into space. Opposition teams simply did not know how to play against a side that swept all before it, winning the 1952 Olympics and scoring 220 goals in 51 matches during the first half of the decade. In 1953, the team earned its nickname – the Magnificent Magyars – by beating a stunned England 6-3 at Wembley. That memorable win was followed by a 7-1 destruction of the English team in Budapest. From June 1950 to November 1955, Hungary's international record read: played 50, won 42, drew seven, lost one. The defeat was heartbreaking, however, as it came in the final of the 1954 World Cup. After taking a 2-0 lead against a West German side they had thrashed 8-3 in the group stages, Hungary – fielding an unfit Puskas – lost 3-2. That single defeat should not detract from one of the finest teams ever to grace the international stage.

> **FACTFILE** The team was still at its peak when the Soviet Union invaded Hungary in 1956. Many of its star players were on tour with their club, Honved, and chose not to return home. Puskas signed for Real Madrid, while Kocsis and Czibor joined Real's great rivals, Barcelona.

WEST GERMANY
Founded: 1900

West Germany staged a major shock when they courageously toppled the favourites, Hungary, to win the 1954 World Cup thanks to two goals from Helmut Rahn. Their side of the mid-1960s finished runners-up at the 1966 tournament and third in 1970. Manager Helmut Schön then rebuilt the team shrewdly, keeping the superb

Sepp Maier in goal and moving Franz Beckenbauer from midfield into defence, where he played alongside Hans-Georg Schwarzenbeck and one of the best full-backs of the 1970s, Paul Breitner. Schön incorporated the talented Günter Netzer into midfield and often played a 4-3-3 formation, with Uli Hoeness in attack alongside goal machine Gerd Müller. West Germany's players had an incredibly strong team spirit because they came almost exclusively from just two clubs – Bayern Munich and Borussia Mönchengladbach. Their self-belief was evident as they powered to the 1972 European Championships title and then went a step further, winning the 1974 World Cup on home soil. By this time, the talented but outspoken Netzer had been replaced by Wolfgang Overath, while midfielder Rainer Bonhof had also played his way into the side. A defeat to Czechoslovakia in the 1976 European Championships final signalled the end of a remarkable period in which West Germany had become the first team to hold the European and World crowns at the same time.

◄ *West German defender Berti Vogts holds the World Cup aloft in 1974, with Hans-Georg Schwarzenbeck (number 4 and Rainer Bonhof (16) to his left.*

USA (WOMEN)
First international match: 1985

Women's international football came of age during the 1990s and early 2000s, with the arrival of World Cup and Olympic competitions. The period's most successful nation was the USA who won two Olympic titles (1996 and 2004) and two Women's World Cups (1991 and 1999). Their record in World Cup matches during the 1990s was remarkable, with 20 wins, two draws and just two defeats. Mia Hamm was considered to be the world's finest female striker, while Kristine Lilly became the first female player to pass 300 international caps in 2006. For a number of the US women's team, 2004 proved a successful swansong, with victory over Brazil to win Olympic gold, a feat that a new generation of US players such as Carli Lloyd, Christie Rampone and Abby Wambach repeated in both 2008 and 2012. The team also finished runners-up in the 2011 World Cup and were unbeaten in 2015 when they defeated Japan 5-2 to become champions for the third time.

▶ *Abby Wambach of the United States is fouled from behind by Homare Sawa of Japan in the second half of the Women's World Cup 2015 final.*

FRANCE
Founded: 1919

France has a long and illustrious football pedigree. It has produced several superb sides, particularly in the late 1950s – the era of Raymond Kopa and Just Fontaine – and in the early 1980s, with an attractive team led by Michel Platini. But it was the side of the late 1990s that finally translated great promise into World Cup success (see pages 92–93). As World Champions, France entered Euro 2000 with the majority of their key players still at their peak, including flamboyant keeper Fabien Barthez and strong, skilled defenders in Marcel Desailly, Lilian Thuram and Bixente Lizarazu. In midfield, a blend of flair and dynamism was headed by the world's best attacking midfielder, Zinedine Zidane. Up front, young livewires such as Sylvain Wiltord and Thierry Henry were intent on making their mark. Five players scored two or more goals in their six-match Euro 2000 campaign, which ended with France beating Italy 2-1 to become the second team (after West Germany in 1974) to hold European and World titles at the same time.

▲ *France celebrate their Euro 2000 triumph after a golden goal from David Trezeguet (centre, with Fabien Barthez's hand on his head) sealed victory.*

SOUTH KOREA
Founded: 1928

At the 2002 World Cup, co-hosts South Korea were given little chance of success by many people. In truth, the country boasted an improving side and had qualified for the previous three World Cups. Under the guidance of Guus Hiddink – a former Real Madrid and Holland coach – the South Koreans beat Poland 2-0 to record their country's first win at the World Cup finals. After a 1-1 draw with the USA, South Korea dumped a strong Portugal side out of the tournament courtesy of Park Ji-Sung's goal. An extraordinary second-round game versus Italy saw South Korea miss a penalty, then go behind, only to equalize two minutes before the final whistle. Urged on by an entire nation, the hardworking side defended resolutely and attacked with energy, skill and surprise. A golden goal three minutes before the end of extra time knocked Italy out of the tournament and sent the country into raptures. The drama was not over, however. A tense quarter-final against Spain ended in a thrilling penalty shootout, with keeper Lee Woon-Jae pulling off a magnificent save from Joaquin before captain Hong Myung-Bo slotted home the winning penalty. A narrow 1-0 defeat to Germany in the semi-final did not dampen the co-host nation's enthusiasm, and attendances at club level rocketed in the following seasons.

FACTFILE Ahn Jung-Hwan struck the goal that knocked Italy out of the World Cup. Ahn played for Italian side Perugia, whose president was so enraged that he terminated the South Korean midfielder's contract.

HIT THE NET

www.fifa.com/associations/
A list of all the national associations linked to FIFA. Clicking on a country gives news and details about their national team.

www.worldfootball.net/
A large website with information and fixtures for all leading league and international competitions.

www.fifa.com/fifa-world-ranking/ranking-table/women/
See the world rankings for women's international teams. Clicking on a country brings up further data and a link to that team's FIFA information page.

▲ *South Korea's Lee Chun-Soo (number 14), Choi Jin-Cheul (4), Hwang Sun-Hong (18) and Park Ji-Sung (21) celebrate their team's penalty shootout victory over Spain in the quarter-finals of the 2002 World Cup.*

SPAIN
Founded: 1904

Spain had been the perennial underachievers on the international stage, producing dozens of world-renowned players – from Ricardo Zamora and Andoni Zubizarreta in goal to Raul and Emilio Butragueño in attack – yet rarely producing the goods at major tournaments. The 2000s, however, saw a major change with the arrival of a clutch of supremely talented, technically-gifted players, many from Barcelona, who thrived on a style of play – dubbed *tika-taka* – where control of the ball, frequent short passing and quick, nimble movement are paramount. Players like Xavi Hernández and Andrés Iniesta in midfield keep possession of the ball in front of no-nonsense defenders such as Carles Puyol and Gerard Piqué. It yielded great results. Between November 2006 and June 2009, Spain went unbeaten in 35 international games until suffering a shock defeat to the USA at the Confederations Cup. Spain won Euro 2008 and became the first champions to successfully defend their European title in 2012. In between came Spain's first ever World Cup triumph, achieved after qualifying with a perfect record (ten wins out of ten) and victories over Portugal, Paraguay, Germany and the Netherlands at the tournament.

◄ *Xavi Hernández unleashes a shot during Spain's comprehensive 4-0 victory over Italy in the final of the 2012 European Championships.*

ITALY
Founded: 1898

Italy and Uruguay emerged as the leading sides during the first decade of the World Cup. The Italians chose not to enter the first tournament, in 1930, but were hosts of the second, where they were managed by Vittorio Pozzo, who was nicknamed the Old Maestro. Pozzo deployed several *oriundi* – Argentinians of Italian descent – including Raimundo Orsi and the captain, Luisito Monti. His side also included one of the world's finest attackers of the inter-war years in Giuseppe Meazza. Italy won the 1934 World Cup under Pozzo's leadership and also triumphed at the 1936 Olympics. Recognizing the fact that his side was ageing, the wily Pozzo introduced more and more youngsters, so that by the time of the 1938 World Cup only two members of the 1934 team,

Meazza and Giovanni Ferrari, remained. Pozzo's overhaul of the side proved a triumph, as Italy beat the highly fancied French, Brazilian and Hungarian teams to reclaim the trophy and make Pozzo the only manager in history to have won two World Cups.

FACTFILE In the semi-final of the 1938 World Cup, the string of Giuseppe Meazza's shorts broke and they fell to the ground just as he went to take a penalty. Holding his shorts up with one hand, Meazza calmly stroked the penalty home past the bemused Brazilian goalkeeper, Valter.

▲ *Italy's national team, including star striker Giuseppe Meazza (front row, centre) pose before the 1938 World Cup. The Italians comfortably beat Hungary 4-2 in the final.*

ENGLAND
Founded: 1863

As an England player, Alf Ramsey's last match had been the 6-3 demolition by Hungary in 1953 – the game that punctured English belief in its footballing superiority. On the back of managing Ipswich Town from the lowly Third Division South to the league championship in 1962, Ramsey was named England manager later that year. By the 1966 World Cup he had assembled a powerful team with a strong spine – Gordon Banks in goal, Jackie Charlton and Bobby Moore in central defence, Bobby Charlton in midfield and, up front, Roger Hunt and the free-scoring Jimmy Greaves (who was injured during the tournament and replaced by Geoff Hurst). Propelled by goals mainly from Hunt and Bobby Charlton, and by a miserly defence that did not concede a goal until the semi-final, England beat Mexico, France, Argentina and Portugal. In the final at Wembley, a memorable hat-trick by Geoff Hurst and a goal from Martin Peters saw England beat West Germany 4-2 to win the trophy (see pages 68–69). After reaching the semi-finals of the 1968 European Championships, England were one of the favourites for the 1970 World Cup. In the quarter-final they were leading 2-0 with just 20 minutes left to play, before West Germany struck back to win 3-2.

▼ *England captain Bobby Moore (left) and keeper Gordon Banks hold aloft the World Cup at Wembley.*

▲ *German striker Birgit Prinz powers away from a North Korean defender during the 2007 Women's World Cup.*

▶ *Nigerian midfielder Sunday Mba.*

NIGERIA
Founded: 1945

In 1985, Nigeria's youngsters captured the World Under-17 Championship to become the first African nation to win a world tournament. Eleven years later, the 'Super Eagles' were the stars of the Atlanta Olympics thanks to their attacking verve, team spirit and will to win. Featuring players such as Celestine Babayaro, Emmanuel Amunike and Daniel Amokachi, Nigeria beat Hungary 1-0 and Japan 2-0, before losing to Brazil 1-0 in the group stages. They then beat Mexico 2-0 in the quarter-finals to set up a second meeting with Brazil. That match is considered to be the finest in Olympic history. With 13 minutes to go Nigeria were losing 3-1, but they pulled one goal back before their captain, Nwankwo Kanu, scored a last-gasp equalizer. In a frenetic period of extra time, Kanu struck again to seal a 4-3 victory. Another great comeback in the final saw Nigeria win gold by defeating Argentina 3-2.

GERMANY (WOMEN)
First international match: 1982

Germany struggled to be competitive in the 1980s, but received a massive boost in 1989 when they won the first of their eight European Championships. The 21st century proved remarkably fruitful for the side as they won the 2003 Women's World Cup and continued their European dominance with their sixth championship crown in a row in 2013. Before retiring in 2011, Germany's goal machine, Birgit Prinz, scored an incredible 128 goals for her country. In the 2007 World Cup, Germany's 11-0 demolition of Argentina and feat of not conceding a goal throughout the tournament were undoubted highlights. Only the Olympics has eluded this powerhouse team, now coached by Silvia Neid, who as an 18-year-old scored two goals in the team's first ever international match, against Switzerland in 1982.

► Johan Neeskens evades the tackle of Argentina's Americo Gallego during the 1978 World Cup final.

HOLLAND
Founded: 1889

Rinus Michels, a former centre-forward for Holland, masterminded a revolution in Dutch football in the mid-1960s. First at club side Ajax, and then with the national team, he developed a system in which all his players were comfortable on the ball and would switch positions, often with devastating results. Called 'total football' (see page 61), the system revolved around such world-class talents as Johan Cruyff, Johan Neeskens and Ruud Krol. With Michels at the helm, the Dutch powered to the 1974 World Cup finals, scoring 14 goals and conceding just one in qualifying. They soared through the rounds, demolishing Argentina 4-0 and beating Brazil 2-0 on the way to the final against West Germany. Despite taking a one-goal lead within 80 seconds, Holland suffered heartbreak, losing 2-1. Two years later, they reached the semi-final of the 1976 European Championships, going out to the eventual winners, Czechoslovakia, in extra time. The Dutch entered the 1978 World Cup without Cruyff, but could still call upon many of the 1974 squad, including Neeskens, Krol and strikers Johnny Rep and Robbie Rensenbrink. They reached the final again, this time losing 3-1 to Argentina. Considered the most talented team never to win the World Cup, the Dutch enthralled millions of fans with their exploits and flair.

MEXICO
Founded: 1927

Having reached the quarter-finals of the two World Cups it has hosted (1970 and 1986), the football-mad nation of Mexico had much to cheer in the 1990s, when its national team dominated the continental championships, the CONCACAF Gold Cup. In the inaugural competition of 1991, Mexico lost to the USA at the semi-final stage, but in the next three competitions they were unstoppable. They were rampant in 1993, beating Canada 8-0 and Jamaica 6-1, before humbling the USA 4-0 in the final. At the 1996 Gold Cup, they defeated invited guests Brazil to win the title and, four years later, beat the USA again to secure a hat-trick of wins. At the heart of Mexico's authoritative displays was the defender Claudio Suarez, nicknamed the Emperor for his commanding performances. Suarez made his national debut in 1992 and played his 177th game in 2006 against Holland. A new generation of Mexico talent has added to this success, winning the Gold Cup in 2009 and 2011, and beating Brazil to grab more gold at the 2012 London Olympics.

FACTFILE
Mexico striker Javier Hernandez, who has grabbed 30 goals from 46 games, was timed as the fastest player at the 2010 World Cup — reaching a speed of 32.15km/h.

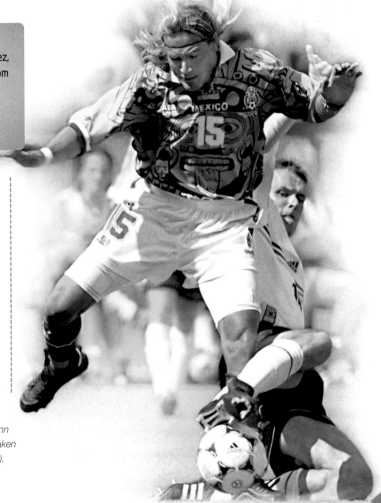

► Mexico's Luiz Hernandez is tackled by Dietmarr Hamann of Germany. His record of 35 goals has since been overtaken by Cuauhtémoc Blanco (39 goals) and Jared Borgetti (46).

BRAZIL
Founded: 1914

The 1958 World Cup signalled the arrival of Pelé and the start of a magnificent era for Brazil, who enchanted fans of the beautiful game as they won three out of four World Cups. The side that claimed the 1970 World Cup is considered by many people to be international football's greatest team. In attack, few nations before or since have been able to field a side so blessed with flair, composure and skill on the ball, as well as superb vision and movement off it. Opposition teams sometimes tried to mark Pelé out of the game, but this would only give space and opportunities to marvellous players such as centre-forward Tostao, the bustling Roberto Rivelino (who had one of the most fearsome shots in world football), the midfield general Gerson or the powerful winger Jairzinho. At the back, high-class players such as Carlos Alberto and centre-back Wilson Piazza maintained a solid defence, but this side was all about attack. After going a goal down to Czechoslovakia in their first match at the 1970 World Cup, Brazil responded by scoring four times. They scored three to beat Uruguay in the semi-final and four in the final, in which they outclassed a strong Italian side with one of the greatest displays of attacking football. Brazil dazzled with their wit and invention, and the 4-1 scoreline was completed by a marvellous team move ending in a thunderous shot by Carlos Alberto (see below). In his last match for

▲ Brazil's team that beat England at the 1970 World Cup. Back row, left to right: Carlos Alberto, Brito, Wilson Piazza, Félix, Clodoaldo, Everaldo, Mario Zagalo (coach); front row: Jairzinho, Roberto Rivelino, Tostao, Pelé, Paulo Cesar.

Brazil, Pelé was chaired off the field by his team-mates after his part in the victory. The departure of other members of the side meant that by the 1974 World Cup, only Rivelino and Jairzinho remained from the team that had captured the imagination of millions.

FACTFILE In 1970, Brazil's manager, Mario Zagalo, became the first person to have both played in and managed a World Cup-winning team. He had played in Brazil's 1958 and 1962 World Cup triumphs.

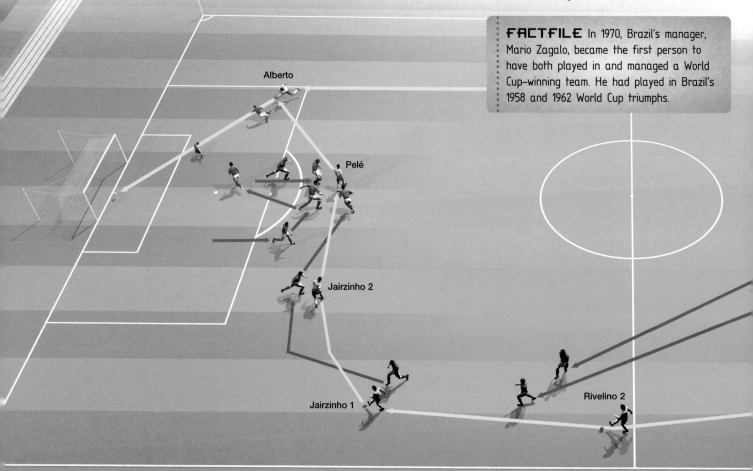

Alberto

Pelé

Jairzinho 2

Jairzinho 1

Rivelino 2

FACTFILE Idriss Carlos Kameni was just 16 when he played in goal for Cameroon in the 2000 Olympic final. He was a hero as early as the fifth minute, when he saved a Spanish penalty. Cameroon went on to win gold in a penalty shootout, making their coach, Jean-Paul Akono, the first African manager to win a major world football competition.

► *Roger Milla runs past Colombian keeper Jose Higuita on his way to scoring during Cameroon's 2-1 victory in the second round of the 1990 World Cup. The Africans were the talk of the tournament, defeating World Cup holders Argentina in the group stage.*

MATCH ACTION

In the 1970 World Cup final against Italy, right-back Carlos Alberto scored one of the finest ever team goals. The move started in the Brazilian half with a series of passes and some highly skilled dribbling from defender Clodoaldo. He released Roberto Rivelino, who fired a pass down the touchline. Jairzinho controlled the ball instantly and cut infield, shielding the ball from Italian defenders before feeding Pelé. Pelé spotted a run by a team-mate on his right and nonchalantly rolled the ball diagonally into the penalty area. Marauding down the right flank, Carlos Alberto met the pass with a booming right-foot shot that sent the ball crashing low into the corner of the net.

FACTFILE Brazil's first international match was in July 1914, when they played English league side Exeter City. In 2004, the 1994 Brazilian World Cup-winning side played a rematch against Exeter, winning the game 1-0.

Clodoaldo 1

Clodoaldo 2

Rivelino 1

CAMEROON
Founded: 1960

Cameroon threatened a major shock at the 1982 World Cup, drawing against Italy (the eventual winners) and Poland, yet failing to reach the second round by a hair's breadth. In 1990, a team led by Roger Milla lit up the tournament, winning a tough group containing the Soviet Union, Argentina and Romania, beating Colombia in round two and taking England to extra time before losing 3-2. Recently, many of Cameroon's footballers have played for Europe's top clubs – Geremi at Real Madrid, Samuel Eto'o at Barcelona and Salomon Olembe at Marseille, for example. After a disappointing 1998 World Cup, Cameroon roared back in 2000. They won the African Nations Cup, beating Nigeria. They then triumphed at the Olympics, stunning Brazil in the quarter-finals, Chile in the semis and Spain in the final to win gold.

LONGEST UNBEATEN INTERNATIONAL RUNS (IN GAMES)

36	Brazil 1993–96	28	South Korea 1977–79
35	Spain 2007–09	27	Colombia 1992–94
31	Argentina 1991–93	26	Spain 2011–13
	Spain 1994–98	25	Italy 2004–06
30	France 1994–96		Netherlands 2008–10
	Hungary 1950–54	24	Brazil 1975–78
29	Brazil 1970–73		Ghana 1981–83

CLUB SIDES

BARCELONA
Spain
Founded: 1899
Stadium: Nou Camp

With their own bank, radio station and one of the most impressive stadiums in the world, Barcelona can easily claim to be one of the world's largest football clubs. Barcelona's domestic achievements are impressive – their sixth-place finish in the Spanish league, La Liga, in 2003 was their worst since 1942. The club have won 23 league titles, finished runners-up 24 times and top the list of Spanish Cup winners, with 27 victories. They have also won the European Cup-Winners' Cup four times – more than any other team. Barcelona smashed the world transfer record in 1973 when they paid £922,000 for Dutch maestro Johan Cruyff. Fifteen years later, he returned as the club's manager. In his first season, Cruyff steered the club to second place in La Liga and to victory over Sampdoria to collect the European Cup-Winners' Cup. Dutchman Ronald Koeman and Denmark's Michael Laudrup were signed to play alongside Spanish stars such as keeper Andoni Zubizarreta and midfielder José Bakero. In 1991, Barcelona won the first of four league titles in a row, and a year later won their first European Cup, beating Sampdoria.

▲ *Barcelona's captain, Carles Puyol, lifts the trophy after his team's 2-1 victory over Arsenal in the final of the 2006 Champions League.*

Their second triumph in the competition came in 2006 along with the Spanish league title. Barcelona have won the prized double of La Liga and Champions League three times (2008–09, 2010–11 and 2014–15).

KASHIMA ANTLERS
Japan
Founded: 1991
Stadium: Kashima Soccer Stadium

The former factory team of Sumitomo Metals Industries, Kashima Antlers were formed in time to enter the inaugural J-League competition in 1993. Their name comes from the literal translation of Kashima, meaning 'deer island'. Little was expected of the side, which lacked the pedigree of Japanese teams such as

▲ *Kashima's Yasuto Honda celebrates with the J-League trophy in 2000.*

Yokohama Marinos and Verdy Kawasaki. The Antlers' management team was ambitious, however, recruiting Brazilian World Cup star Zico, first as a player and later as technical director. Zico's fellow countrymen Mazinho, Jorginho and Bismarck – along with talented Japanese players such as Atsushi Yanagisawa, Tomoyuki Hirase and Yasuto Honda – helped take the Antlers to four J-League titles and three Japanese Cups between 1996 and 2002.

AL-AHLY
Egypt
Founded: 1907
Stadium: Mukhtar El-Tetsh

Cairo-based Al-Ahly are the dominant football club in Egypt and one of the most successful teams in North Africa. Having won the first Egyptian league competition in 1949, they held on to the title until 1960, when they lost out to fellow Cairo side and fierce rivals Zamalek. The 1980s were glorious for Al-Ahly. At home, they won five of the seven Cup of Egypt trophies and seven out of a possible ten league titles between 1980 and 1989. Abroad, Al-Ahly won the African Champions League twice, in 1982 and 1987, and also won the African Cup-Winners' Cup three times in a row. Al-Ahly were named as the CAF African Club of the 20th Century before going on to win the African Champions League in 2001, 2005, 2006, 2008, 2012 and 2013, and winning seven Egyptian league titles in a row (2005–11).

FACTFILE Two of Al-Ahly's youngest stars during the 1990s were the twins Hossam and Ibrahim Hassan, the most-capped players in Egyptian football. The brothers were idolized as they helped Al-Ahly to four league titles, but turned from heroes to villains when they sensationally quit the club to join rivals Zamalek in 2000.

▲ Flamengo's Ze Carlos da Silva performs a spectacular overhead kick during the 2003 Brazilian Cup final against Cruzeiro.

FLAMENGO
Brazil
Founded: 1895
Stadiums: Gávea, Maracana

Brazil is full of famous football sides, including Vasco da Gama, São Paulo, Botafogo and Corinthians. Flamengo are the most heavily supported of them all, having recorded 42 attendances of 100,000 or more at their games. Many gifted players have worn the side's distinctive black-and-red striped shirts. One of the greatest was Léonidas da Silva, known as the Black Diamond and the star of the 1938 World Cup. After a successful period in the 1950s, when the team won three Rio state league titles and earned the nickname the Steamroller, Flamengo had to wait more than 25 years for their next great era. Inspired by Zico and his strike partner, Nunes, the side won the Rio Championship (the Carioca) in 1978, 1979 and 1981, and the Brazilian National Championship in 1980, 1982 and 1983. In 1981, they captured the Copa Libertadores and a month later went on to claim the World Club Cup, beating Liverpool 3-0.

MANCHESTER UNITED
England
Founded: 1878
Stadium: Old Trafford

Sir Alex Ferguson, the Premiership's longest-serving and most successful manager, led Manchester United to a unique treble in English football when they won the Premiership, the FA Cup and the Champions League in 1999. Forty years earlier, a Manchester United side managed by Sir Matt Busby – another Scot who became a knight – had captured the hearts and minds of supporters everywhere. The story began in the mid-1950s. Great things were expected of the young 'Busby Babes' side that had won two league titles (in 1956 and 1957) and included, among other talents, the young England stars Roger Byrne and Duncan Edwards. But in 1958, a tragic plane crash in

◄ Bobby Charlton (left) celebrates after scoring the opening goal in Manchester United's defeat of Benfica to win the European Cup in 1968.

Munich killed 23 people on board, including eight members of the Manchester United first team. Busby had to build a new side, which contained tough defenders like Nobby Stiles, young midfielders such as Brian Kidd, and two survivors from the Munich crash, Bobby Charlton and central defender Bill Foulkes. Although often playing in midfield, Charlton formed a glittering attacking trio with Denis Law and George Best. Busby's side won the league title in 1965 and 1967, but the pinnacle of their achievements came in the 1968 European Cup. After beating Real Madrid in the semi-final, Manchester United faced Benfica in the final. Two goals from Charlton, one from Best and one from the 19-year-old Kidd secured a memorable 4-1 victory. The Red Devils, as the team is nicknamed, had become the first English side to win the European Cup.

◄ Ryan Giggs (left) in action during a friendly match in 2009. Giggs played four Champions League finals (1999, 2008, 2009 and 2011) and scored in each of the first 21 seasons of the English Premier League.

INTERNAZIONALE (INTER MILAN)
Italy
Founded: 1908
Stadium: Giuseppe Meazza (San Siro)

Also known as Inter Milan, Internazionale were formed by a group of former AC Milan players. During the rule of dictator Benito Mussolini, the club was forced to change its name to Ambrosiana-Inter, but switched it back in 1942. Argentinian coach Helenio Herrera joined Inter in 1960 and pioneered a new tactical system, playing a sweeper behind a back four and using fast-moving defenders to build attacks. Known as the *catenaccio* (doorbolt) system, it was seen as negative and defensive by some. But Inter won Serie A in 1963, 1965 and 1966 and also triumphed over Real Madrid in 1964 and the mighty Benfica in 1965 to win the European Cup twice. They added the World Club Cup to their list of honours in 1964 and 1965, but did not add to their European tally until the 1990s, when they won the UEFA Cup three times. In 2006, Inter were controversially awarded the Italian league title when Juventus were stripped of the trophy. They followed up with four further Serie A titles in 2007, 2008, 2009 and 2010.

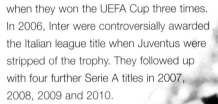

▲ *Sparta Prague's Radoslav Kovac is challenged by Michael Chrysostomos of Cypriot side APOEL Nicosia during a Champions League qualifier.*

SPARTA PRAGUE
Czech Republic
Founded: 1893
Stadium: Letná

One of the grand clubs of Eastern European football, Sparta have been known by a series of different names, from Kralovske Vinohrady (King's Vineyard) through AC Sparta, Spartak Sokolovo and Sparta Bratrstvi. The club have dominated the domestic game winning over 30 league championships, the latest being in 2013–14 with the side finishing runners-up in 2014–15. The first great Sparta side competed admirably in Europe in the late 1920s and 1930s, winning the Mitropa Cup (the forerunner of the European Cup) in both 1927 and 1934. A number of Sparta players also featured in the Czechoslovakia side that finished runners-up in the 1934 World Cup. These included star striker Oldrich Nejedly, who was the tournament's leading scorer with five goals. Sparta had several more great eras, notably in the early 1960s and the beginning of the 1990s, when they competed in the first Champions League competition in 1991–92. Despite memorable victories over Olympique Marseille, Dynamo Kiev and Barcelona, Sparta narrowly failed to qualify for the final.

◀ *Luiz Suarez, Inter Milan's elegant midfielder, on the ball in 1967. Inter broke the world transfer record to buy the Spaniard, paying £142,000 in 1961.*

SANTOS
Brazil
Founded: 1912
Stadium: Vila Belmiro

Santos are most famous as being Pelé's club. They had won few honours before he began playing for them in 1956, aged only 15. During his 19 years at the club, Santos won the São Paulo Championship ten times and the Copa Libertadores twice, in 1962 and 1963. They also won the World Club Cup in those years, the first with an extraordinary 5-2 win away at Benfica, which included a sensational hat-trick from Pelé. Santos have fared less well in the years since, but a number of bright young stars emerged at the turn of the century. The club took a gamble on many of these players in the 2002 Brazilian National Championship, fielding a side with an average age of just 22. With 17-year-old midfielder Diego and 18-year-old striker Robinho especially prominent, Santos rolled back the years and delighted many neutral fans by winning the competition.

◀ *Brazilian star Neymar runs with the ball for Santos during a 2012 Brazilian league match versus Palmeiras. Neymar scored more than 130 goals for Santos by the time he was 21 years old. In 2013 he transferred to Barcelona for £48.6 million.*

BOCA JUNIORS
Argentina
Founded: 1905
Stadium: La Bombonera

Best known in Europe as the club for which Diego Maradona played, Boca Juniors were founded by a group of Italian immigrants and an Irishman, Patrick MacCarthy. With their Buenos Aires neighbours River Plate, they form one of the fiercest rivalries in world football. Boca have the edge in the derby matches and have won three more Copa Libertadores than River. Boca had a strong resurgence at the end of the 20th century. Beginning in May 1998, they went 40 league games unbeaten to set an Argentinian record. The run helped them to win the Clausura and Apertura league titles in 1999, a feat followed by an incredible four Copa Libertadores triumphs in 2000, 2001, 2003 and 2007, as well as two Intercontinental Cups in 2000 and 2003.

DICK, KERR LADIES
England
Founded: 1917
No stadium

W. B. Dick and John Kerr owned a rail and tram equipment-making factory in Preston, northwest England. During World War I, women began to work in factories, taking the jobs of the men serving in the war. In 1917, the women at Dick, Kerr challenged their male colleagues to a game of football and went on to organize matches against male and female opposition to raise money for war charities. By 1920, Dick, Kerr Ladies were playing matches to sell-out crowds. One fixture against St Helen's Ladies attracted 53,000 spectators to Everton's Goodison Park. In 1921, at the peak of their popularity, Dick, Kerr Ladies played 67 games and a tour of the USA the following year saw the team win three and draw three out of nine matches against male sides. The Football Association felt threatened by a team which, in some cases, was drawing bigger crowds than the men's game. In 1921, the FA banned all women from playing football on the pitches of its member clubs. Incredibly, the ban remained in force for 50 years. As a result, support for women's football dwindled, and by 1926 Dick, Kerr Ladies had disbanded. Yet the team left an important legacy by showing that women could play football in a competitive, entertaining fashion.

◀ *The Dick, Kerr Ladies attack the penalty area during a floodlit game against Heys of Bradford in 1919.*

AC MILAN
Italy
Founded: 1899
Stadium: Giuseppe Meazza (San Siro)

AC Milan's first period of notable success came in the 1950s, when a trio of Swedish stars – Gunnar Gren, Nils Liedholm and Gunnar Nordahl – followed by Uruguayan striker Juan Alberto Schiaffino, helped them to four Serie A titles. Nordahl remains the club's highest scorer, with an amazing 210 goals in 257 games. The 1960s saw AC Milan emerge as one of the leading clubs in Europe, winning two European Cups and a Cup-Winners' Cup trophy. A period of decline followed, which included an enforced relegation in 1980 as a result of a betting scandal. Milan's fortunes were revived by the arrival of a new chairman, Silvio Berlusconi, in 1986. The wealthy media tycoon and future Italian prime minister appointed Arrigo Sacchi as coach the following year. An exciting team was assembled, which included the superb Dutch trio of Ruud Gullit, Marco van Basten and Frank Rijkaard, alongside the home-grown talents of Franco Baresi, Roberto Donadoni and Paolo Maldini. Milan won Serie A in 1988 and went on to win it five times during the 1990s. Starting in 1991, Milan went unbeaten in Serie A for an incredible 58 games, a run that included thrashings of Foggia (8-2) and Fiorentina (7-3). The side also put five goals past Sampdoria, Lazio, Pescara and

▲ *Kaka sprints away from Liverpool's defence during the 2007 Champions League final. Milan beat Celtic, Bayern Munich and Manchester United on the way to the final.*

Napoli (twice). In Europe, Milan beat Real Madrid 5-0 and then Steaua Bucharest 4-0 in the final to collect the European Cup in 1989 – a competition they also won in 1990, 1994 and 2003, and in which they were runners-up in 1993, 1995 and 2005. They won their seventh Champions League title in 2007. In Italy, Milan claimed the Serie A title for the 18th time in 2011.

RIVER PLATE
Argentina
Founded: 1901
Stadium: Monumental

River Plate are one of Argentina's leading sides. In the late 1930s, they moved to a wealthy suburb of Buenos Aires which, along with a team of expensive players, led to their nickname, the Millionaires. River are renowned for their attacking style. In the late 1940s, their powerful forward line became known as *La Maquina* (the Machine), and the club has produced a succession of world-class attackers, including Omar Sivori, Mario Kempes, Hernan Crespo, Javier Saviola and the legendary Alfredo di Stefano. River Plate have won a total of 36 Argentinian league titles, yet it was not until 1986 that they triumphed in the Copa Libertadores. The team had made the final twice previously (in 1966 and 1976) before a side featuring Norberto Alonso, Juan Gilberto Funes and the great Uruguayan striker Enzo Francescoli beat America Cali of Colombia. River continued their habit of making the Copa Libertadores final in years ending in six with their second win, again versus America Cali, in 1996.

◀ *Paraguayan striker Nelson Cuevas (left) is congratulated by Gaston Fernandez after scoring River Plate's first goal in a 3-2 victory over Colón in 2004.*

KAIZER CHIEFS

South Africa
Founded: 1970
Stadium: Johannesburg Athletics Stadium

Kaizer Motaung played for South Africa's oldest and most famous club for black footballers, the Soweto-based Orlando Pirates. In 1968, he moved to the USA to play for the Atlanta Chiefs in the newly formed NASL. On returning to South Africa, he founded the Kaizer Chiefs (named after Motaung and his former US team) with ex-Orlando Pirates team-mates Zero Johnson, Ratha Mokgoatlheng, Msomi Khoza and Ewert Nene. Featuring a mixture of promising youngsters and experienced veterans, the Chiefs soon made their mark. They won the Life Cup in 1971 and 1972, and the BP Top Eight Cup in 1974. In the same year, they claimed their first South African league title. Tragedy struck in 1976, with the death of captain Ariel Kgongoane in the Soweto uprising and the killing of Ewert Nene, but the Chiefs went on to win the league in 1977 and 1979.

▲ *Patrick Mabedi (left) of Kaizer Chiefs tackles Vikash Dhorasoo of Olympique Lyonnais during the 2003 Peace Cup competition, held in South Korea.*

MOST CONSECUTIVE LEAGUE CHAMPIONSHIPS

15	Tafea FC (Vanuatu)	1994-2008
14	Skonto Riga (Latvia)	1991-2004
13	Al-Faisaly (Jordan)	1959-66, 1970-74
13	Rosenborg (Norway)	1992-2004
13	Lincoln (Gibraltar)	2003-15
11	Nauti (Tuvalu)	1980-90
11	Al-Ansar (Lebanon)	1988, 1990-99
11	Loto Ha'apai FC (Tonga)	1998-2008
10	BFC Dynamo (Germany); Dinamo Tblisi (Georgia); Pyunik Yerevan (Armenia); Sheriff Tiraspol (Moldova); Taipower (Taiwan)	

▼ *Eluding Red Star Belgrade's Miodrag Belodedici (left), Jean-Pierre Papin of Marseille powers upfield during the 1991 European Cup final.*

OLYMPIQUE MARSEILLE

France
Founded: 1899
Stadium: Vélodrome

One of France's biggest clubs, Olympique Marseille boast an intensely passionate support. After a flurry of league titles at the start of the 1970s (helped by Yugoslavian striker Josip Skoblar, who scored a record 44 goals in the 1970–71 season), Marseille found success hard to come by. New chairman Bernard Tapie arrived in 1985 and invested heavily, bringing in expensive stars

such as Enzo Francescoli, Jean-Pierre Papin, Didier Deschamps and the Ghanaian midfielder Abedi Pele. Papin had the greatest impact, showing an incredible appetite for goals and becoming the French league's leading scorer for an astonishing

five consecutive seasons from 1988 to 1992. The team rampaged through the domestic league, winning five championships in a row from 1989 to 1993. Marseille were agonizingly close to becoming the first French club to win the European Cup, going out in the semi-finals to Benfica in 1990 and losing on penalties in the final to Red Star Belgrade the following year. In 1993, a header by Basile Boli sent Marseille fans into ecstasy as they beat AC Milan 1-0 to win the trophy. Then it all went horribly wrong, as Marseille were found guilty of match-fixing a French league game against Valenciennes. They were stripped of their 1993 league title and relegated, as well as being denied the right to defend the Champions League trophy the following season. Tapie was eventually imprisoned for corruption. Marseille spent the rest of the 1990s battling to regain their status, with a certain degree of success – in 1999 they were runners-up in both the French league and the UEFA Cup.

FLUMINENSE
Brazil
Founded: 1902
Stadiums: Laranjeiras, Maracanã

Founded in 1902, Fluminense have traditionally been supported by the middle classes, while their fierce Rio de Janiero rivals Flamengo drew support from the working class. Derby games between the two always guarantee big crowds. One 'Flu v Fla' derby in 1963 attracted a world-record attendance for a club match, with 177,656 supporters crammed inside the enormous Maracanã Stadium. Fluminense also contest Rio's oldest derby, the *Classico Vovô* (Grandpa Derby), with Botafogo, co-founders of the Rio league.

Despite being the home club of a series of Brazilian footballing legends, including Didi during the 1950s and Carlos Alberto and Roberto Rivelino in the 1960s and 1970s, Fluminense have always disappointed on the international stage. They have never won a major South American competition. However, they have achieved much in Brazil, winning the Rio Championship 31 times. One of their most impressive runs came when the Tricolores – so nicknamed for their green, red and white colours – won three Rio Championships in a row from 1983 to 1985. Fluminense have also won the Brazilian National Championship four times, the last domestic title being won in 2012.

◀ *Brazilian legend Romario (right), in Fluminense colours, celebrates with his team-mates during a league match against Goias in 2004.*

ARSENAL
England
Founded: 1886
Stadium: Emirates

First known as Dial Square FC, Arsenal were formed by workers from the Royal Arsenal munitions factory in Woolwich, south London – hence their nickname, the Gunners. After a move to the north of the city in 1913, the club's rise to the top of the English game coincided with the appointment of Herbert Chapman as manager in 1925. Chapman was innovative both on and off the pitch, and he built a counter-attacking team featuring inside-forwards Alex James and David Jack, and winger Cliff Bastin, whose 178 goals for the club remained a record for over half a century. Arsenal were league runners-up in Chapman's first season and won the title in 1931 with a points total that would not be beaten for 30 years. Runners-up in 1932, they then claimed three league titles in a row (1933–35) and two FA Cups (1930 and 1936). Despite a league and FA Cup double in 1971,

FACTFILE Under Herbert Chapman, 'The Arsenal' became just 'Arsenal', allegedly to make them appear at the top of an alphabetical list of Division One clubs. Chapman also successfully campaigned for Gillespie Road underground station, close to the ground, to be renamed Arsenal.

▲ *Arsenal players congratulate Thierry Henry after his goal against Fulham. Henry scored 37 goals in all competitions in both 2002–03 and 2003–04.*

the closest Arsenal have come to their earlier dominance has been under French manager Arsène Wenger. With a team boasting Thierry Henry, Dennis Bergkamp and Patrick Vieira, they won three Premier League titles and four FA Cups from 1998 to 2005. Arsenal were unbeaten through the 2003–04 season, recording a total of 49 league games without defeat, a record in English football. They have won the FA cup in total a record 12 times.

STEAUA BUCHAREST
Romania
Founded: 1947
Stadium: Ghencea

Formed by the Romanian Army, Steaua Bucharest had built a formidable team by the mid-1980s. The side included the superb goalkeeper Helmut Ducadam, Miodrag Belodedici (one of the finest sweepers in Europe), goal machine Marius Lacatus in attack and Romania's greatest player, Gheorghe Hagi. In August 1986, the club began an unbeaten run that is unique in Romanian football. They did not suffer a defeat for three league seasons, conceding 63 goals but scoring a staggering 322. The team made history abroad too, beating Spanish giants Barcelona in the final of the 1986 European Cup to become the first East European club to lift the prestigious trophy. In the early 1990s, after three seasons as runners-up in the Romanian league, Steaua began another incredible run, winning six consecutive domestic titles between 1993 and 1998.

GALATASARAY
Turkey
Founded: 1905
Stadium: Ali Sami Yen

Turkey's three biggest clubs – Galatasaray, Fenerbahçe and Besiktas – are all based in Istanbul and their passionate supporters are fierce and occasionally violent rivals. Galatasaray have won the league title 19 times (one more than Fenerbahçe), the latest being in 2013, as well as the Turkish Cup 14 times (nine more than Fenerbahçe). They are the best-known Turkish club abroad, partly through their competitive performances in Europe during the 1990s. Visiting foreign teams often encounter an intimidating atmosphere – from 'Welcome to Hell' banners displayed at the airport by fans, to a stadium that turns into a cauldron of colour and noise on match nights. Galatasaray went unbeaten at home in Europe from 1984 to 1994,

▲ *Striker Hakan Sükür made more than 500 appearances for Galatasaray, scoring more than 290 goals.*

the year in which they drew 3-3 at Old Trafford to knock Manchester United out of the Champions League. In 2000, they won their first major European trophy by beating Arsenal to win the UEFA Cup.

JUVENTUS
Italy
Founded: 1897
Stadium: Delle Alpi

▲ *Alessandro del Piero lines up an overhead kick. He spent 20 years at Juventus before moving to A-League side, Sydney FC in 2012.*

Formed by high-school students in the city of Turin, Juventus used to play in pink shirts until they switched to black-and-white striped ones in 1903. The club has enjoyed successful spells, including five consecutive league titles from 1931 to 1935 and a 1980s team that won Serie A four times. Juve beat Liverpool to win the 1985 European Cup, but the victory was overshadowed by the Heysel Stadium tragedy in which 39 fans died. Financed by the wealthy Agnelli family, owners of the Fiat car company, Juventus spent lavishly on top-class players in the 1990s, including Roberto Baggio, Gianluca Vialli, Attilio Lombardo, Angelo di Livio, Fabrizio Ravanelli and Christian Vieri. After capturing the UEFA Cup twice in the early 1990s, Juve won an Italian league and cup double in 1995, and beat Ajax to win the Champions League in 1996. They lost the final of that competition in 1997 and 1998, but their fans could console themselves with Serie A titles in both years. Following a match-fixing scandal, Juventus were stripped of the 2005 and 2006 Serie A titles and relegated to Serie B for the first time. They bounced back into Serie A in 2009 and built a new era of dominance, winning their fourth Serie A championship in a row in 2014–15 and reaching the final of the Champions League the same season.

BAYERN MUNICH
Germany
Founded: 1900
Stadium: Allianz Arena

Germany's most famous club was formed in 1900 from rebels who had split from their former club, MTV 1879. The new team beat their old side 7-1 in the first match between the clubs. Although Bayern won a league title in 1932, by the early 1960s they were one of West Germany's less fashionable clubs and did not merit a place in the Bundesliga when it was formed in 1963. They achieved promotion soon after, and by the late 1960s were a dominant force in the domestic game. At the helm were future footballing legends such as Sepp Maier, Franz Beckenbauer and Gerd Müller, who was the Bundesliga's top scorer in seven seasons (1967, 1969–70, 1972–74 and 1978). With that squad, Bayern won German Cups in 1966 and 1967, and a European Cup-Winners' Cup in 1967. In the early 1970s, Bayern's stars were joined by more world-class players such as Paul Breitner and Uli Hoeness. The team won three Bundesliga titles in a row and three consecutive European Cups from 1974 to 1976. Success has continued with 2012–13 proving a stellar season, with a notable Bundesliga, German Cup and Champions League treble under outgoing coach Jupp Heynckes. Futher success came so that in 2014–15, Bayern celebrated winning their 25th Bundesliga title, their third league title in a row, two years after a league, cup and Champions League treble in 2012–13.

▶ *This header by Jerome Boateng helped give Bayern Munich one of their 29 wins out of 34 games in the 2012–13 Bundesliga.*

▲ *Werner Roth rounds the Atlético Madrid goalkeeper as Bayern Munich power to a 4-0 victory to win the 1974 European Cup final replay. Bayern had salvaged a 1-1 draw in the first match with a goal in the last minute of extra time.*

BENFICA
Portugal
Founded: 1904
Stadium: Estadio da Luz

Benfica remain Portugal's most famous and successful club, despite the long periods of glory enjoyed by rivals Porto and Sporting Lisbon. Their greatest era was undoubtedly the 1960s, which began under the management of Hungarian Bela Guttmann. The side played with a mix of pace, power and skill, typified by the midfielder Mario Coluna and the brilliant Eusebio. Benfica began the decade by defeating Barcelona 3-2 to win the 1961 European Cup. The following year, facing the mighty Real Madrid in the final, they found themselves 3-1 down to a Ferenc Puskas hat-trick, but fought back to beat the Spanish giants 5-3. They featured in five European Cup finals during the 1960s and won eight out of ten league championships. Defending another league title in the 1972–73 season, Benfica went unbeaten through 30 league matches, scoring 101 goals in the process.

▲ *Benfica pose before the 1968 European Cup final, having beaten Juventus in the semi-finals. Amazingly, their toughest opponents were Northern Irish side Glentoran in the first round – Benfica sneaked through on the away goals rule.*

ZENIT SAINT PETERSBURG
Russia
Founded: 1925
Stadium: Petrovsky Stadium

Founded by a group of local metal workers, Zenit originally played in the Soviet league and in the 1950s could count on the support of famous classical composer Dmitri Shostakovich in the stands. The break-up of the Soviet Union saw Zenit, known as the Blue-and-Whites, enter the Russian league, which it won for the first time under Dick Advocaat in 2007 – with Andrei Arshavin the team's standout performer. Three further league titles came in 2010, 2011–12 and 2014–15. The club frequently competes in the Champions League but in 2008 Zenit won the UEFA Cup for the first time and beat Manchester United later the same year to lift the UEFA Super Cup.

LOS ANGELES GALAXY
USA
Founded: 1995
Stadium: StubHub Center

A founder member of Major League Soccer (MLS), the Los Angeles Galaxy are one of its most successful sides, with five MLS Cups (2002, 2005, 2011, 2012, 2014) and four MLS Supporters' Shields trophies (1998, 2002, 2010, 2011). In addition, they have won the Lamar Hunt US Open Cup twice (2001, 2005) and, in 2000, the CONCACAF Champions League. Attracting homegrown talents such as Cobi Jones and Landon Donovan, the Galaxy have also bought in foreign stars including David Beckham and, in 2015, Steven Gerrard. After previously playing at the Rose Bowl and Titan Stadium, since 2005 the Galaxy's games have been held at the StubHub Center, a ground they share with MLS rivals CD Chivas USA.

◄ *Juninho of the LA Galaxy competes for the ball with Chivas USA's Oswaldo Minda during their 2013 MLS match, which ended in a 1-1 draw.*

ANDERLECHT
Belgium
Founded: 1908
Stadium: Constant vanden Stock

▲ *Belgian striker Enzo Scifo on the ball for Anderlecht against PSV Eindhoven – the team for which Luc Nilis, Scifo's World Cup team-mate, played.*

It took 39 years from the club's formation for Anderlecht to win their first Belgian league championship. Since then, the Brussels-based side have made up for lost time, winning a staggering 33 league titles – 20 more than the second most successful side in Belgium, Club Brugge. In addition, Anderlecht have been runners-up 20 times. Such consistency has seen the club qualify to play in a major European competition every year from 1964 to 2007. The 1970s were a golden era for Anderlecht. They were runners-up in the 1970 Inter-Cities Fairs Cup, losing 4-3 over two legs to Arsenal. By the mid-1970s, under the management of Raymond Goethals, Anderlecht's team boasted many quality players. A strong midfield, featuring Frankie van der Elst, Ludo Coeck and Arie Haan, played behind talented attacking duo Benny Nielsen and Robbie Rensenbrink. The club contested three European Cup-Winners' Cup finals in a row, beating West Ham 4-2 in 1976, but losing to Hamburg the following year. Anderlecht bounced back to knock the same German side out of the 1977–78 competition on their way to the final, where they thrashed Austria Vienna 4-0. The team also added two European Supercups to their trophy cabinet by beating Bayern Munich in 1976 and Liverpool in 1978.

HIT THE NET

www.soccerlinks.net/pages/index.html
A huge collection of web links to more than 5,000 official and unofficial club websites, searchable by continent and country.

www.eurotopfoot.com/indexgb.php3
This website ranks 475 football clubs according to their performances in European competitions and provides profiles of each of the featured clubs.

www.soccerbase.com/teams/home.sd
A great database of clubs and national teams, searchable by competition or region, which gives details of teams, their players and results.

ESPERANCE SPORTIVE TUNIS

Tunisia
Founded: 1919
Stadium: El–Menzah

With a distinctive strip that gave them their nickname – the Blood and Golds – Esperance have long been one of the leading clubs in Tunisia and North Africa. Back-to-back Tunisian league wins in 1993 and 1994 paved the way for their 1994 African Champions

▲ *Esperance's Issam Jomaa vies with Nigerian team Enyemba's Musa Aliyu in the semi-finals of the 2004 African Champions League.*

League triumph where, in front of a delirious home crowd, they beat the Egyptian holders Zamalek 3-1. In 1997, Esperance began a record-breaking league run. Seeing off the challenge of leading rivals such as Etoile Sportive du Sahel and Club Africain, the team captured an incredible seven straight league championships. Before this feat, no Tunisian club had won more than three league titles in a row. They also won four more league titles in a row (2009–12), a further title in 2014 and a second African Champions League in 2011. Many of the side's best players were part of the Tunisian national side that won the 2004 African Nations Cup on home soil.

▼ *Peñarol players celebrate their winning goal against fierce rivals Nacional to claim the 1999 Uruguayan Championship.*

SPARTAK MOSCOW

Russia
Founded: 1922
Stadium: Lokomotiv

Although Moscow Dynamo are the most famous Russian team outside the country, their local rivals Spartak Moscow have claimed more silverware, winning 12 Soviet league titles and ten Soviet Cups. They also made the semi-finals of European competitions twice in the early 1990s. Unfortunately, Spartak's greatest team (of the late 1940s and early 1950s) peaked in the days before major European competitions existed. Spartak dominated the first ten years of the Russian League (1992–2001), winning nine league titles, but have since been overtaken by Rubin Kazan and Zenit Saint Petersburg.

▲ *Spartak Moscow's Senegalese defender Baye Ali Ibra Kebe (right) tackles Liverpool's Jamie Carragher during a Champions League match in 2002.*

PEÑAROL

Uruguay
Founded: 1891
Stadium: Centenario

Along with Nacional, Peñarol dominate Uruguayan football. Peñarol are marginally the more successful, with more than 45 league titles. In head-to-head meetings up to the spring of 2012, Peñarol lead their rivals by 182 wins to 166. The club's first golden era came in the 1960s. Led by Ecuadorian striker Pedro Spencer, the side won three Copa Libertadores (1960, 1961 and 1966) and two World Club Cups (against Benfica in 1961 and Real Madrid in 1966). Peñarol's side of the 1980s added to this tally, winning two more Copa Libertadores and, in 1982, beating Aston Villa to win a third World Club Cup. Peñarol hold a number of Copa Libertadores records: the largest win (11-2 against Valencia of Venezuela in 1970), the highest aggregate win (14-1 versus Everest of Ecuador in 1963) and the most consecutive participations in the competition (15 between 1965 and 1979).

AJAX
Holland
Founded: 1900
Stadium: Amsterdam ArenA

Coach Rinus Michels arrived at Ajax in the 1964–65 season, just in time to save them from relegation. (The team finished 13th out of 16.) Michels went on to develop the concept of 'total football' (see page 61), which would have a major impact at both club and international level. Signs of a renaissance at Ajax began to show as early as 1966, when the team won the Dutch league and shocked Liverpool 5-1 in the European Cup. Three years later, Ajax became the first Dutch side to reach the final of that competition, where they lost to AC Milan. Spurred on by Dutch rivals Feyenoord winning the European Cup in 1970, Ajax went on to claim the trophy for the next three years with the help of such legends as Johan Cruyff, Arie Haan, Ruud Krol and Johan Neeskens. Playing an electric style of fluid football with the emphasis firmly on attack, they were crowned Dutch league champions six times in eight seasons (1966–68, 1970, 1972–73) and won the European Supercup and World Club Cup, both in 1972. Ajax also supplied the bulk of the players for the Dutch side that finished runners-up at the 1974 World Cup. By the mid-1970s, however, Neeskens, Cruyff and the coach Michels had moved to Spain and Ajax entered a period of decline. But through a comprehensive and much-copied youth system, they were eventually able to replace their former stars with several new waves of talent, including Dennis Bergkamp, Jan Vertonghen, Wesley Sneijder and Christian Eriksen.

▼ *Twins Frank and Ronald de Boer, together with strikers Nwankwo Kanu and Finidi George, take a lap of honour after Ajax's 1-0 victory against AC Milan in the final of the 1995 Champions League.*

LIVERPOOL
England
Founded: 1892
Stadium: Anfield

In 1959, Liverpool were struggling in the English second division and had been knocked out of the third round of the FA Cup by amateur side Worcester City. Then Bill Shankly arrived as manager.

He was a passionate, no-nonsense Scot who went on to build a successful Liverpool side that won the league championship three times and lifted the UEFA Cup in 1973. A year later he resigned, and Bob Paisley – Shankly's assistant for 15 years – was promoted to manager. Paisley's Liverpool won 19 major trophies in nine years, making him the most successful British manager of the 20th century.

FACTFILE
Between January 1978 and January 1981, Liverpool set an all-time record of 85 home games unbeaten in all competitions. Included in this run were an incredible 63 home league matches in a row.

The club won six league titles and three League Cups thanks to a watertight defence, a quick, accurate passing game and intelligent attacking by players such as Kevin Keegan, Steve Heighway, John Toshack and Kenny Dalglish. A UEFA Cup win in 1976 was followed by European Cup triumphs in 1977 and 1978, making Liverpool the first British side to successfully defend the trophy. In 1981, the club beat Real Madrid to win the European Cup for a third time, and a fourth win came (after penalties) in 1984 against Italian side Roma.

◀ *Liverpool's Ray Kennedy (far left), Graeme Souness and Alan Hansen close down Flamengo star Zico during the 1981 World Club Cup.*

CELTIC
Scotland
Founded: 1888
Stadium: Celtic Park

Celtic, along with their Glasgow-based rivals Rangers, have dominated Scottish football for decades. However, Celtic had not won the league title for 11 years before the arrival of Jock Stein as manager in 1965. Stein developed a home-grown side, all of whom hailed from Glasgow and the surrounding area. The team was full of youth and pace, and had an adventurous style of play. These qualities were typified by the tricky winger Jimmy Johnstone, marauding full-back Tommy Gemmell, prolific strikers Steve Chalmers, Bobby Lennox and Willy Wallace, and a defensive rock in Billy McNeill, the captain. Celtic began an astonishing run from 1966, winning nine Scottish league championships in a row and completing a Scottish Cup and league double five times during that period. Yet they contested the 1967 European Cup final as underdogs to a powerful Internazionale side that had won two of the previous three European Cups. Against the odds, Celtic recovered from a goal down to beat the Italians 2-1, becoming the first British side to win the biggest club prize in European football. The 'Lions of Lisbon' narrowly failed to repeat their achievement when they reached the 1970 European Cup final, going down 2-1 to Dutch side Feyenoord. It would be 33 years before the Scottish club reached their next European final, losing 3-2 to Porto in the 2003 UEFA Cup final.

▶ *Winger Jimmy Johnstone (left) scored 130 goals for Celtic on the way to nine league championships, five League Cups and four Scottish Cups with the club.*

▲ *Colo Colo's Jose Domingo Salcedo gets ahead of Sebastian Battaglia of Argentinian side Boca Juniors during a Copa Libertadores match in 2008.*

COLO COLO
Chile
Founded: 1925
Stadium: David Arellano

With around 60 per cent of the country's football fans following them, Colo Colo are easily the most heavily supported and successful of all the Chilean club sides. The team has won a record 30 league championships (13 more than fierce rivals Universidad de Chile) as well as the Chilean Cup – the *Campeonato de Copa* – ten times. Under their coach Arturo Salah, Colo Colo captured league titles in 1986 and 1989, before former Yugoslavia under-20 coach Mirko Jozic took up the manager's post during the 1990 season. The team completed a sequence of three league titles in a row in 1991, the same year that they enjoyed fantastic success abroad. In 1973, Colo Colo had been the first Chilean side to contest a final of the premier South American club cup competition, the Copa Libertadores. In 1991, the club went one stage further, beating the mighty Argentinian side River Plate in the semi-finals and the cup holders Olimpia 3-0 on aggregate to win the trophy. Whilst further international success has been restricted to a runners-up spot in the Copa Sudamericana in 2006, the club won league titles in 2006, 2007 and 2008.

▲ *Dynamo Kiev pose with the 2003 Ukrainian Cup after beating the holders – and Kiev's most competitive rivals in Ukrainian football – Shakhtar Donetsk.*

DYNAMO KIEV
Ukraine
Founded: 1927
Stadium: National Sport Komplex Olimpiyskiy

Originally the football team of the Soviet secret police, Dynamo Kiev were the first club outside Moscow to win the Soviet league championship. A player in that 1961 side, Valery Lobanovsky, became Kiev's coach 13 years later. He led the club through its greatest era, which began spectacularly with back-to-back Soviet league titles. In 1975, Kiev won the Cup-Winners' Cup, becoming the first Soviet side to win a European competition. They also beat Bayern Munich 3-1 to win the European Supercup. In total, Lobanovsky (in three separate spells) managed Kiev to eight league titles, six Soviet Cups and two European Cup-Winners' Cups. In 1991, after the break-up of the Soviet Union, Kiev played in the newly formed Ukrainian league. They have dominated there, winning 14 league titles including the 2014–15 competition.

REAL MADRID
Spain
Founded: 1902
Stadium: Bernabeu

Real Madrid are one of the world's most famous and successful sides. They have won 32 Spanish league titles, nine more than rivals Barcelona and 22 more than their neighbours, Atlético Madrid. They have also captured 11 European trophies and three World Club Cups. In the 1940s and 1950s, Real's president, Santiago Bernabeu, began to transform the club with foreign signings and a huge desire to win the newly formed European Cup competition. Real did not disappoint, capturing the first European Cup, in 1956, and the next four as well. The team included two of the world's outstanding attacking talents in Ferenc Puskas and Alfredo di Stefano, as well as pacy winger Paco Gento, central defenders Marcos Marquitos and Juan Zarraga, and attacking midfielder Hector Rial. From 1957 to 1965, Real remained unbeaten at home in 121 Spanish league matches and won five La Liga titles in a row (1961–65). A new-look side captured the European Cup for a sixth time in 1966. Today, Real are one of the world's richest clubs, with a habit of buying football's most famous and expensive players, such as Zinedine Zidane and David Beckham, and more recently Cristiano Ronaldo and Gareth Bale. With stars such as these, Real have won four La Liga titles in the 21st century, including the 2007–08 competition, and have taken their European Cup and Champions League triumphs to ten.

▲ *Real Madrid's victorious team pose with the 1960 European Cup after one of the greatest ever displays of attacking football (see pages 14–15).*

▼ *Pepe and Ronaldo hold the Supercopa trophy after Real Madrid won it for the ninth time in 2012.*

THE WORLD CUP COMES HOME

France entered the 1998 World Cup under intense pressure. The tournament was to be held on French soil, they had failed to qualify for the previous World Cup and critics claimed that the squad lacked a striker of true international class. What they did have, however, was the world's most creative midfielder in Zinedine Zidane, a strong defence and a battery of hard-working midfielders and attackers. France powered through their group, winning all three games. In the second round, veteran defender Laurent Blanc scored the first golden goal at the World Cup, to beat Paraguay. Further victories over Italy and Croatia took *Les Bleus* to a final against the mighty Brazil, led by Ronaldo. More famous for his mesmerizing ball skills on the ground, Zidane scored two headed goals against a subdued Brazilian team, and an injury-time strike by Emmanuel Petit completed a 3-0 victory. The World Cup had been the brainchild of a Frenchman back in the 1920s. Now, at last, the cup had come home. *Les Bleus* were on top of the world.

France's Zinedine Zidane (number 10) rises high to score with a header in the 1998 World Cup final.

FOOTBALL DREAMS

From Beijing to Buenos Aires, Manchester to Mexico City, millions of children, teenagers and adults play football for fun, sport and exercise. Many are content to take part at an amateur level, but for some, the dream of emulating the stars they read about, watch and worship is a passion.

YOUNG DREAMS

Promising players often emerge at an early age in school and local teams. In most countries, young footballers can play at a regional, county or state level in organized youth team competitions. Major football clubs run youth sides and football academies, and also send scouts to watch games in the hope of spotting new talent. Young players may be invited to an open day or trial, where scouts and coaches can observe them in action at close hand. A club may then offer a contract or a place at its youth academy to a promising player. Famous academies exist at clubs such as Bayern Munich, Manchester United and Porto. The most famous is De Toekomst, the youth academy of Dutch side Ajax. It has been responsible for producing truly great footballers such as Johan Cruyff, Marco van Basten, Dennis Bergkamp and – more recently – Wesley Sneijder, Elijero Elia, Toby Alderweireld and Luis Suarez.

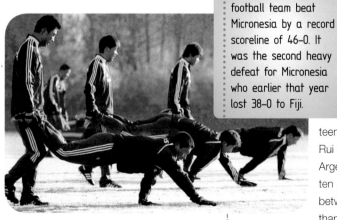

▲ Young Chinese footballers perform wheelbarrow exercises. According to FIFA, there are more than 28 million registered players in China with the numbers of young footballers rising.

▲ Freddy Adu was born in Ghana, but is now a US citizen. Here, aged 14, he shoots past Sierra Leone's keeper at the 2004 Under-17 World Championship.

YOUTH TEAMS AND COMPETITIONS

As young players approach the pinnacle of the game, there are international matches for schoolboys and schoolgirls as well as under-17 and youth competitions. These reach a peak with FIFA's Under-17 World Championship and the FIFA U-20 World Cup. The latter competition began in 1977; at the 1991 tournament, Portugal swept to the title with a midfield containing teenagers João Pinto, Rui Costa and Luis Figo. Argentina won five of the ten competitions held between 1993 and 2011 thanks to goals from players such as Javier Saviola, Lionel Messi and Sergio Aguero, who was top scorer at the 2007 tournament. Serbia won the 2015 tournament, beating Brazil in the final. FIFA's Under-17 World Cup has also thrown up a number of stars. Landon Donovan was the 1999 tournament's Most Valuable Player, an award given to Cesc Fàbregas in 2003, Anderson in 2005 and Mexico's Julio Gómez González in 2011. Some young players are thrown into action with the adults in the reserve side or first team at a professional club. One of the youngest was Freddy Adu, who in 2004 came on as a substitute for US club DC United in their game against San Jose Earthquakes. He was just 14 years old.

FACTFILE
In 2015, Vanatu's U23 football team beat Micronesia by a record scoreline of 46–0. It was the second heavy defeat for Micronesia who earlier that year lost 38–0 to Fiji.

HANDLING REJECTION

For millions of wannabes, the hope of playing professional football remains just a dream. As players rise through the footballing ranks, the vast majority find that their talents are surpassed by others and they are unable to progress further. Some talented young footballers are rejected because coaches believe their slight build or lack of height would put them at a

disadvantage. As youngsters, Kevin Keegan and Allan Simonsen were rejected by major clubs for being too small, yet both went on to star for club and country and win the coveted European Footballer of the Year award. Other players are turned down because their levels of fitness are not high enough. As a 16-year-old, the great Michel Platini was rejected by French club Metz after medical checks revealed he had poor breathing and a weak heart.

Rejection is hard to take for many junior players, but some are able to use such a setback to spur themselves on and prove their doubters wrong. Dino Zoff trialled at Internazionale, whose coaches were unimpressed. The same thing happened at Juventus, but the young keeper was not put off – he worked hard at his game and was eventually signed by Udinese. More than 20 years later, he captained Italy to the World Cup trophy. In 2009, Lassana Diarra, who had been rejected by Nantes for being too small and lightweight, moved from Portsmouth to Spanish giants Real Madrid for almost £20 million.

▶ In the final of the men's blind football tournament at the 2004 Paralympics, held in Greece, Argentina's Oscar Moreno (right) holds off Sandro Soares of Brazil.

◀ Brazil's Oscar (left) chases the ball down at the FIFA U-20 World Cup. He scored a hat-trick in the final.

FOOTBALL FOR ALL

Football can be enjoyed in all climates and conditions and by people of all ages and abilities. It is also played competitively by footballers with disabilities that range from being wheelchair-bound to having impaired hearing. In 2014, Russia, Ukraine and Germany were the medal winners at the Deaflympics, held in Bulgaria. Amputee football is played by outfield players using crutches, but no artificial leg, and by goalkeepers who are single-arm amputees. Since 1984, the Paralympics has included a seven-a-side football competition for people suffering from cerebral palsy and brain injuries.

The game is played largely according to FIFA's seven-a-side rules, but with bigger goals, no offsides and two 30-minute halves. Football for blind and visually impaired athletes uses a special ball. It contains a noise-making device that makes a distinctive sound as the ball moves. Teams consist of four blind outfield players, a keeper (who can be partially sighted) and five substitutes. In 2004, the sport made its debut at the Paralympics. Brazil have proven to be the true masters of this 50-minute-long game at the Paralympics, winning all three events so far, including the one held at London 2012.

FACTFILE
In 2014, Gloriana Villalobos made her debut for Costa Rica at the age of 14. The following year she appeared at the 2015 Women's World Cup.

▶ Eric Cantona controls the ball during a beach football match. The sport has its own FIFA World Cup. The 2013 tournament, held in Tahiti, was won by Russia. They beat Spain 5-1 in the final.

A PRO'S LIFE

Viewed from the outside, a professional footballer's life appears glamorous, exciting and rewarding. But behind the appearances in top matches, on television shows and at celebrity events, lies much hard work and sometimes frustration and disappointment.

MAKING THE FIRST TEAM

Signing as a youngster for a big club is every aspiring footballer's dream, but, in truth, a young player in this position is only halfway towards his or her goal. Competition for one of the 11 starting places is intense. Many young players do not make the grade and have to move elsewhere – often down a division or two – to play first-team football. 'If you're good enough, you're old enough' is a motto used by some coaches who have thrust exceptionally talented youngsters into first-team action for their club or country. Cameroon striker Samuel Eto'o first played for his country the day before his 16th birthday. In 2012, a product of Samuel Eto'o's soccer school in Cameroon, Fabrice Olinga became the Spanish La Liga's youngest ever goalscorer at 16 years and 98 days. Four days later he found himself playing in a UEFA Champions League match for Malaga, and within two months was playing and scoring for his national team, Cameroon. Most young players have to wait far longer for their first-team debut.

LOANED OUT

Increasingly, in many leagues, young players are loaned out to other clubs to gain experience. At the start of the 2014–15 season, Chelsea had more than 25 players out on loan with other clubs, including Christian Atsu, Marko Marin and Tomáš Kalas. Loan spells can be relatively short and to a lower-division club in the same country, such as David Beckham's six-week loan spell at Preston North End when he was a Manchester United youngster. They can also be for longer periods and to a club in a different country, as with Fernando Torres who in 2015 went on an 18-month loan to Atlético Madrid. Many players who are frustrated by a lack of opportunities seek a loan or permanent move elsewhere to play first-team football. This is not just limited to young, inexperienced footballers. In 2013, American MLS side DC United obtained experienced Panama midfielder Marcos Sánchez on loan. Others agree to a loan move to put them in the shop window for a future permanent transfer, either to the club that has taken them on loan or to another in that league.

◀ *English striker Andy Carroll has twice gone on loan, firstly with Preston North End then a season-long loan with West Ham United in 2012, for whom he signed permanently in 2013.*

TRAINING, INJURIES AND RECOVERY

A typical week for a footballer involves training, resting, going to club functions and travelling to one or more games. Training usually involves a mixture of fitness, strength and flexibility exercises to boost a player's stamina, pace and sharpness. Players also practise skills and tactics – improving their heading or working on free kicks, for example. In Europe, footballers have for years eaten a healthy, scientifically managed diet. Britain, in contrast, was slow to catch on. Even in the 1970s and 1980s, a pre-match meal was often as heavy as steak, egg and chips.

Injuries occur fairly often in football. An English FA study of the 1997–98 and 1998–99

> **FACTFILE** Spanish goalkeeper Santiago Canizares missed the 2002 World Cup after dropping a bottle of aftershave on his foot.

▲ *Romelu Lukaku trains with Chelsea. He was loaned to West Bromwich Albion for the 2012–13 season and then Everton for 2013–14.*

▲ *Whilst playing for Malaga in 2012, Fabrice Olinga became La Liga's youngest goalscorer at the tender age of 16 years and 98 days.*

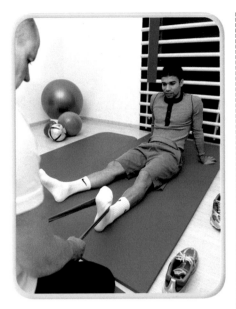

▲ *Eduardo da Silva works with a physiotherapist in the gym to help him recover from a broken leg. Recovery from an operation or a serious injury can be a difficult time, as players miss key games and face a long period of training.*

seasons recorded over 6,000 injuries, mostly to knee and ankle joints or leg muscles. In April 2013, more than 70 players were out injured in the 18-team Bundesliga, and around 50 in Italy's Serie A league. Arsenal suffered 25, Everton 37 and Manchester United 39 significant injuries to players during the 2014–15 season.

Injured players are treated by a club's doctor and physiotherapist. They are sent to the best consultants and surgeons to ensure as quick a recovery as possible. This can take weeks or months and usually involves long days in the gym, gentle training and intensive sessions with the physio. Injured players are painfully aware that their place in the team has been filled. A young footballer may have seized the chance well, making it harder for the injured player to return.

A career in football can be short, with players retiring by their early thirties (although goalkeepers can play on into their late thirties). Serious injuries are what professional footballers fear most. Every year, an average of 50 English league players are forced to retire because of injury.

REWARDS AND RESPONSIBILITIES

Football's top players are paid handsomely and treated as celebrities in a similar way to music and movie stars. Some use their celebrity to publicize good causes, to help coach and inspire young people or to visit hospitals, schools and charities. Just like showbusiness stars, footballers have to deal with the media. A club may ask players to give interviews for website features or to co-operate with newspapers and television companies to promote an upcoming game or new kit, for example. What can be harder for young footballers to handle is the way in which the press can invade their private lives. Photographers and reporters may besiege a player's home and follow their family and friends. Footballers are seen as important role models for young people and any wrongdoing, such as being fined for speeding, snubbing autograph hunters or partying, attracts much negative television and newspaper attention.

FACTFILE Blackburn Olympic spent a week at a health spa before the 1883 FA Cup final. The players' daily diet included a glass of port and two raw eggs for breakfast, a leg of mutton for lunch and 12 oysters for dinner.

FACTFILE In 2004, QPR manager Ian Holloway took his team to train with ballet dancers. The aim was to improve the players' flexibility and balance, helping them to avoid injuries.

◀ *Top players are constantly in the public eye. Here, David Beckham signs autographs at an open training session. To attend, each fan donated £4 to charity.*

▼ *Lionel Messi holds the FIFA Ballon d'Or trophy, awarded to the world's best footballer each year. The sumptuous skills and goalscoring exploits of the mesmeric Argentinean helped him win the award four years in a row (2009–12).*

THE PLAYERS' STAGE

Without stadiums, football would still be played, but games would be far quieter, less passionate and exciting affairs. Stadiums spring into life on match days, when they are transformed from empty, silent steel and concrete structures into a seething sea of noise and colour.

GREAT STADIUMS

England and Scotland boasted the world's first great stadiums. Glasgow's Hampden Park was built in 1903; in 1937, almost 150,000 spectators were admitted to watch an international match between Scotland and England. The biggest crowd at London's Wembley Stadium – which was built in just 300 days – was its first, for the 1923 FA Cup final. More than 150,000 people crammed inside, spilling onto the pitch and forcing the kick-off to be delayed.

The mighty Maracanã Stadium in Rio de Janiero, Brazil, is almost completely round. It holds the official world record for a football crowd – in 1950, around 199,850 people watched a World Cup game there between Brazil and Uruguay. In 2014, Brazil's Maracanã Stadium joined Mexico City's

▲ A staggering 114,000 spectators, all standing, cram into London's Crystal Palace to watch the 1901 FA Cup final between Tottenham Hotspur and Sheffield United.

Azteca stadium as the only venues to twice hold World Cup final games. Many of the world's biggest football arenas were built to host the World Cup or European Championships – from the Centenario in Uruguay, the venue for the first World Cup in 1930, to Poland's National Stadium that

hosted Euro 2012 matches. Ten venues, both new and old, will be used for Euro 2016 from Parc des Princes (which first opened in 1897) to Lyon's Stade des Lumières, completed just months before the beginning of the tournament.

BEHIND THE SCENES

The forgotten people of football are often the staff who run a stadium and ensure that the day of a match goes smoothly. We tend to think of them only when there is a problem such as crowd trouble or a pitch that is unfit for play. The club or stadium owner liaises with police and local authorities and employs stewards to prevent pitch invasions, violence and other problems. Box office staff do their best to ensure that tickets are sold and distributed correctly, while turnstile operators and sellers of programmes and food and drink all work at a ground on a match day. At the 2006

▼ At Euro 2004, Fabien Barthez saves a David Beckham penalty in the Estadio da Luz in Lisbon, Portugal. The 65,000-capacity arena is Benfica's home ground.

▶ Groundstaff in traditional dress prepare the goal nets at the National Stadium in Lagos, Nigeria, before the opening game of the 1999 World Youth Championship.

World Cup, tickets contained tiny microchips that could be read by scanners, easing crowd congestion and helping to prevent ticket fraud.

The groundstaff are in charge of the goals, the pitch and its markings. They work especially hard when the pitch is in poor condition because of bad weather – clearing snow, thawing out the pitch or soaking up excess moisture. On the day of the game, or sometimes earlier, the match referee examines the pitch carefully and talks to the groundstaff before deciding whether the game can go ahead.

▲ A groundsman gives the pitch a close cut at Newcastle United's St James Park stadium. Pitch care is vital at all top-level clubs.

STADIUM INNOVATION

Stadium tragedies have occurred all over the world (see pages 104–105), prompting many governments and football authorities to bring in far stricter rules on stadium design, capacities and crowd control. In the past 30 years, new safety laws and innovations in architecture have led to major changes in the design of football stadiums. Despite fans feeling a strong emotional attachment to a ground, dozens of clubs have abandoned their old stadium in or near the centre of a town or city. The money raised from the sale of the land is used to build a new stadium on the outskirts. Many of these stadiums form part of a hotel, leisure or shopping complex. A famous example is the Stade

FACTFILE The Timsah Arena stadium is green and shaped like a giant crocodile's head. Completed in 2015, it's the home of Turkish club Bursapor and seats approx 45,000.

FACTFILE At the 1986 World Cup, eagle-eyed officials spotted that the pitch markings at the edge of the penalty area for the France-Hungary game were in the wrong place. They had to be hastily repainted.

de France in Paris, which was built to host the final of the 1998 World Cup. It features 17 shops and 43 cafes and restaurants for its 80,000 spectators.

Notably, the USA staged the first indoor World Cup qualifier (at the Seattle Kingdome) and the first indoor World Cup finals match (at the Pontiac Silverdome). Stadiums with a sliding roof have become more and more popular, allowing the venue to host music concerts and other indoor events. The Amsterdam ArenA was opened in 1996 as Ajax's new ground. The first European stadium with a retractable roof, it seats 51,859 spectators. The Millennium Stadium in Cardiff, Wales, and London's Wembley Stadium also have sliding roofs. Inside a new stadium, fans may find a removable pitch, corporate boxes for business entertaining and giant screens that replay action from the game. Germany's Arena Auf Schalke, opened in 2001, has 540 video screens throughout the stadium and a giant video cube suspended from the roof. With four 36m^2 video screens, it is the first of its kind in Europe.

TOP TEN LARGEST FOOTBALL STADIUMS

POPULAR NAME	LOCATION	CAPACITY
Azteca	Mexico City, Mexico	106,000
Nou Camp	Barcelona, Spain	95,500
FNB Stadium	Soweto, South Africa	94,736
Wembley Stadium	London, UK	90,000
Gelora Bung Karno	Jakarta, Indonesia	88,083
Borg El Arab	Alexandria, Egypt	86,000
Santiago Bernabéu	Madrid, Spain	85,454
Azadi	Tehran, Iran	84,412
Signal Iduna Park	Dortmund, Germany	80,667

▲ The Estádio do Maracanã (Maracanã Stadium), refurbished for the 2014 World Cup. In June 2013, the 78,800 capacity stadium hosted its first official game, a friendly between Brazil and England that ended 2-2.

SUPPORTERS AND TEAMS

Dreams are not only held by players and coaches. Everyone connected to a club or national side dreams that their team will achieve glory and success, and this especially includes the most loyal, passionate and vocal group of all – the fans.

FOLLOWING A TEAM

For millions of supporters, following their club or national side is a lifelong passion. Fans may chant for a manager to leave or be unhappy with certain players or the team's form, but their love of the club tends to remain. Dedicated fans go to great lengths to follow their side, putting up with poor weather and long hours of travelling to away games. Many fans spend much of their income every season on getting to as many games as possible and buying replica shirts and other merchandise – from T-shirts and scarfs to club-branded toothpaste and credit cards. Do these supporters get a fair deal for their time, effort and expenditure? To many casual or non-fans, the answer appears to be no. Entertainment and the 'right' result are never guaranteed, and ticket prices have soared at all-seater

▼ *Mascots are a feature at many football games. These British mascots are taking part in the 2002 Mascot Grand National, which was won by Oldham Athletic's Chaddy the Owl.*

stadiums, sometimes pricing ordinary fans out of the game. Yet, being a loyal football fan is rarely a decision made with the head. It is all about heart and emotion. Every loyal fan loves to feel the rush of excitement as they approach their home ground, chant with the crowd and witness the start of a match. What comes next is a 90-minute rollercoaster ride of highs and lows, ending at the final whistle and followed by a post-match examination of what went right and wrong, before hope and expectancy build for the next game.

◄ *A facepainted Greek fan shows support for his team at the 2004 European Championships.*

TOP TEN AVERAGE LEAGUE ATTENDANCES (2012–13)		
1	Borussia Dortmund	80,463
2	Barcelona	77,632
3	Manchester United	75,335
4	Real Madrid	73,081
5	Bayern Munich	72,882
6	Schalke 04	61,578
7	Arsenal	59,992
8	Hamburg	53,252
9	Marseille	52,917
10	VfB Stuttgart	50,801

HIT THE NET

www.stadiumguide.com
Information on the leading football stadiums in Europe and elsewhere, including the venues for Euro 2016.

http://expertfootball.com/wp/?p=754
A pair of webpages looking at some of the world's greatest derby matches.

www.fifa.com/worldcup/destination/stadiums
Check out all the stadiums that were used to host the 2014 World Cup in Brazil.

FACTFILE With a Dutch mother and a Belgian father, fan Raymond Brul had a problem at Euro 2000. In the end, he showed his support for both nations by painting half his car in Dutch team colours and half in Belgian colours.

FANS AND THE MEDIA

Few stadiums hold more than 60,000 spectators, but the rise of television coverage has opened up the game to millions of new fans. Some supporters, however, criticize TV for concentrating on the top teams and moving matches to different days and new starting times. TV companies spend a fortune on buying the rights to show live games and highlights from the top leagues. Back in the studio, famous ex-players and managers comment on the action, while

▲ *Pelé's 1970 World Cup shirt was auctioned in 2002 for a record £157,750, beating the sum paid for Geoff Hurst's 1966 World Cup shirt by £66,000.*

reporters and statisticians provide interviews and highly detailed analysis of matches.

Coverage of football in other media has boomed, too. Fans manage their own sides in computer simulations or fantasy football leagues, while results, news and video clips are sent to their smartphones and tablets. They can read about their club in books, magazines, fanzines and blogs. The rise of radio phone-ins and online messageboards has allowed fans to voice their opinions on games, players, managers and referees.

MORE THAN A GAME

Fans look forward to certain matches in particular – a clash between two teams at the top of the league table, for example. A game between a small club and a top side allows fans to dream of a famous giantkilling victory. In 2008, Luxembourg fans (who had seen 59 defeats in the last 60 competitive matches) were delirious when their side beat Switzerland.

Sometimes, even results in friendly matches can surprise, such as Cape Verde beating Portugal 2-0 in an April 2015 game.

FACTFILE In 1998, Newcastle United fans draped the giant Angel of the North statue with a 9m-high Alan Shearer football shirt that cost £1,000 to be specially made.

▶ *Fans of Turkish club Galatasaray drum up a fearsomely loud atmosphere before the 2000 UEFA Cup final against Arsenal.*

The most anticipated and passionate of all games tend to be derby matches between two neighbouring sides. Most clubs have some form of derby match, but certain rivalries have passed into football folklore. Among them are the Milan derby between Internazionale and AC Milan and, in Greece, the battle between Olympiakos and Panathinaikos. One of the most intense derbies in South America is between the two great Argentinean sides, Boca Juniors and River Plate. For some fans, beating their rivals in a derby can be even more important than league or cup success.

Some of the biggest derbies are not between neighbouring sides, but between the top clubs in the country. Spain's *Superclassico*, for example, is contested by two teams 500km apart – Real Madrid in the heart of the country and Barcelona on the east coast.

WHEN FANS TURN BAD

Sometimes, the passion of fans at a derby or other match can turn violent. Fighting between fans has occurred since football's early days, but it became known as the 'English disease' in the 1960s and 1970s as hooliganism flared up around the country. At the 1998 World Cup and Euro 2000, England supporters fought running battles with other nationalities. More recently, hooliganism at English clubs has declined dramatically thanks to CCTV cameras, undercover police operations, all-seater stadiums and police forces working with clubs to identify, ban and even jail hooligans. Such techniques are being adopted in other countries where fan violence is a problem. In 2012, Tottenham fans were attacked in Rome, a Leeds United fan was jailed for attacking a goalkeeper (Chris Kirkland) on the pitch, and 24 fans were injured during violent clashes between Polish and Russian fans at the Euro 2012 tournament. Also in 2012, a terrible pitched battle between Al-Ahly and Al-Masry supporters in Port Said, Egypt, left 74 people dead. This tragic and unpleasant series of events should not mask the fact that the vast majority of football fans are peaceful and never cause any trouble.

◀ *AC Milan keeper Dida is struck by a flare thrown by Internazionale supporters during a Champions League quarter-final in 2005. Referee Markus Merk abandoned the game and AC Milan were awarded a 3-0 win.*

THE FOOTBALL INDUSTRY

Football is extremely big business with clubs valued in their hundreds of millions. In 2014–15, the 20 richest teams generated a staggering 6.1 billion euros of income. But the pressure to achieve success has seen many clubs fall deeply into debt with some facing the threat of going out of business altogether.

BIG BUSINESS

In 2009, Manchester City's new owners, members of the Abu Dhabi royal family, made an audacious bid of almost £100 million to lure Kaka to the club. Money is no guarantee of success, however. Liverpool's last league title was in 1990, while the last European trophy of one of the richest clubs, Manchester City, was in 1970. Less wealthy clubs can still succeed in football. In 1997, Spain's Villareal were bottom of the second division, had just three members of staff and a stadium capacity of 3,500. The club, based in a small town with only 40,000 people, has since reached the Spanish first division and the semi-finals of the 2004 UEFA Cup and 2006 Champions League. Porto do not figure in the list of the world's top 20 richest clubs, but in 2004 they won the biggest club prize in Europe, the Champions League. More recently, in 2011, they added the UEFA Europa League crown to their achievements.

FACTFILE
In 1991, Manchester United were valued at £18 million. In 2005, to buy control of the club, American businessman Malcolm Glazer had to spend £790.3 million.

FACTFILE
In 1999, Romanian club Nitramonia Fagaras were so cash-stricken that they could not pay a £14,000 gas bill. They had to transfer two players, Gabor Balazs and Ioan Fatu, to Gazmetan Medias (the gas company's football club) as payment.

▲ *From his 2005 move to Corinthians in Brazil until being signed by Manchester City in 2009, Argentinean attacker Carlos Tevez was, unusually, 'owned' by two companies, MSI and Just Sport Limited.*

MONEY MATTERS

In the past, football clubs received most of their money from selling programmes, tickets and food and drink. Today, these items often contribute less than a third of all the money a club generates in a year. Sales of merchandise and deals with advertisers may make up around a third of a club's income (sometimes more for the biggest clubs). The largest part of a club's income comes from the sale of broadcasting rights to television in particular, but also to radio and the internet. In 2014–15, Real Madrid earned 204.2 million euros from broadcasting rights, a huge sum.

Some clubs have succeeded through the backing of a wealthy company or individual who spends many millions on the team. Since 2003, it is estimated that Roman Abramovich has spent over £1,000 million on Chelsea, while the Agnelli family – owners of car-makers Fiat – have spent almost as much on Juventus. Some clubs sell shares in the company that runs them, with mixed success. When Borussia Dortmund were knocked out of the Champions League

TRANSFER MILESTONES

YEAR	FEE	PLAYER
1905	£1,000	Alf Common (Sunderland to Middlesbrough)
1952	£52,000	Hans Jeppson (amateur to Napoli)
1961	£142,000	Luis Suarez (Barcelona to Internazionale)
1968	£500,000	Pietro Anastasi (Varses to Juventus)
1975	£1.2m	Giuseppe Savoldi (Bologna to Napoli)
1985	£5m	Diego Maradona (Barcelona to Napoli)
1992	£10m	Jean-Pierre Papin (Marseille to AC Milan)
1998	£21m	Denilson (São Paolo to Real Betis)
1999	£32m	Christian Vieri (Lazio to Internazionale)
2001	£45.62m	Zinedine Zidane (Juventus to Real Madrid)
2009	£80m	Cristiano Ronaldo (Manchester United to Real Madrid)
2013	£85.3m	Gareth Bale (Tottenham to Real Madrid)

▲ Fans survey the wide range of merchandise for sale at the Nihondaira Stadium, one of the two homes of Japanese J-League side Shimizu S-Pulse.

FACTFILE
Lionel Messi can leave Barcelona if another team bids more than £205 million for him!

◄ Cristiano Ronaldo plays in his first game for Real Madrid after his £80 million signing in 2009. Between 2013 and 2015, Real spent over £250 million on new players.

in 2003–04, for example, the value of the club fell by over 15 per cent.

Many clubs have run up huge debts through excessive transfer fees and wages, the collapse of TV deals or bad management. In 2014, the debt of Premier League clubs was thought to total over £2 billion. In Spain, the debt of Real Madrid alone is believed to be more than £160 million. Many clubs in all leagues have been forced to sell their best players to raise money. Others, such as Glasgow Rangers, have been forcibly relegated to a lower division by their footballing authority (in this case the Scottish FA) due to financial problems, or they have officially gone bankrupt.

PLAYER POWER

Players have always moved from club to club, and for a century the best players have often cost some sort of transfer fee. During the 2012–13 season, Chelsea could field a side including Juan Mata, Oscar, Eden Hazard and Fernando Torres, which cost more than £250 million in transfer fees alone. Fees spiralled from the mid-1980s,

with peaks including the 2001 transfer of Zinedine Zidane (£45 million), Cristiano Ronaldo (£80 million) in 2009, and in 2013 Gareth Bale's £85.3 million transfer to Real Madrid. In summer 2013 alone, English Premier League clubs spent over £620 million. For many other clubs, growing debts mean that they are less able to splash out on such big-money signings. Partly, these debts are due to spiralling player wages. In 1995, a ruling by the European Court of Justice – the Bosman ruling – made it easier for players to move from club to club at the end of their contracts on a free transfer. Clubs were forced to offer higher wages to lure or to keep star players. Lionel Messi, for example, is believed to earn more than £750,000 per month at Barcelona.

RICH REWARDS?

More of a football club's money is spent on buying and paying players than on any other expenditure. In 2014–15, Manchester United spent £215 million on wages, more than any other Premiership team, while Paris Saint-Germain paid its players an average of over £5.2 million each per year. The rewards for top players are similar in the world's richest leagues, which are all in Europe. Players employ agents to handle transfer moves, from which they may receive five per cent or more of the overall fee plus a signing-on bonus. Advertising and endorsing products, sponsorship deals and writing books and newspaper columns can greatly boost the income of a player. In 2014, Lionel Messi was believed to be earning over £47 million per year, some of that from endorsements. But in the lower divisions of the top leagues and in smaller leagues around the world, the rewards are much smaller and job security for players can be poor.

◄ Walter Strutz, chairman of Mainz, despairs as his side misses out on promotion to the German Bundesliga. For clubs everywhere, playing in the top division – where the financial rewards are greatest – is a major goal.

FOOTBALL NIGHTMARES

Football has a dark side. With passions running high on and off the pitch and with so much at stake in big matches, the game has sometimes lurched into a nightmare world of cheating, abuse, violence and even death.

CUT OFF IN THEIR PRIME

A number of players have died suddenly through on-pitch collisions or because of a medical problem. In 1973, Pedro Berruezo died of heart failure while playing for Sevilla. Thirty years later, during a Confederations Cup match against Colombia, Cameroon's 28-year-old midfielder Marc-Vivien Foe collapsed, and died shortly afterwards. In 2015, whilst playing for Club Atlético Paraná in Argentina, Cristian Gómez died of heart failure.

Plane crashes have wiped out entire football teams, including Bolivia's most popular team, The Strongest, in 1969, the Soviet (now Uzbek) team of Pakhtakor Tashkent in 1979, and 18 members of the Zambian national squad in 1993. Other air crashes have devastated club sides, such as the 1958 Munich disaster that killed eight Manchester United players and 11 officials and journalists.

▲ In the 1940s, Torino won four league titles in a row. When their aircraft crashed in 1949, 18 players died, comprising most of the Italian national side.

MATCH-FIXING AND CHEATING

In 1909, George Parsonage was banned for life after asking for a £50 signing-on fee when he joined Chesterfield (the maximum allowed was £10). This looks quaint compared to today's examples of corruption, bribery and match-fixing. In 1999, the former head coach of Romania's Dynamo Bucharest, Vasile Ianul, was sentenced to 12 years in prison for stealing £1.6 million from the club. German football was rocked in 2004 when referee Robert Hoyzer owned up to fixing matches. He was sentenced to more than two years in prison. In 2006, after a match-rigging scandal, Juventus were relegated to Serie B while AC Milan, Lazio, Fiorentina and Reggina Calcio were fined, removed from European competitions and had league points deducted. An attempt to fix a game on the pitch occurred when Chile were being outplayed by Brazil in a 1989 World Cup qualifier. Goalkeeper Roberto Rojas cut himself with a razor blade hidden in his glove and pretended to have been injured by an object thrown from the crowd. The game was called off, but video footage proved Rojas' cheating. He was banned and Chile were prevented from qualifying for the 1994 World Cup. In 2013, Europol, the European Union's police, announced an investigation into more than 300 football matches in Europe.

STADIUM DISASTERS

Crumbling stadiums, overcrowding, poor safety rules and bad crowd control have caused many stadium disasters. The worst ever football tragedy occurred in Lima, Peru, in 1964 when over 300 fans were killed and more than 500 injured in panic stampedes and riots. In a 1982 European Cup match in Moscow, 340 people died, most by

FACTFILE
In 1999, the owner of Doncaster Rovers, Ken Richardson, was sent to prison for four years for conspiring to burn down the club's main stand.

▲ Fans pay tribute to Colombian defender Andrés Escobar. The scorer of an own goal in a 2-1 loss to the USA at the 1994 World Cup, Escobar was murdered in his home country ten days later, shot 12 times by an unknown gunman.

ANDRÉS ESCOBAR 1967 - 1994

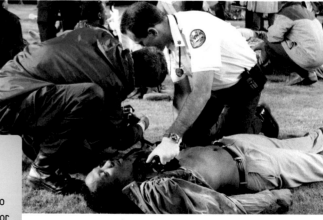

▲ Emergency workers tend to a victim of a tragedy at South Africa's Ellis Park in 2001. Four major stadium disasters occurred in Africa in that year. Altogether, they took the lives of more than 200 people.

Newcastle United players and Aston Villa's Gareth Barry try to separate brawling team-mates Kieron Dyer and Lee Bowyer in April 2005. Both players had fallen foul of the authorities before and been criticized as poor role models for youngsters.

FACTFILE In November 2004, the mother of Brazilian star Robinho was kidnapped and only released 41 days later. The mothers of two more Brazilian star players were kidnapped shortly afterwards.

crushing, when police tried to force fans out of a crowded section of the stadium and down an icy staircase. Two major disasters occurred in 1985 – a wooden stand at Bradford City's ground caught fire, killing 56 people, while the European Cup final also ended in tragedy. A wall collapsed at the Heysel Stadium in Belgium and a riot flared when some Liverpool fans charged at Juventus supporters. One Belgian and 38 Italian spectators died as a result.

POOR ROLE MODELS?

Footballers are highly esteemed as role models to the young, but some have abused their position and been convicted of crimes. In 2013, Manchester City's Courtney Meppen-Walter was jailed for 16 months for causing death by dangerous driving. Other players have behaved violently on and off the pitch. In November 2005, a huge brawl begun by Turkish players in a World Cup qualifier against Switzerland led to the country having to play its next six home

▲ *At Liverpool's Anfield ground, fans lay tributes to the 96 people who died during the 1989 FA Cup semi-final at Hillsborough Stadium.*

games in other countries. Footballers have also fought with fans. Manchester United's Eric Cantona, for example, kung-fu kicked a Crystal Palace supporter in 1995.

Like athletes in other sports, footballers are tested for illegal drug use. In 2011, Manchester City's Kolo Touré was banned for six months for failing a drugs test, while in 2007, Ecuador's Michael Arroyo was banned for two years after testing positive for using marijuana. Diego Maradona remains football's most notorious drugs

cheat. He was sent home from the 1994 World Cup after testing positive for the stimulant ephedrine; in recent years, Maradona has fought an addiction to cocaine. Many other footballers have battled against alcohol addiction, from former England captain Tony Adams to Brazilian legend Garrincha.

RACISM AND INTIMIDATION

Some fans, players and managers have been found guilty of racially insulting or abusing opponents. Racism in football was thought to be on the wane, with non-white footballers making up a fifth or more of the total number of players in many European leagues. Anti-racism campaign work has been carried out by many clubs, governments and groups such as FARE (Football Against Racism in Europe). However, incidents of racist chanting still occur. In January 2013, AC Milan's Kevin-Prince Boateng walked off the pitch followed by the rest of both teams after he and other black players were targets of racial abuse from some supporters. Violence and intimidation can occur on and off the pitch; sometimes, match officials are the target. In 2005, referee Luiz Carlos Silva was drawn into a fist fight after being attacked on the pitch by a fan during the Brazilian derby between America MG and Atlético Mineiro. In 2012, a Dutch referee's assistant was attacked by teenagers from Nieuw Sloten B1, one of the teams taking part in the game. He died the next day.

▲ *Referee Anders Frisk was hit by an object thrown by Roma fans during a 2004 Champions League match against Dynamo Kiev. Frisk abandoned the game at half time and UEFA awarded Kiev a 3-0 victory. In 2005, Frisk retired from refereeing after he and his family received death threats.*

SNAPSHOT

SPAIN WIN AT LAST

A fourth place World Cup finish and a single European Championship in 1964 was a poor return for a team of Spain's incredible calibre. Spain entered Euro 2008 with a skilful side, packed with talents such as Xavi Hernández, Andrés Iniesta, goalkeeper Iker Casillas and predatory striker Fernando Torres. Spain purred through their group, mauling Russia 4-1 and beating Sweden and reigning champions Greece. They endured a tense battle against world champions Italy, going through 4-3 on penalties, before brushing aside Russia again in the semi-final. Spain met Germany in the final, with Torres striking the game's only goal in the 33rd minute. At last, Spain's attacking flair and intricate passing play had turned them into worthy tournament winners. The team built on this European success to become the world's most dominant side, winning the 2010 World Cup and Euro 2012.

Iker Casillas, Spain's goalkeeper and captain, punches the ball away during the final of Euro 2008. Casillas had earlier been the hero of Spain's quarter-final win over Italy, saving two penalties in a shootout.

THE WORLD CUP

Friendlies or charity matches are entertaining, but for a football match to have meaning it has to be part of a wider competition. Football has spawned hundreds of different competitions, but none can compete in global interest and prestige with the World Cup. From small beginnings with 13 competing countries, it has grown to the point where 203 nations attempted to qualify for the 2014 competition.

▲ *Sepp Blatter announces the hosts of the 2018 and 2022 World Cups on TV.*

HOPING TO HOST

Six nations expressed an interest in hosting the first World Cup, held in 1930, and ever since, countries prepare their bid many years in advance to try and secure the World Cup within their borders. Only one tournament has ever been co-hosted (Japan/South Korea, in 2002), whilst in 2010 the tournament was held in Africa for the first time. In December 2010, the hosts of two future World Cups were announced, with Russia the location for the 2018 tournament and the Middle Eastern nation of Qatar the destination for the 2022 competition.

▲ *Argentina's goalkeeper, Juan Botasso, makes a despairing dive, but fails to stop Hector Castro scoring Uruguay's fourth goal in the 1930 final.*

URUGUAY 1930

Final
Uruguay 4 • Argentina 2
Semi-finals
Uruguay 6 • Yugoslavia 1
Argentina 6 • USA 1
Games 18 **Goals** 70
Goals per game 3.89

It took 19 minutes for France's Lucien Laurent to write his name in the record books as the scorer of the first World Cup goal. France beat Mexico 4-1, but it was their only victory and, like Belgium and Romania, they went out at the group stage. Four European sides made the long trip to South America by boat, but only Yugoslavia reached the semi-finals. They and the USA were thrashed in the semis, by Uruguay and Argentina respectively. Argentina boasted the best forward of the competition, Guillermo Stabile, but Uruguay – on home soil and as reigning Olympic champions – were firm favourites. In the final, they came back strongly after Argentina had taken a 2-1 lead, to become the first World Cup winners.

ITALY 1934

Final
Italy 2 • Czechoslovakia 1
Semi-finals
Italy 1 • Austria 0
Czechoslovakia 3 • Germany 1
Games 17 **Goals** 70
Goals per game 4.12

In 1934, the South American teams had not forgotten the lack of European entrants for the first World Cup. As a result, world champions Uruguay chose not to defend their title, while Brazil and Argentina sent understrength sides to Italy. Yet 32 nations, mostly European, were keen to enter the competition. With 16 places available, qualification matches began in June 1933. Italy's 4-0 win over Greece marked the first and only time that a World Cup host has had to play a qualifier to get into the finals. Egypt were the first nation outside of the Americas or Europe to qualify, but following one round of knockout games, the eight remaining teams were all European. After a 7-1 thrashing of the USA, Italy's goals dried up and they only just sneaked past Spain and Austria on their way to the final. In that match, Italy's Luisito Monti (formerly of Argentina) became the only player to have appeared in a World Cup final for different countries. Against a battling Czech side, a goal five minutes into extra time from Italy's Angelo Schiavio secured the Jules Rimet trophy for the hosts.

▼ *Coach Vittorio Pozzo is carried aloft by triumphant Italian players after masterminding their 1934 World Cup campaign.*

FRANCE 1938

Final

Italy 4 • Hungary 2

Semi-finals

Italy 2 • Brazil 1

Hungary 5 • Sweden 1

Games 18 **Goals** 84

Goals per game 4.67

With the threat of war looming over Europe, Spain and Austria were forced to pull out of the tournament. But the 1938 World Cup did feature the first team from Asia, the Dutch East Indies (now Indonesia), as well as a Cuban side that sprang a major shock by beating Romania in a replay. Sweden thrashed Cuba 8-0, but were then on the receiving end of a 5-1 semi-final mauling by the first great Hungarian side. The other semi-final saw one of the great managerial blunders when the Brazil coach, Adhemar Pimenta, either because of arrogance or through injury fears, rested his star player, Léonidas da Silva. Léonidas had lit up the tournament, most notably in an epic 6-5 thriller against Poland in which he became the first player to score four goals in a World Cup finals match, only for Poland's Ernest Wilimowski to do the same five minutes later. Without the tournament's top scorer, Brazil crashed to defeat against Italy, who went on to become champions for the second time.

▶ *Léonidas da Silva twists and turns at the 1938 World Cup. An outrageously skilful attacker, the Brazilian was one of the first players to master the overhead kick.*

> **FACTFILE** Dr Ottorino Barassi, the vice president of the Italian FA, smuggled the World Cup out of a bank in Rome and hid it to prevent the Nazis from stealing the trophy. For much of World War II, football's greatest prize lay in a shoebox under Barassi's bed.

BRAZIL 1950

Final pool

Uruguay 5 pts • Brazil 4 pts

Sweden 2 pts • Spain 1 pt

Games 22 **Goals** 88

Goals per game 4.00

The only World Cup to feature a final pool of four instead of a final, the 1950 tournament started poorly. Scotland and Turkey withdrew, only 13 nations attended and the mighty Maracanã Stadium was not ready to host the first match. But the competition built in excitement and drama as the goals flowed, often from the boots of the hosts who, after topping their group, ran rampant in the final pool stages, scoring seven against Sweden and six against Spain. Before that point, there had been several notable shocks, including the USA's 1-0 defeat of a highly rated England team. The final pool format could have been an anticlimax, but the outcome went down to the very last game, with Uruguay and Brazil separated by one point and playing in front of around 199,850 fans. Despite falling a goal behind to the favourites, Uruguay won the match 2-1 to lift the World Cup once more.

> **FACTFILE** At the 1930 World Cup, not one of the 18 games was drawn. Neither was there a play-off game to decide third place.

▲ *Brazilian keeper Moacir Barbosa gathers the ball during a 1950 group game against Yugoslavia. The match, watched by more than 142,000 spectators in the Maracanã, ended in a 2-0 victory to Brazil.*

WORLD CUP GOLDEN BOOT WINNERS (GOALS)

1930	Guillermo Stabile, Argentina (8)
1934	Oldrich Nejedly, Czech. (5)
1938	Léonidas da Silva, Brazil (8)
1950	Ademir Menezes, Brazil (9)
1954	Sandor Kocsis, Hungary (11)
1958	Just Fontaine, France (13)
1962	Garrincha, Brazil; Vava, Brazil; Valentin Ivanov, USSR; Leonel Sanchez, Chile; Florian Albert, Hungary; Drazan Jerkovic, Yugoslavia (4)
1966	Eusebio, Portugal (9)
1970	Gerd Müller, West Germany (10)
1974	Gregorz Lato, Poland (7)
1978	Mario Kempes, Argentina (6)
1982	Paolo Rossi, Italy (6)
1986	Gary Lineker, England (6)
1990	Salvatore Schillaci, Italy (6)
1994	Hristo Stoichkov, Bulgaria; Oleg Salenko, Russia (6)
1998	Davor Suker, Croatia (6)
2002	Ronaldo, Brazil (8)
2006	Miroslav Klose, Germany (5)
2010	Thomas Müller, Germany; Wesley Sneijder, Holland; Diego Forlán, Uruguay; David Villa, Spain (5)
2014	James Rodriguez, Columbia (6)

SWITZERLAND 1954

Final

West Germany 3 • Hungary 2

Semi-finals

West Germany 6 • Austria 1

Hungary 4 • Uruguay 2

Games 26 **Goals** 140

Goals per game 5.38

As home to the headquarters of FIFA, which was celebrating its 50th birthday, Switzerland was an obvious host for the 1954 tournament. It featured newcomers such as Turkey, South Korea and the western half of a divided Germany (which had been barred from the 1950 competition). The fans saw plenty of drama and goals, none more than in Austria's 7-5 defeat of Switzerland (the highest-scoring game in the history of the World Cup finals). Hungary, boasting the incredible talents of Ferenc Puskas, Sandor Kocsis and Nandor Hidegkuti, were the most rampant side, scoring an incredible 27 goals in just five matches. At their third World Cup, Uruguay thrashed Scotland 7-0 and beat England 4-2 to reach the semi-finals. They were the only team never to have been beaten in the World Cup until they came up against Hungary, who won 4-2 and went into the final as favourites. West Germany, however, overturned the odds to record a highly emotional victory.

Pelé chases the ball during Brazil's exciting semi-final against France. The tie was poised at 2-1 to Brazil before Pelé scored three goals in 21 minutes.

first ever 0-0 draw. Yet it was the two smaller British nations, Wales and Northern Ireland, who qualified for the quarter-finals, with the Irish sensationally beating a strong Czechoslovakian team. Free-scoring France and Brazil quickly emerged as the favourites, and their semi-final clash was an epic in which the 17-year-old Pelé blasted a hat-trick in Brazil's victory. France had to be content with a 6-3 mauling of West Germany to secure third place. Just Fontaine's four goals in that game propelled him to the Golden Boot with 13 goals in total, a record to this day. The hosts, Sweden, had quietly and efficiently seen off some very strong sides – including Hungary, the Soviet Union and West Germany – to reach the final, but they were no match for Brazil. In a rematch of the pair's third-place play-off at the 1938 World Cup, Brazil triumphed 5-2 to win the tournament for the first time.

FACTFILE Vava's goal in the 1962 final (to add to his pair of goals in the 1958 final) make him the only player to have scored in the finals of successive World Cups.

SWEDEN 1958

Final

Brazil 5 • Sweden 2

Semi-finals

Brazil 5 • France 2

Sweden 3 • West Germany 1

Games 35 **Goals** 126

Goals per game 3.60

Fifty-five countries entered the 1958 qualifying tournament and some big names, including Italy, Holland, Spain and Uruguay, failed to qualify. All four UK home nations (Scotland, England, Northern Ireland and Wales) reached the finals – the only time this has happened. England had lost key players in the Munich aircrash (see page 79), but were the only team to hold a rampant Brazilian side to a draw and to stop them scoring. It was the World Cup's

Hungary's Zoltan Czibor outjumps Ottmar Walter of West Germany in the 1954 final. Czibor scored to put Hungary 2-0 up, but found himself on the losing side after a heroic comeback by the Germans.

Argentina's Jorge Albrecht (left) and Uwe Seeler of West Germany struggle for the ball in 1966. Seeler played in each of the four World Cups sandwiched between West Germany's victories in 1954 and 1974.

CHILE 1962

Final

Brazil 3 • Czechoslovakia 1

Semi-finals

Brazil 4 • Chile 2

Czechoslovakia 3 • Yugoslavia 1

Games 32 **Goals** 89

Goals per game 2.78

Chile was a controversial choice to host the World Cup, with its small population and its infrastructure damaged by an earthquake in 1960. As it turned out, most of the problems happened on the pitch. A series of bad-tempered matches occurred in the first round, including the infamous 'Battle of Santiago', during which armed police invaded the pitch three times to split up warring Chilean and Italian players. Chile made it through to a semi-final against Brazil by beating the Soviet Union, while two strong Eastern European sides, Yugoslavia and Czechoslovakia, battled it out in the other semi-final. The Brazilians lost Pelé to injury after only two games, but in Garrincha and Vava they had two of the best players of the tournament. Brazil duly won the final with a team featuring eight World Cup-winners from the 1958 tournament.

ENGLAND 1966

Final

England 4 • West Germany 2

Semi-finals

England 2 • Portugal 1

West Germany 2 • Soviet Union 1

Games 32 **Goals** 89

Goals per game 2.78

The 1966 World Cup was a well-organized tournament and the first to feature a mascot (World Cup Willie). West Germany and Portugal were the most free-scoring sides in a competition characterized by defensive play. Two enormous shocks occurred early on – Brazil were eliminated by Portugal and newcomers North Korea knocked out Italy with a stunning 1-0 victory. The North Koreans won the support of many neutral fans, and their quarter-final meeting with Portugal was a classic. North Korea were 3-0 up within 20 minutes before Portugal, inspired by the tournament's eventual top

▲ *Portugal's star striker, Eusebio, walks off in tears after his team is eliminated from the 1966 World Cup following a 2-1 defeat by England.*

scorer, Eusebio, hit back to win 5-3. In the semi-final, Eusebio's 82nd-minute strike could not stop England going through to meet West Germany in what proved to be an epic final. The Germans went ahead, then England scored twice to lead until a surprise last-minute German goal took the game into extra time. Geoff Hurst scored two more goals to secure a dramatic victory for the host nation (see pages 68–69).

FACTFILE Two pairs of brothers have played on winning sides in a World Cup final – Fritz and Ottmar Walter of West Germany (1954) and England's Jack and Bobby Charlton (1966).

MEXICO 1970

Final

Brazil 4 • Italy 1

Semi-finals

Brazil 3 • Uruguay 1

Italy 4 • West Germany 3

Games 32 **Goals** 95

Goals per game 2.97

For many seasoned football observers, the 1970 World Cup remains the best. Much of the brutal, physical play seen in the 1962 and 1966 tournaments was absent. In its place were fascinating tactical and skilful contests between the world's greatest sides. Although the tournament was the first to feature red and yellow cards, no player was sent off, and some of the games have passed into football legend. These include a chess-like battle between Brazil and England that the South Americans narrowly won 1-0; Italy's 4-1 defeat of Mexico; and the Italians amazing 4-3 victory against West Germany in the semi-final. But the final tops the list. Brazil had powered through the rounds, with star players such as Jairzinho (who set a record by scoring in all six of Brazil's games), Pelé and Rivelino exhibiting great attacking flair. In the final they were unstoppable, recording their third World Cup win and claiming the Jules Rimet trophy for good.

▼ *Brazilian striker Tostao holds off Italy's Roberto Rosato during the 1970 World Cup final. Tostao suffered a freak eye injury before the tournament and only last-minute surgery enabled him to play.*

WEST GERMANY 1974

Final

West Germany 2 • Holland 1

Third-place play-off Poland 1 • Brazil 0

Games 38 **Goals** 97

Goals per game 2.55

Ninety-nine nations attempted to qualify for the 1974 tournament, which would see the winners lift a new trophy – the FIFA World Cup. Spain, France and England all failed to reach the tournament, while Zaire, Haiti, East Germany and Australia made their debuts. Changes to the competition format meant that there would be no semi-final games. Instead, the winners of the two second-round groups would contest the final and the group runners-up would play off for third place. Holland, exhibiting their brand of 'total football', swept aside Bulgaria (4-1), Uruguay (2-0), Brazil (2-0) and Argentina (4-0) to top Group A and reach the final. Poland were the surprise team of the tournament. Propelled in part by the goals of striker Gregorz Lato, they came second in Group B after narrowly losing 1-0 to West Germany. The West Germans had taken time to reach top gear, but with Franz Beckenbauer pulling the strings and the prolific Gerd Müller in fine form, they made the final. There, they overcame the setback of a first-minute Dutch goal from a penalty to win the World Cup for a second time.

> **FACTFILE** On 14 June 1974, Carlos Caszely of Chile became the first player to receive a red card in a World Cup tournament.

▼ Peru's Teofilo Cubillas (centre) runs at Argentina's defence during his side's controversial 6-0 defeat. Cubillas scored five goals at the 1978 World Cup, matching his tally at the 1970 competition.

ARGENTINA 1978

Final

Argentina 3 • Holland 1

Third-place play-off Brazil 2 • Italy 1

Games 38 **Goals** 102

Goals per game 2.68

A colourful and at times controversial tournament, the 1978 World Cup may have lacked some standout stars, but it was rarely short of footballing drama. The hosts found themselves in the toughest of groups with France, Hungary and a young Italian side that beat them, but Argentina made it through to the second group stage. Tunisia caused a shock by drawing with holders West Germany and beating Mexico 3-1 to become the first African side to win a World Cup finals game. Austria, with their star striker Hans Krankl, played strongly in the early stages, beating Spain, Sweden and West Germany. But they were crushed 5-1 by a Dutch squad lacking Johan Cruyff, who had pulled out of the tournament for family reasons. Scotland's campaign promised much, but went badly wrong when they failed to beat Iran and lost to Peru. They then roused themselves, however, to beat Holland 3-2. In the second group stage, Italy, Argentina, Brazil and Holland emerged as frontrunners. Much controversy centred on the Argentina-Peru game. The last match in Group B, it would determine whether Argentina or Brazil reached the final. Peru had played well in the early stages of the tournament, winning their group ahead of Holland. Their 6-0 loss to Argentina was suspicious and meant that Brazil were knocked out without having suffered a defeat, while Argentina progressed to the final, in which they beat Holland.

◄ Germany's defence, marshalled by legendary goalkeeper Sepp Maier and the incomparable Franz Beckenbauer (far right), holds firm against a Dutch attack in the 1974 World Cup final.

SPAIN 1982

Final

Italy 3 • West Germany 1

Semi-finals

Italy 2 • Poland 0

West Germany 3 • France 3 (5-4 penalties)

Games 52 **Goals** 146

Goals per game 2.81

In 1982, the format of the tournament changed again so that 24 countries would appear at the finals. Teams played in six groups of four, with the top 12 sides playing in four groups of three to determine the semi-finalists. Belgium surprised the holders, Argentina, beating them and El Salvador to win their group, while England topped theirs ahead of France. The two surprise teams were Northern Ireland, who beat Spain to reach the second round, and Algeria, who had stunned fans by winning their match with West Germany. Poland made the semi-finals, but the hosts went out after winning just one match. The toughest second-round group, containing Brazil, Argentina and Italy, saw the Italians go through, beating Brazil in a 3-2 thriller. At the semi-final stage, West Germany beat France in an equally exciting encounter, but could not stop the Italians from winning their third World Cup.

▶ *In 1982, an Algerian fan waves banknotes in protest as West Germany and Austria conspire to achieve a result which took both European teams through at the expense of Algeria. All final group matches are now played simultaneously to give teams an equal chance.*

MEXICO 1986

Final

Argentina 3 • West Germany 2

Semi-finals

Argentina 2 • Belgium 0

West Germany 2 • France 0

Games 52 **Goals** 132

Goals per game 2.54

Colombia had been due to host the 1986 World Cup, but troubles in that country meant they had to withdraw. When Mexico stepped in, they became the first nation to host the tournament twice. More than 120 nations battled for the 24 places in the finals, in which Canada and Iraq both made their debuts. Morocco became the first African nation to reach the second round when they won a group that

contained Portugal, Poland and England. Denmark looked promising until they were thrashed 5-1 by Spain, while Belgium squeezed past the Soviet Union 4-3 in one of the best games of the tournament. The quarter-finals were extremely tight affairs. Three went to penalty shootouts, while the fourth game saw England face Argentina. Maradona arrived at the World Cup as the world's most expensive player and a heavily marked man. His incredible dribbling and scoring skills made him the best player of the tournament. In the quarter-final, his two goals (one a deliberate handball, the other a magnificent solo effort – see pages 56–57) sank England and he repeated the feat against Belgium in the semi-final. In the final, West Germany went 2-0 down, rallied to 2-2, but were beaten by an 88th-minute goal from Argentinian midfielder Burruchaga.

FACTFILE The fastest sending-off in World Cup history occurred in 1986, when Uruguay's José Batista was dismissed against Scotland after just 55 seconds.

▲ *Marco Tardelli (left) charges away after scoring Italy's second goal in the 1982 World Cup final against West Germany. Team-mates Claudio Gentile and Gabriele Oriali are equally jubilant.*

◀ *Argentina's Diego Maradona celebrates as his side triumphs over West Germany in the 1986 World Cup final.*

ITALY 1990

Final

West Germany 1 • Argentina 0

Semi-finals

West Germany 1 • England 1 (4-3 penalties)

Argentina 1 • Italy 1 (4-3 penalties)

Games 52 **Goals** 115

Goals per game 2.21

This well organized and attended World Cup is remembered for moments of great theatre, from veteran Cameroon striker Roger Milla's dance at the corner flag to Costa Rica's joy at defeating both Scotland and Sweden to qualify for the second round. Sadly, the tournament also saw much negative football and a record number of bookings (164), as well as 16 sendings-off. Every previous winner of the World Cup made it through the group stages, with Cameroon the talk of the tournament after their defeats of Romania and Colombia set up a quarter-final against England. Cameroon went 2-0 up, but two Gary Lineker penalties and a third England goal in extra time saw every neutral's favourite team go out. Holland arrived as European Champions, but failed to win a match, while Brazil and the Soviet Union had similarly disappointing tournaments. Both semi-finals were tense games that went to penalty shootouts, but the final was deeply forgettable. West Germany beat Argentina courtesy of an 85th-minute penalty, while Pedro Monzon was the first of two sendings-off for Argentina and the first player to be red-carded in a World Cup final.

▼ Italian goalkeeper Walter Zenga concedes a headed goal to Argentina's Claudio Caniggia in the 1990 semi-final.

USA 1994

Final

Brazil 0 • Italy 0 (3-2 penalties)

Semi-finals

Brazil 1 • Sweden 0

Italy 2 • Bulgaria 1

Games 52 **Goals** 141

Goals per game 2.71

Some feared that the crowds at the 1994 World Cup would be small in a country where male football is not a dominant sport. But they were proved wrong by a lively tournament attended by an average of 70,000 spectators per game. Attacking play had been encouraged by the adoption of both the backpass rule (see page 24) and three instead of two points for a win in the group games. Despite losing many players since the break-up of the Soviet Union, Russia recorded the biggest win, 6-1 against Cameroon, with Oleg Salenko scoring five goals – the most by one player in a World Cup match. Maradona went home after he failed a drugs test, and the Republic of Ireland caused the biggest shock of the group stages by beating Italy 1-0.

◀ Bulgaria's Iordan Letchkov (left) beats Germany's Thomas Hassler to score a spectacular diving header at the 1994 World Cup.

The Bulgarians had a marvellous World Cup, beating Argentina, knocking out Germany and finishing fourth overall. European sides dominated the quarter-finals, taking seven out of the eight places, yet it was Brazil who beat Holland, Sweden and Italy to lift the World Cup trophy for a record fourth time.

FRANCE 1998

Final

France 3 • Brazil 0

Semi-finals

France 2 • Croatia 1

Brazil 1 • Holland 1 (4-2 penalties)

Games 64 **Goals** 171

Goals per game 2.67

More countries from outside Europe and South America attended the last World Cup of the 20th century, as the number of places rose from 24 to 32. Newcomers included Jamaica, Japan and South Africa. Iran caused a shock in their first World Cup for 20 years by beating the USA. Nigeria upset the odds with a 3-2 defeat of Spain that effectively knocked out the European side. Despite 22 red cards, the football was enthralling, with Croatia, Denmark, Brazil, France and Holland playing attacking football. England narrowly went out, losing on penalties to Argentina in one of the games of the tournament. Croatia were the dark horses, progressing quietly and then beating Germany 3-0 in the quarter-final.

For the second World Cup in a row, Italy were knocked out on penalties, this time to France at the quarter-final stage. A France-Brazil final was an exciting prospect, but Ronaldo was ill before the game and was extremely subdued, as were his team-mates. France won with relative ease, aided by two goals from Zinedine Zidane (see pages 92–93).

SOUTH KOREA AND JAPAN 2002

Final
Brazil 2 • Germany 0
Semi-finals
Brazil 1 • Turkey 0
Germany 1 • South Korea 0
Games 64 **Goals** 161
Goals per game 2.52

The 2002 competition was the first to be held in Asia and the first to be hosted by two nations. An amazing 193 countries attempted to qualify for the 32 places on offer and there were surprise failures to reach the finals by Holland, Yugoslavia, Uruguay and Colombia, while China appeared at their first tournament. The shocks began in the opening game, when France – the World Cup holders and European Champions – were sensationally beaten 1-0 by Senegal. France then lost to Denmark and went out of the World Cup with just one point. They were joined by Russia and also by European heavyweights Poland and Portugal, who finished in the bottom two places of Group D behind the USA and South Korea. Cheered on by passionate home crowds,

the South Koreans were the story of the tournament, knocking out Italy, Spain and Portugal on the way to the semi-finals. The USA beat Mexico to make the quarter-finals, as did Senegal, who beat Sweden before losing to Turkey. The Turks lost narrowly to Brazil in the semi-final, but claimed third place overall. In the final, Brazilian striker Ronaldo put memories of 1998 behind him, scoring two goals against Germany and winning the Golden Boot.

GERMANY 2006

Final
Italy 1 • France 1 (5-3 penalties)
Semi-finals
Italy 2 • Germany 0 (after extra time)
France 1 • Portugal 0
Games 62 **Goals** 147
Goals per game 2.3

The opening match was a thriller – Germany beating Costa Rica 4-2 – and set the scene for an enthusiastically-hosted tournament. On the pitch, things were not so friendly with a record card count (345 yellow and 28 red) and games in which defences dominated, especially in the knockout, stages.

Africa had five teams at the tournament for the first time, although only Ghana progressed from the group stage. Ivory Coast were desperately unlucky, narrowly losing to Argentina and Holland in a tough group. Oceania's first representative for many years, Australia, were a surprise, qualifying from a group featuring Brazil, Japan and Croatia and only losing to Italy via a controversial last-gasp penalty.

France scraped through the group stage, but their ageing side then beat highly-fancied Spain, Brazil and Portugal to reach the final. There they faced Italy and a defence led by Fabio Cannavaro that had only conceded a single goal during the competition.

▼ *Senegal beat France 1-0 in the opening match of the 2002 World Cup, the first in a series of surprise results. Here, French midfielder Patrick Vieira (left) fights for the ball with Senegalese defender Papa Bouba Diop.*

The first all-European final since 1982 was all about two men, Zinedine Zidane – playing in his last competitive match – and Italian defender Marco Materazzi. Zidane scored a penalty only for Materazzi to equalize from a corner. Both men tussled during extra time, and Zidane was sent off for head-butting the Italian in the chest. During the tense penalty shootout, David Trezeguet, who had scored the golden goal that beat Italy in the final of Euro 2000, missed as Italy won their fourth World Cup.

▶ *Turkey's Hakan Sukur (right) tangles with Lee Min-Sung of South Korea during the 2002 third-place play-off.*

▲ *Fabio Grosso, scorer of Italy's winning penalty in the final against France, kisses the World Cup.*

SOUTH AFRICA 2010

Final

Spain 1 • Netherlands 0 (after extra time)

Semi-finals

Netherlands 3 • Uruguay 2

Spain 1 • Germany 0

Games 64 **Goals** 145

Goals per game 2.27

The first tournament to be held on the African continent will be remembered as a noisy, colourful affair with some 3.18 million spectators attending matches in the ten stadiums, many purpose-built for the tournament. Whilst teams such as Russia and Turkey failed to qualify, Serbia and Slovakia made their debuts at the tournament. Fans of Bafana Bafana (the nickname of the South African team) got the first chance to cheer as Siphiwe Tshabalala scored the opening goal of the tournament for the hosts as they drew 1-1 with Mexico, but they went out at the group stage as did France, Cameroon, Denmark and defending champions, Italy.

The Germans would score the most goals (16) in the tournament but would finish in third place after being knocked out in the semi-finals. The Netherlands were also on a roll, taking their World Cup and World Cup qualifying winning run to 13 games when they knocked out Brazil in the quarter-finals. Spain lost their very first game, 1-0 against Switzerland, but they won each of their four knockout games 1-0, including a tense final against the Netherlands, to claim their first ever World Cup.

▶ *Mesut Özil of Germany kicks the ball away from Lucas Biglia of Argentina during the 2014 World Cup final game.*

▲ *Xabi Alonso of Spain lifts the World Cup after a tense 1-0 win over the Netherlands in the 2010 final.*

BRAZIL 2014

Final Germany 1 • Argentina 0 (a.e.t.)

An enthusiastic Brazilian fanbase welcomed the World Cup back after a gap of 64 years. It was the first to feature goal line technology and vanishing foam used by referees to mark 9.1m distances for defenders to stand at free kicks. Bosnia & Herzegovina were the one nation making their first World Cup appearance. Defending champions, Spain, crashed out at the group stage after being thrashed 5-1 by the Netherlands and losing 2-0 to an impressive Chile. In Group D, England and Italy were knocked out as

Uruguay and Costa Rica progressed, while Algeria qualified for the knockout stages for the first time in their history. A total of 171 goals were scored in the 64 matches played, eight coming in an extraordinary semi-final where Germany demolished the hosts 7-1, scoring five of their goals in less than 20 first half-minutes. Their opponents, Argentina, defeated the Netherlands in the semi-final and took Germany into extra time where a goal from Mario Gotze made Germany the first team from Europe to win a World Cup held in the Americas. Colombia's James Rodriguez won the Golden Boot for top scorer with six goals, while Lionel Messi was awarded the Golden Ball as the tournament's best player.

THE WOMEN'S WORLD CUP

CHINA 1991

Final USA 2 • Norway 1

The first Women's World Cup was a great success and proof that women's football had a major global audience. China, Denmark, Chinese Taipei and Italy were all knocked out in the quarter-finals, leaving the USA, Norway, Sweden and Germany in the semi-finals. Around 65,000 spectators watched the final, in which the USA beat Norway with a goal from Michelle Akers just three minutes from full time.

SWEDEN 1995

Final Norway 2 • Germany 0

The tournament's 26 games saw plenty of goals. Brazil were thrashed 6-1 by Germany, who then lost a 3-2 thriller to Sweden. The USA and China shared the spoils in an epic 3-3 encounter and Norway powered through their group, putting 17 goals past Canada, England and Nigeria, before knocking out the USA at the semi-final stage. Sweden's Ingrid Jonsson became the first woman to referee a FIFA final, in which Norway scored two first-half goals to secure the world crown.

▼ *Brazil's Marta was the top scorer, with seven goals, at the 2007 Women's World Cup, held in China.*

USA 1999

Final USA 0 • China 0 (5-4 penalties)
Expanded to 16 teams, the tournament was a huge success and saw Nigeria become the first African side to reach the quarter-finals. The USA, with Mia Hamm, Brandi Chastain and Tiffeny Milbrett all playing superbly, had to come from behind against a strong German team, before overcoming Brazil in the semi-finals. In contrast, China cruised to the final, mauling cup-holders Norway 5-0. The final, played in front of more than 90,000 fans at the Rose Bowl, was a very tense affair. The game went to penalties, with Briana Scurry saving Ying Liu's spot kick to see the USA win the shootout 5-4.

USA 2003

Final Germany 2 • Sweden 1
An epidemic of the SARS virus prevented China from hosting the World Cup, which moved to the USA at the last minute. The 2003 tournament was predicted to be a successful swansong for many of the

USA's veteran players. However, a vibrant, attacking German side – headed by the tournament's leading scorer, Birgit Prinz – knocked them out at the semi-final stage. In a memorable final, a golden goal by subsitute Nia Kuenzer secured Germany their first Women's World Cup.

CHINA 2007

Final Germany 2 • Brazil 0
The tournament got off to a record start with Germany thrashing Argentina 11-0 in Group A whilst Brazil, led by top scorer Marta, mauled New Zealand 5-0 and China 4-0 in Group D. These two teams, along with Norway and the USA, made it out of their groups and into the semi-finals, where Brazil handed a surprise 4-0 defeat to the USA to join Germany in the final. Two second-half goals from Birgit Prinz and Simone Ladehr propelled Germany to their second World Cup final victory in a row.

GERMANY 2011

Final Japan 2 • USA 2 (3-1 penalties)
A successful, exciting, well-staged tournament saw almost a million spectators watch matches between the 16 teams, which included Colombia and Equatorial Guinea for the first time. Two of the quarter-finals went to penalty shootouts, with France prevailing over England after a 1-1 draw and Brazil losing to the US team after an epic match in Dresden. The Americans went down to ten players after a red card in the 65th minute, but managed to take the game into extra time and equalized in the 122nd minute. The US went through to the final where they came up against the newest force of women's football. Japan, led by the tournament's best player, Homare Sawa, became the first team from Asia to win a World Cup.

CANADA 2015

Final USA 5 • Japan 2
Canada hosted the tournament which was expanded to include 24 teams, up from 16 from 2011. The six stadiums all featured artificial turf instead of grass which caused controversy and complaints from some players, but otherwise the tournament was considered a success and showcased elite women's football with some compelling matches and stunning displays. Switzerland defeated Ecuador 10-1 in a game where Ecuador's Angie Ponce scored two own goals, whilst Germany thrashed the Ivory Coast 10-0. Many other games, though, were close, tense affairs with eight of the 12 Round of 16 and quarter-final games being decided by 1-0 or 2-1 scorelines. England knocked out the hosts at the quarter-final stage whilst Australia defeated a highly rated Brazilian team at the same stage, lost narrowly to Japan but beat Germany in the play-off game to finish third overall. Former champions USA met current holders Japan in the final where a spectacular hat-trick from US midfielder, Carli Lloyd, included an incredible shot from the halfway line. Lloyd was awarded the Golden Ball as player of the tournament in which she scored six goals, tied with Germany's Célia Šašic as the top scorer.

▲ *Homare Sawa, captain of the Japanese team, lifts the trophy awarded to the winners of the 2011 Women's World Cup. Sawa was the tournament's leading goalscorer with five goals.*

THE EUROPEAN CHAMPIONSHIPS

The European Championships started life in 1958 as the UEFA European Nations Cup, but struggled to find enough nations to compete. Today, however, the competition is the largest international football competition behind the World Cup. Like that tournament, it is held every four years.

HUMBLE BEGINNINGS

Henri Delaunay, secretary of the French FA and the first general secretary of UEFA, had suggested a European tournament back in 1927. Regionalized European competitions such as the Balkan Cup and the Home Internationals for the four countries that comprise the UK took place, but a complete European-wide competition did not begin until 1958, with the final held in France in 1960. The early tournaments saw teams play a series of qualifying rounds, with the four winners progressing to play a mini tournament consisting of semi-finals and a final. The standout match in the first competition was the semi-final between France and Yugoslavia. France were ahead 4-2 when Yugoslavia scored in the 75th, 78th and 79th minutes to win 5-4. The Yugoslavs lost to the Soviet Union in the final and would also lose to Italy in the 1968 final. Strong teams from Eastern Europe dominated the early competitions – the Soviet Union reached the semi-final or final of each tournament between 1960 and 1972, while Hungary, Yugoslavia and Czechoslovakia also performed well. The Czechs had a sparkling 1976 competition. In just four days, they beat the two 1974 World Cup finalists, West Germany and Holland, to win the title.

FACTFILE Midfielder Michel Platini holds the record for the most goals scored in a European Championships. He scored nine of France's 14 goals in the 1984 competition.

CHANGING FORMATS

From 1968, qualifying took place in groups rather than rounds of knockout matches; the format of the competition has continued to change since. By the 1980 tournament in Italy, eight teams were taking part in the finals. Belgium were the story of that competition, winning a very tough group containing England, Italy and Spain before losing narrowly to West Germany in the final. The 1980s saw two highly gifted and entertaining sides, France and Holland, win the European Championships. Throughout the 1980s and early 1990s, however, many top sides failed to reach the finals, which dented the competition's prestige. England, Holland and Italy all failed to make the 1984 tournament; France failed to qualify for the 1988 Championships; and neither Italy nor Spain were present in 1992. With the countries of Eastern Europe dividing into smaller states in the early 1990s, the numbers of competing sides boomed and UEFA expanded the format so that 16 teams contested the finals of Euro 96.

► Gaizka Mendieta (left) of Spain and Goran Djorovic of Yugoslavia compete for a header during the European Championships 2000. Spain secured a 4-3 victory in injury time after they had been 3-2 down with just moments to play.

HOSTS AND WINNERS

YEAR	HOST	FINAL
1960	France	USSR 2-1 Yugoslavia
1964	Spain	Spain 2-1 USSR
1968	Italy	Italy 2-0 Yugoslavia (after replay)
1972	Belgium	West Germany 3-0 USSR
1976	Yugoslavia	Czechoslovakia 2-2 W. Germany (5-3 pen)
1980	Italy	West Germany 2-1 Belgium
1984	France	France 2-0 Spain
1988	West Germany	Holland 2-0 USSR
1992	Sweden	Denmark 2-0 Germany
1996	England	Germany 2-1 Czech Republic
2000	Belgium / Holland	France 2-1 Italy
2004	Portugal	Greece 1-0 Portugal
2008	Austria / Switz.	Spain 1-0 Germany
2012	Poland / Ukraine	Spain 4-0 Italy

EURO 1992

The 1992 tournament saw perhaps the biggest surprise win in the competition's history. Denmark had failed to qualify, most of its players were on holiday and the team's manager was decorating his kitchen when news emerged of Yugoslavia's disqualification and Denmark's invitation to join. In a dramatic semi-final against Holland, a heroic penalty save by Peter Schmeichel saw them through to the final, where they beat Germany to win the most unlikely of European Championship crowns.

▲ *Denmark's players line up before their Euro 92 match against Sweden, which they lost 1-0. The under-prepared Danes rallied superbly, however, qualifying from their group and winning the title.*

FACTFILE Spanish leader General Franco, a critic of communism, refused the Soviet team entry into Spain to play their qualifying game for the 1960 competition. The Soviets were awarded a win.

▲ *Czech Republic striker Milan Baros was the top scorer at Euro 2004, with five goals.*

EURO 96 AND 2000

Euro 96 got off to a strong start, with England's Paul Gascoigne scoring the goal of the tournament against Scotland, the Czech Republic stunning Italy with a 2-1 win and Croatia effectively knocking the holders, Denmark, out of the competition. In the final, Germany defeated the Czech Republic with a golden goal, the first to decide a major football competition.

Euro 2000 was co-hosted (for the first time) by Holland and Belgium. The Dutch side scored the highest number of goals in a finals match, thrashing Yugoslavia 6-1. The Spanish impressed, but fell to the eventual winners, France, in the semi-final.

EURO 2004

Euro 2004 began with 50 nations in qualifying. The first round at the finals threw up a series of surprises as Spain and Italy were knocked out; the same fate befell Germany, who drew with minnows Latvia in their group. In Group A, Russia beat Greece thanks to a Dmitri Kirichenko goal scored after just 67 seconds – the fastest in the history of the European Championships. The Czech Republic and France topped their groups unbeaten, but both were knocked out by a hard-working, well-organized, defensively orientated Greek team. The Greeks also beat Portugal twice (in the first and last games of the competition) to win the trophy.

EURO 2008

Held jointly in Austria and Switzerland, the tournament was packed with flowing football, particularly from the eventual winners, Spain, who beat Russia twice— they also beat Greece, Sweden, Italy and, in the final, Germany. Russia, who supplied two players to the team of the tournament in Arshavin and Zhirkov, had looked in good form beforehand, knocking the Netherlands out 3-1, whilst Turkey impressed with their never-say-die spirit but were beaten 3-2 by Germany in a thrilling semi-final. A total of 1.14 million spectators watched the 31 matches played.

► *Spanish striker Fernando Torres is on the attack during the Euro 2012 final against Italy. Torres scored Spain's third goal of four after coming on as a 75th-minute substitute. The match was watched by 63,170 spectators at the Gdansk Arena in Poland.*

EURO 2012

The third tournament to be jointly held, this time in Poland and Ukraine, Euro 2012 set an attendance record with more than 1.4 million spectators (46,481 per game). Shocks included the Netherlands failing to win a game and Russia losing out to Greece in qualifying for the quarter-finals. Only Germany qualified from the groups with a perfect three wins out of three games. Two of the other group winners, the Czech Republic and England, both went out at the quarter-final stage, England losing on penalties to Italy. The Italians, propelled by two goals from Mario Balotelli, beat Germany to reach the final, but had no answer to a Spanish side fully intent on attack. With player of the tournament Andrés Iniesta pulling the strings, Spain won 4-0, a record margin of victory in a European Championships final.

THE OLYMPICS

Until the emergence of the World Cup, the Olympics provided football's leading world competition. Football appeared in the 1896 games as an exhibition event and became a full Olympic sport 12 years later. With the exception of the 1932 Los Angeles games, it has featured at every Olympics since. The competition was boosted in the 1990s by the admittance of professional stars and the emergence of African football, which produced two Olympic gold medallists in Nigeria and Cameroon.

EMERGING PLAYERS

Great professional players have emerged from the Olympics. For example, French midfielder Michel Platini and Mexican legend Hugo Sanchez burst onto the international scene at the 1976 Montreal games. The 1996 Brazil team included Rivaldo and Ronaldo. The 1952 Olympics in Helsinki, Finland, saw the arrival of a stunningly good Hungarian side. Featuring players such as Ferenc Puskas, Nandor Hidegkuti and Sandor Kocsis, the Hungarians conceded two goals but scored 20 on their way to the gold medal. These players went on to form the core of the Hungarian side that lit up international football through the 1950s (see page 70).

▲ Celestine Babayaro of Nigeria in action during the gripping 1996 Olympic semi-final against Brazil. Nigeria won 4-3 and went on to beat Argentina 3-2 in the final to become the first African side to win a major international tournament.

AMATEURS ONLY

For most of its history, Olympic football was played by amateurs only. The rise of professional football in the 1920s meant that many of the world's best professionals were unable to appear at the games. State-run teams from Eastern Europe dominated the Olympics after World War II – from 1952 to 1988, every Olympic winner came from Eastern Europe with the exception of the 1984 French side, while Hungary remain the only team to have won football gold three times. But as the Olympics began to accept professional athletes in other sports, so it changed the rules for football. Professionals who were part of their national under-23 team appeared at the 1992 games. In 1996, the rule was relaxed to allow each side to field three professional players over the age of 23. At Sydney 2000, Chile, led by 33-year-old striker Ivan Zamorano, won bronze. Zamorano's six goals made him top scorer at the games.

FACTFILE The 1952 Olympics produced three amazing games. Egypt caused a shock by beating Chile 5-4. Luxembourg eclipsed that with a 5-3 win over England. Yugoslavia led the Soviet Union 5-2 with just 14 minutes to go, but the game ended as a thrilling 5-5 draw.

FACTFILE Records of the first games at the 1896 Olympics are vague. It may be that games between a Greek teams and a Danish team took place. One source suggests a Greek team fielded five British men all with the surname Whittal.

◄ Mexico's Oribe Peralta is mobbed after scoring the winner at the 2012 Olympic final against Brazil.

OLYMPIC WOMEN

Women's football finally became part of the Olympics at the 1996 Atlanta games, after many years of lobbying for inclusion. With no time for a qualifying competition, the top eight nations at the 1995 Women's World Cup were invited to take part, with the exception of England, who were ineligible to compete. The final saw China beaten 2-1 by the USA in front of 76,481 spectators, a world record for a women's sporting event at that time. Five nations – the USA, China, Germany, Norway and Brazil – shared all the medals until 2012, when powerful Canadian and Japanese teams emerged. But the qualification system now in place will ensure that Asia, Africa and Oceania are all represented at future Olympics.

▲ *The US team celebrate winning gold at the 2004 Olympics. Mia Hamm (front row, second from right), the most famous player in women's football, announced her retirement shortly after receiving the gold medal.*

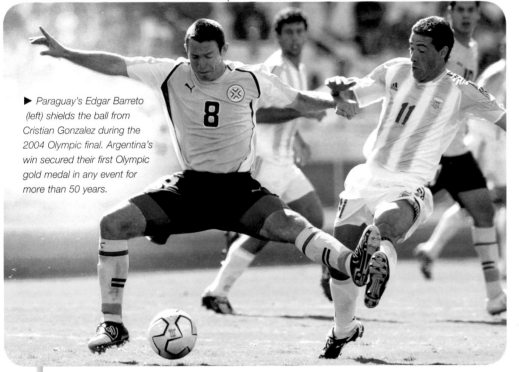

▶ *Paraguay's Edgar Barreto (left) shields the ball from Cristian Gonzalez during the 2004 Olympic final. Argentina's win secured their first Olympic gold medal in any event for more than 50 years.*

OLYMPIC GOLD MEDALLISTS

MEN

1908	Great Britain
1912	Great Britain
1920	Belgium
1924	Uruguay
1928	Uruguay
1936	Italy
1948	Sweden
1952	Hungary
1956	Soviet Union
1960	Yugoslavia
1964	Hungary
1968	Hungary
1972	Poland
1976	East Germany
1980	Czechoslovakia
1984	France
1988	Soviet Union
1992	Spain
1996	Nigeria
2000	Cameroon
2004	Argentina
2008	Argentina
2012	Mexico

WOMEN

1996	USA
2000	Norway
2004	USA
2008	USA
2012	USA

2008 AND 2012 GAMES

The 2008 games saw Italy impress before being knocked out by Belgium. Argentina beat a strong Brazilian side and narrowly defeated Nigeria in the final to win their second Olympic gold in a row. In the women's tournament, Japan came a surprising fourth and the USA defeated Brazil in the final, in extra time – exactly as they had done in 2004. The 2012 tournament saw Great Britain appear for the first time since 1960 and Honduras deliver a giant-killing, beating Spain 1-0. Mexico and Brazil despatched Asian opponents (Japan and South Korea) to meet in the final, which Mexico won. In the women's matches, Japan beat Brazil and France to meet reigning champions USA in the final, where two goals from Carli Lloyd saw the USA win gold again.

THE COPA AMERICA

The oldest continental cup competition, the Copa America has been played under a bewildering array of names and formats ever since the first competition, a three-way affair between Argentina, Uruguay and Chile in 1910. One thing has remained constant – its status as a major footballing prize for the nations of South America.

▲ The Brazil team celebrate with the Copa America trophy after beating Argentina in a penalty shootout in 2004.

CUP DOMINATION

The Copa America has had to contend with clubs reluctant to release players and the increasing popularity of international club competitions. Yet it still maintains a strong appeal. There have been 44 Copa America competitions, eight of which have been unofficial but are counted for the records. The tournament has been dominated by the big three South American nations of Argentina, Brazil and Uruguay. Fifteen Copas passed until another country, Peru, won it. Since then, Argentina and Uruguay (both with 15 titles) have maintained a strong grip. Brazil have won eight times; Paraguay and Peru twice and Bolivia, Chile and Colombia have each won once.

FACTFILE Two players have scored 17 Copa goals – Norberto Mendez (Argentina) and Zizinho (Brazil).

INVITED GUESTS

In 1993, the Copa was expanded to 12 sides. Teams are invited from outside South America including Mexico (runners up twice), USA, Costa Rica and Honduras—who caused a sensation in 2001 by beating Brazil 2-0 in the quarter-finals. Mexico appeared for the sixth time at the 2015 Copa, drawing 3-3 with hosts Chile who progressed to the final after beating Uraguay and Peru in the quarters and semis. Chile defeated Argentina 4-1 on penalties to win their first-ever Copa.

◀ Uruguay's Egido Arevaldo (right) battles for the ball during the 2011 Copa America final against Paraguay. Uruguay knocked out Argentina in the quarter-finals, and Peru in the semis.

COPA AMERICA WINNERS

Year	Winner	Year	Winner
1910*	Argentina	1955	Argentina
1916*	Uruguay	1956*	Uruguay
1917	Uruguay	1957	Argentina
1919	Brazil	1959*	Argentina
1920	Uruguay	1959	Uruguay
1921	Argentina	1963	Bolivia
1922	Brazil	1967	Uruguay
1923	Uruguay	1975	Peru
1924	Uruguay	1979	Paraguay
1925	Argentina	1983	Uruguay
1926	Uruguay	1987	Uruguay
1927	Argentina	1989	Brazil
1929	Argentina	1991	Argentina
1935*	Uruguay	1993	Argentina
1937	Argentina	1995	Uruguay
1939	Peru	1997	Brazil
1941*	Argentina	1999	Brazil
1942	Uruguay	2001	Colombia
1945*	Argentina	2004	Brazil
1946*	Argentina	2007	Brazil
1947	Argentina	2011	Uruguay
1949	Brazil	2015	Chile
1953	Paraguay	*unofficial tournament	

THE AFRICAN NATIONS CUP

The first African Nations Cup, held in 1957, was contested by just three of Africa's nine independent nations at the time – Sudan, Ethiopia and the eventual winners, Egypt. Since then, the number of independent African countries has risen sharply. At the 2015 tournament, 51 teams competed to qualify for 16 places at the finals.

AFRICAN NATIONS CUP WINNERS

Year	Winner	Year	Winner
1957	Egypt	1988	Cameroon
1959	Egypt	1990	Algeria
1962	Ethiopia	1992	Ivory Coast
1963	Ghana	1994	Nigeria
1965	Ghana	1996	South Africa
1968	Congo–Kinshasa	1998	Egypt
1970	Sudan	2000	Cameroon
1972	Congo–Brazzaville	2002	Cameroon
1974	Zaire	2004	Tunisia
1976	Morocco	2006	Egypt
1978	Ghana	2008	Egypt
1980	Nigeria	2010	Egypt
1982	Ghana	2012	Zambia
1984	Cameroon	2013	Nigeria
1986	Egypt	2015	Ivory Coast

◄ Samuel Eto'o and Hosny Abd Rabou battle for possession during the 2008 African Nations Cup final.

FACTFILE In 1998, Egyptian coach Mahmoud al-Gohari became the first person to have won the African Nations Cup as both a player and as a manager.

WINNERS AND LOSERS

A qualifying stage for the African Nations Cup was introduced in 1968, with eight places up for grabs. This was increased to 12 in 1992 and 16 for the 1998 competition. Champions have come from around the continent – from Africa's northernmost country, Morocco (winners in 1976), to its southernmost nation, South Africa, who returned from the international wilderness to win an emotional competition in 1996. Eight tournament finals have ended in penalty shootouts, including the 2015 tournament when the Ivory Coast defeated Ghana 9-8 despite missing their first two penalties. One of the most unlucky nations has to be Zambia, who lost an entire team in a tragic 1993 plane crash (see page 104), yet miraculously reached the final the following year. Zambia finally triumphed at the 2012 tournament, after a period of dominance by Egypt – three wins in a row – which took them to the top of the winners' table with seven cups. The 2013 competition threw up plenty of surprises as lowly Burkina Faso reached the final, won by Nigeria's 'Super Eagles'.

UPS AND DOWNS

The African Nations Cup has had to endure its ups and downs, with poor playing facilities in some countries, hostilities between nations and major controversies. These continue into the modern era. Nigeria, one of Africa's top sides, were expelled from the 1998 tournament after they had refused to travel to the 1996 competition. Since the early 1990s, the best teams in the competition have relied on calling back as many of their foreign-based stars as possible. In 2006, for example, not one player in the Ivory Coast and Cameroon squads was based in his home country. Four years later, Cameroon striker Samuel Eto'o notched his 18th goal, making him the tournament's all-time leading goal scorer.

► Mahamadou Diarra of Mali (left) goes past Senegal's Henri Camara at the 2004 African Nations Cup.

THE ASIAN GAMES AND ASIAN CUP

Asia is the one continent that has two major football competitions for its nations – the Asian Games and the Asian Cup. Both tournaments are held every four years, but in cycles that keep them two years apart.

THE ASIAN GAMES

The Asian Games is a multi-sport competition in which football is just one of a number of events. In the first tournament, football featured alongside weightlifting, cycling and basketball, and was played in games lasting 80, not 90, minutes. India, Burma (now Myanmar) and Taiwan dominated the early competitions. The South Koreans have shared the title twice, after the final was drawn. Penalty shootouts were later introduced to decide the winner and Iran beat North Korea 4-1 on penalties to capture the 1990 title. After a self-imposed exile from the Asian Games in the mid-1990s, Iran powered to victories

▲ Iran's Yahya Golmohammadi (left) and keeper Ebrahim Mirzapour run a lap of honour after a shock defeat of Japan to win the 2002 Asian Games.

in 1998 and 2002. By the 2002 games, the tournament had been altered to become an under-23 competition, with sides allowed to field up to three over-age players. The 2014 competition was held in South Korea and saw the home team win, beating North Korea in the final with Iraq third.

THE ASIAN CUP

First held in Hong Kong with just four teams, the Asian Cup has grown in importance. Qualification for the 12-team tournament held in Lebanon in 2000 attracted 42 countries. The footballing gap between rich and poor Asian nations was highlighted when Kuwait recorded the highest ever victory in qualifying, trouncing Bhutan 20-0. However, the

◄ Zheng Zhi (left) of China and Japan's Takayuki Suzuki jump for a header during the 2004 Asian Cup final, held in Beijing. Japan took the trophy with a 3-1 victory.

gradual emergence of higher-quality sides from the former Soviet Republics, smaller Gulf states such as Bahrain and Qatar, and countries in southeast Asia promises to make future tournaments more competitive. Iran, Japan and Saudi Arabia are the competition's most successful teams, winning the cup three times each, while Israel were a major force in the early years. They were in the final of the first four Asian Cups, winning in 1964. In 1975, however, Israel were expelled from the Asian Football Confederation, and joined UEFA in 1992.

China became hosts for the first time in 2004, when the tournament was expanded to include 16 teams. The Japan versus China final attracted enormous interest. The match was broadcast live to 60 nations; in China alone, the television audience was more than 250 million.

The 2007 tournament was jointly hosted by four nations in Southeast Asia and saw Australia compete for the first time. They were beaten by Iraq, who sensationally went on to win the tournament for the first time in their history. Australia would finish runners-up in 2011 but in 2015 triumphed as champions for the first time. The Socceroos scored the most goals (14) and deafeated South Korea 2-1 in the final.

ASIAN GAMES AND ASIAN CUP WINNERS

GAMES WINNERS			
1951	India	2014	South Korea
1954	Taiwan		
1958	Taiwan	**CUP WINNERS**	
1962	India	1956	South Korea
1966	Burma	1960	South Korea
1970	Burma and	1964	Israel
	South Korea	1968	Iran
1974	Iran	1972	Iran
1978	North Korea	1976	Iran
	and South Korea	1980	Kuwait
1982	Iraq	1984	Saudi Arabia
1986	South Korea	1988	Saudi Arabia
1990	Iran	1992	Japan
1994	Uzbekistan	1996	Saudi Arabia
1998	Iran	2000	Japan
2002	Iran	2004	Japan
2006	Qatar	2007	Iraq
2010	Japan	2011	Japan
		2015	Australia

THE CONCACAF CHAMPIONSHIP

Of all the footballing regions of the world, North America, Central America and the Caribbean Islands have had the most complex history of competitions. Five different tournaments have been open to them, starting with the CCCF Championship in 1941.

▲ *Manley Junior Tabe of Vanuatu releases the ball ahead of New Zealand's Aaron Lines in the 2002 Oceanian Nations Cup.*

THE GOLD CUP

For a number of years, competition in the CONCACAF zone was used as a direct way of qualifying for the World Cup. In 1991, the tournament was renamed the Gold Cup, which today features 12 teams at the finals. Every Gold Cup has been hosted by the USA, either alone or jointly with Mexico. Teams from outside CONCACAF have often been invited to play. In 1996, the Brazilian under-23 side lost to Mexico in the final. South Korea were guests in 2000, but they lost out on a quarter-final place to Canada on the toss of a coin. Canada went on to beat another guest, Colombia, in the final. At the 2002 competition, lots were drawn in a three-way tie for two quarter-final places. Canada and Haiti progressed at the expense of Ecuador, but the tournament was eventually won by the USA for the first time since 1991. In 2011, Jamaica surprisingly topped Group B, but lost to the United States in the knockout rounds. The US team battled in a hugely entertaining final, losing 4-2 to Mexico. Mexico won the 2015 Gold Cup beating Jamaica 3-1 in the final.

THE OCEANIAN NATIONS CUP

Oceania's competition is the smallest and youngest of the continental championships. It has been held nine times since 1973, and is now held every four years. The 2004 tournament saw a major surprise as the Solomon Islands defeated New Zealand to make the final, losing that match to Australia. The 2012 tournament saw further surprises, with New Caledonia knocking out New Zealand and Tahiti emerging as the champions.

GOLD CUP WINNERS

Canada	2000
Mexico	1993, 1996, 1998, 2003, 2009, 2011, 2015
USA	1991, 2002, 2005, 2007, 2013

▲ *Wilmer Lopez (left) of Costa Rica kicks the ball between the legs of Cobi Jones of the United States during the first half of the championship match. Costa Rica were Gold Cup runners-up in 2002.*

▲ *Mexican captain Pavel Pardo celebrates with the CONCACAF Gold Cup in 2003 after his side's 1-0 victory over Brazil in the final.*

FOOTBALL LEAGUES

Clubs compete in leagues that are made up of several divisions. Rules, numbers of teams and the length of a league season vary around the world. Many top leagues – in Spain, Italy, France and Germany, for example – have 18 or 20 teams.

NUMBERS AND BREAKS

The top divisions of Sweden and Russia each contain 16 teams, whilst Australia and Latvia feature just ten sides. In most leagues the sides play each other twice, home and away, during a season. In Denmark, the 12 teams play each other three times. Scotland's top division has an unusual format – there are 12 teams, but the season lasts for 38 games. Sides play each other three times, before the league turns into two groups of six for a further round of matches. Some leagues – in Argentina and Mexico, for example – are split into two short seasons every year. League teams in Spain, France, Bulgaria, Hungary and some other countries take a midwinter break, while in northern European nations, such as Norway and Finland, the league season begins in the spring.

PROMOTION AND RELEGATION

While leagues in Australia and the USA guarantee each team a place for the following season, most leagues have a system of promotion and relegation, with top and bottom sides switching places for the new season. In Uruguay, relegation and promotion are determined by the performance of teams over two seasons. In Austria, one side is promoted and one relegated each season. In Hungary, the Czech Republic and the Ukraine, two

▲ PSV Eindhoven's Philip Cocu fights for the ball with Feyenoord's Shinji Ono (right) during a Dutch premier league match in 2004.

▼ Toluca (in yellow) battle with Tigres in the Mexican league. Toluca won the 2002–03 Clausura, or winter, championship – their fourth league title since 1998.

▲ South Korean Ahn Jung-Hwan, playing for Japanese side Yokohama F Marinos, celebrates his winning goal in a J-League encounter against Kashima Antlers.

▶ Shinji Ono (left) of the Western Sydney Wanderers in action in the A-League Grand Final in 2013, a game won 2-0 by their opponents – the Central Coast Mariners.

HARD FALLERS

Just as clubs can rise, so can they fall. In the 2014–15 season, 11 former champions of the English league (with 25 titles between them) played outside the top division. A slide down the divisions can be gradual or sudden. Napoli were home to Diego Maradona and one of Italian football's aristocrats, winning the league title in 1987 and 1990 and finishing runners-up in the two intervening years. Yet, by the early 2000s they were bankrupt and playing in Serie C, two divisions down from the top flight.

Rarely, however, has a downturn been more dramatic than that experienced by Manchester City or Tasmania 1900 Berlin. In 1937, Manchester City were the English league champions. In the following season, they scored 80 league goals, more than any other side, but were relegated. Tasmania 1900 Berlin were joint first in the early stages of the 1965–66 Bundesliga season. By the end, they were bottom and holders of a series of unenviable records for a season, including: fewest wins (two), most losses (28), most goals against (108) and lowest points total (eight).

teams go up and down, while in Germany, France, Spain and Portugal it is three.

In Germany, the third-place team in the second division contests a two-game play-off with the team finishing 16th in the Bundesliga, to determine who will play in the top division the following season. Other nations, such as Italy and England, hold a play-off series featuring semi-finals and a final to determine which of four teams will be promoted along with others that won automatic promotion above them. In Italy, play-offs are also used to determine which side joins three other relegated teams from Serie A. Play-off systems are criticized for turning a whole season into a lottery over one, two or three games, but many people think they maintain interest and add drama.

FAST RISERS

Some leagues have been dominated by a small number of teams throughout their history. For 43 seasons from 1932, the Uruguayan league title was won by either Peñarol or Nacional (Defensor were champions in 1976). Scotland's Glasgow Rangers hold the world record for the most league championships, with a staggering 54 titles, eight more than their arch rivals, Celtic. In some leagues, small teams have

risen dramatically from humble beginnings to become champions or contenders. In Europe, the now mighty Bayern Munich were not considered successful enough to join the Bundesliga in the early 1960s, but since then they have become one of the pillars of German football.

> **FACTFILE**
> The Isles of Scilly, off the coast of southwestern England, are home to the Scillonian League, the world's smallest. Woolpack Wanderers and Garrison Gunners are the only two sides to contest the league, as well as two cup competitions.

▶ River Plate's Paraguayan striker Nelson Cuevas is challenged by defender German Re of Newell's Old Boys during an Argentinian first division match in Buenos Aires.

SERIE A

Serie A has a reputation as the ultimate test for the world's top players. For decades, South American stars have played for its clubs; they were joined in the 1990s by talents from Africa and Asia. Some clubs are now struggling financially as a result of their lavish spending on players. Winning Serie A is sometimes referred to as the *scudetto* (small shield), as the champion's strip the following season bears a small coat of arms in Italian colours. Sometimes, the quality of Serie A has meant that a team which is successful in Europe has struggled at home. Internazionale, for example, won the UEFA Cup in 1994, but could only manage 13th place in the league. Juventus are the most successful Serie A club, with 31 titles, followed by AC Milan and Internazionale (both 18) and Genoa (nine). In 2004, Serie A expanded from 18 to 20 teams, but was rocked two years later by a match-fixing scandal. Juventus were stripped of the 2005 and 2006 titles, leading to Inter being awarded the 2006 *scudetto*.

LA LIGA

The Spanish league banned foreign players between 1963 and 1973, but since then it has been the home of some of the world's greatest footballers, from Johan Cruyff and Diego Maradona to current stars Neymar, Lionel Messi and Cristiano Ronaldo. While Barcelona and Real Madrid have dominated in recent seasons, the league is highly competitive.

La Liga has two professional divisions and a series of amateur divisons. Unlike other national leagues, the reserve sides of the major clubs play in the lower divisions, not in a separate reserves league. Real Madrid and Barcelona remain La Liga's most wealthy and successful clubs, with more than 55 league titles between them.

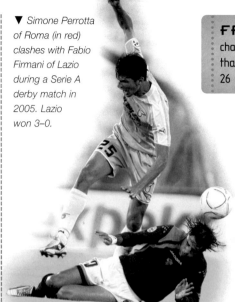

▼ Simone Perrotta of Roma (in red) clashes with Fabio Firmani of Lazio during a Serie A derby match in 2005. Lazio won 3–0.

▼ Barcelona's Argentinian striker Lionel Messi (right) is one of the stars of La Liga.

FACTFILE In the 1998 Swedish league championship, AIK Solna scored fewer goals than any of their 13 opponents (just 25 in 26 matches), yet still managed to win the title.

THE BUNDESLIGA

After the division of Germany into East and West following World War II, the West German Bundesliga was first contested in 1965. In 1991, after reunification, two sides from the former East Germany were admitted into the top division. Since then, eastern sides have struggled to maintain a regular presence in the Bundesliga. Bayern Munich are by far the most successful Bundesliga club, with 24 titles, followed by Borussia Mönchengladbach and Borussia Dortmund (five each), Werder Bremen (four) and Hamburg and VfB Stuttgart (three).

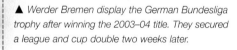

▲ Werder Bremen display the German Bundesliga trophy after winning the 2003–04 title. They secured a league and cup double two weeks later.

The Bundesliga was one of the last major leagues to adopt a system of three points for a win (in 1995) and Bayern Munich's totalled a record 91 points in 2012–13. In 2008–09, the Bundesliga took a fascinating twist when VfL Wolfsburg, who had never won a major German competition, scooped the league, propelled by 54 goals from strikers Grafite and Edin Dzeko. Grafite's tally of 28 goals was the highest since the early 1980s, but still short of the record 40 goals Gerd Müller scored for Bayern in 1971–72. Müller's total of 365 Bundesliga goals is unlikely to be beaten for many years.

HIT THE NET

www.european-football-statistics.co.uk/
A great resource for learning more about the performances and placings of clubs in many European leagues.

http://www.worldfootball.net/winner/champions-league
Global lists of league champions and cup winners.

◄ Man United's Robin van Persie competes against a former team-mate, Kieran Gibbs (left) and Laurent Koscielny of Arsenal, during a 2013 league game.

THE ENGLISH PREMIER LEAGUE

In the early 1990s, England's first division clubs broke away from league control to form the Premier League. Money has flooded into the top clubs' coffers and a wide gap has opened up between established sides and newly promoted teams, who find it very hard to stay up. At the top of the table, Manchester United have won 13 out of a possible 21 titles. Their battle for league supremacy was mainly fought with Arsenal and Chelsea in the 2000s, whilst Manchester City – bolstered by stars David Silva and Sergio Aguero – took the title in both 2011–12 and 2013–14. Matches are often very exciting and attract massive worldwide TV audiences, making it the most watched domestic league on the planet.

LIGUE 1

Despite having produced some of the world's greatest players, the French league has traditionally not been as well funded as others in Europe. Its home-grown stars, such as Yohan Cabaye and Franck Ribery, usually move abroad. Despite this, French teams appear to be on the up, reaching the final of both the Champions League and the UEFA Cup in 2004. The French league is highly competitive. Between 1983 and 2003, only three sides – Auxerre, Monaco and Paris Saint Germain – played in the top division

▼ WUSA, the world's only pro women's league, ran for just three seasons in the USA. In 2009, it was replaced by the WPS, featuring seven teams.

every season. AS Saint-Étienne and Marseille have each won the league ten times, but in recent years Lyon (Olympique Lyonnais) and Paris Saint-Germain have won. PSG achieved three titles in a row in 2015.

ASIAN LEAGUES

The first professional league in Asia was South Korea's K-League, which began with just five teams in 1983. Featuring no relegation, it now has 14 teams. The league's most successful side is Seongnam Ilhwa Chunma, with seven titles. Japan's J-League kicked off in 1993 and now has two divisions. In 2004, Yokohama F Marinos became the first club to win three J-leagues in a row, while Kashima Antlers are the most successful side with seven titles. The Chinese Super League has been won by Guangzhou Evergrande four times since it began in 2004.

MAJOR LEAGUE SOCCER (MLS)

Early attempts at setting up a professional league in the USA included the heavily financed North American Soccer League (NASL), which ran from 1968 to 1984 and featured global superstars such as Pelé, albeit near the end of their careers. The MLS celebrated the start of its 20th season in 2015 and mixes home-grown players with international stars such as Thierry Henry and Bradley Wright-Phillips. In 2012, the league grew to 19 teams with the arrival of the Montreal Impact. Teams play in two divisions, Eastern and Western. Unlike most leagues, there is no relegation and promotion. The LA Galaxy with five championships and DC United with four are the most successful sides in MLS history.

CLUB CUP COMPETITIONS

In 1872, Wanderers beat Royal Engineers by one goal to nil to win the first FA Cup – the oldest surviving major cup competition. Since that time, hundreds of cup competitions have been introduced all over the world. Some, such as the Asian Supercup and the African Supercup, are contested between the winners of other cup competitions.

CONTINENTAL CUP COMPETITIONS

Every continent has one or more cup competitions for its best clubs. The two most famous are the Copa Libertadores and the European Champions League (see pages 132–133). The winners of these two competitions play each other to determine the world's best team in the World Club Cup (previously called the Intercontinental Cup). Often seen as a curiosity by neutrals, the World Club Cup has suffered from withdrawals and bad-tempered games, but its staging in Japan from 1980 has kept the competition alive, despite the arrival of the World Club Championship in 2000–01.

In Africa, the African Cup-Winners' Cup and the CAF Cup are only exceeded in prestige by the African Champions League, which was first played for in 1964. Egyptian side Al-Ahly have won the competition eight times, while Algerian team ES Setif won in 2014, their first triumph since 1988. The Asian Cup-Winners' Cup ran from 1991 to 2002 and was won by Saudi Arabian teams six times. In contrast, the AFC Champions League has seen winners from nine countries. South Korean clubs, such as 2012 winners Ulsan Hyundai, have triumphed in the competition ten times; Japanese clubs – such as 2008 champions Gamba Osaka – have won the title five times.

COPA LIBERTADORES

South America's first international club competition was staged by Chilean club Colo Colo in 1948 and won by Brazil's Vasco da Gama. However, it was not until 1960 that a regular competition, the Copa Libertadores, was set up. Peñarol of Uruguay won the first two contests, but were defeated in the final of the third by Santos, courtesy of two goals from Pelé. Today, the Copa Libertadores begins with nine groups of four teams and culminates in a second round, quarter-finals, semi-finals and a pair of games – home and away – between the finalists. It is open to the top sides of each South American nation, but Mexican teams were also invited to compete from 1999–2001. The Copa Libertadores has always outshone the national team competition – the Copa America – and

▲ Boca Juniors celebrate their penalty shootout victory over AC Milan in the 2003 World Club Cup. Argentinian clubs have won the competition nine times, more than any other nation.

◄ Action from a 2005 AFC Champions League match between Al-Ain of the United Arab Emirates and Saudi Arabian side Al-Ittihad, who won the title in both 2004 and 2005.

other South American cups in popularity and passion. This intensity has led to flare-ups on the pitch and in the stands. In the 1971 Copa match between Boca Juniors and Sporting Cristal, a brawl ended in the arrest of most of the players, while Colombia's Atletico Nacional were banned in 1990 after a referee received death threats.

The Copa Libertadores has mainly been won by teams from Brazil, Argentina and Uruguay. Independiente hold the record of seven victories; the only teams to have reached the final more often are Peñarol and Boca Juniors (both ten times). Uruguay's Nacional have won three Copas. Colombia's clubs lost seven out of eight finals before in 2004, minnows Once Caldas beat Brazilian giants Santos and São Paulo to become unexpected champions, a feat matched by Ecuador's LDU Quito in 2008, Atlético Mineiro in 2013 and Argentinian outsiders, San Lorenzo, in 2014.

▶ *Rubin Kazan's Salomon Rondon (right) tries to shield the ball from Levante defender Sergio Ballesteros during their Europa League encounter. Former Russian league champions, Rubin Kazan beat Inter Milan in the group stages and then knocked out Spanish sides Levante and Atlético Madrid, before falling to Chelsea at the quarter-final stage.*

CUPS IN EUROPE

Most leagues in Europe have one or more cup competitions for their teams to contest. Among the best known domestic cup competitions are the English FA Cup; the Scottish Cup, which started in 1874; the Spanish Cup, which began in 1902; and the French Cup, which was first played for in 1918. From 1960 until 1999, the winners of national cup competitions in Europe played in the Cup-Winners' Cup. The first and last Cup-Winners' Cups were won by Italian sides (Fiorentina and Lazio), but the most successful team was Barcelona, who lifted the trophy four times. They suffered a surprising loss in the 1969 final to Slovan Bratislava (now in Slovakia), who became the first Eastern European club to win a major continental cup. Since the Cup-Winners' Cup was scrapped, cup winners in Europe's strongest nations have competed for the UEFA Cup.

The UEFA Cup's forerunner began in 1955 as the Inter-Cities Fairs Cup, a competition that took two years to complete. By 1960, the Fairs Cup was played over the course of a year and, for the 1971–72 season, a new trophy and new name – the UEFA Cup – were introduced. In 1972, the European Supercup arrived, and was contested between the victors of the European Champions Cup and the Cup-Winners'

◀ *CSKA Moscow's Venaumin Mandrikin celebrates with the 2005 UEFA Cup as his side become the first Russian club to win a major European trophy, beating Sporting Lisbon 3-1 in the final.*

Cup. UEFA Cup winners have so far come from 11 nations, with Italian clubs taking the title on nine occasions, German and English sides winning six times, and Spanish teams five times. More than 100 teams now enter the first stages of the competition and places are granted through winning a national cup, a high league finish, or being knocked out of the Champions League group stage. In 2009, the UEFA Cup was renamed as the Europa League, with a group stage containing 12 mini-leagues of four clubs each.

◀ *São Paulo's Ricardo Oliveira (left) fights for the ball with Internacional's Fabiano Eller during the final of the 2006 Copa Libertadores. Internacional won the trophy and went on to stun Barcelona four months later, beating them 1-0 in the World Club Cup.*

EUROPEAN CHAMPIONS

European club competitions date back to 1927, when the Mitropa Cup was first contested by the leading clubs of central Europe. Sparta Prague were its first winners. The last Mitropa Cup was won by Yugoslav side Borac Banja Luka in 1992, but by then the glamour of the Mitropa had long been eclipsed by the mighty European Cup, a competition that is now known as the European Champions League.

◀ Real Madrid keeper Rogelio Dominguez claims the ball during the 1959 European Cup final against French club Stade de Reims. The game ended 2-0 to Real, who lifted their fourth European Cup in a row.

▶ Julius Aghahowa of Shakhtar Donetsk is challenged by Barcelona's Fernando Navarro in a 2004–05 Champions League game. Aghahowa's two goals gave the Ukrainian side a surprise victory.

EARLY DAYS

The European Champion Clubs' Cup, usually known as the European Cup, developed out of a meeting set up by Frenchman Gabriel Hanot. Italian, Spanish, French and Portuguese club sides were keen to take part, as were teams from many other nations. The first European Cup, held in 1955–56, featured major names such as Real Madrid, Sporting Lisbon, Anderlecht and AC Milan. Clubs that are less well known today also entered – Århus GF and FC Saarbrucken, for example. English league champions Chelsea, however, were forbidden from entering, but Scottish club Hibernian reached the semi-final. The first winners of the trophy were Real Madrid.

CHANGING CHAMPIONS

Real won the first five European Cups, before the tournament hit a golden age of competition in the 1960s, with Benfica, Internazionale and AC Milan all winning the trophy. The 1970s saw both Ajax and Bayern Munich crowned champions three years in a row. English clubs won six European Cups in succession from 1977, but were banned from European competition for five years after the 1985 Heysel Stadium disaster (see page 105). There have been 15 Spanish winners, and 12 English and 12 Italian champions.

As the European Cup grew in intensity, it became harder to successfully defend the title. The last back-to-back winners of the trophy were AC Milan in 1989 and 1990. The first year that the final went into extra time was 1958, while the first penalty shootout in the final was in 1984. The two finals won by Eastern European sides, Steaua Bucharest (1986) and Red Star Belgrade (1991), both went to nail-biting penalty shootouts.

EXPANSION AND DOMINATION

The format of the European Cup remained almost unchanged for its first 35 years. Teams competed in knockout rounds, playing one match at home and one away. If the scores were tied after the two games, the team with more away goals would go through. For many years, the competition was open only to the league champions of each country. Today, as many as four sides from each top league take part.

▲ Nottingham Forest celebrate winning their second European Cup title in a row after winger John Robertson's single goal was enough to defeat German side Hamburg in the 1980 final.

EUROPEAN CUP / CHAMPIONS LEAGUE WINNERS

1956	Real Madrid	1976	Bayern Munich	1996	Juventus
1957	Real Madrid	1977	Liverpool	1997	Borussia Dortmund
1958	Real Madrid	1978	Liverpool	1998	Real Madrid
1959	Real Madrid	1979	Nottingham Forest	1999	Manchester United
1960	Real Madrid	1980	Nottingham Forest	2000	Real Madrid
1961	Benfica	1981	Liverpool	2001	Bayern Munich
1962	Benfica	1982	Aston Villa	2002	Real Madrid
1963	AC Milan	1983	Hamburg	2003	AC Milan
1964	Internazionale	1984	Liverpool	2004	Porto
1965	Internazionale	1985	Juventus	2005	Liverpool
1966	Real Madrid	1986	Steaua Bucharest	2006	Barcelona
1967	Celtic	1987	Porto	2007	AC Milan
1968	Manchester United	1988	PSV Eindhoven	2008	Manchester United
1969	AC Milan	1989	AC Milan	2009	Barcelona
1970	Feyenoord	1990	AC Milan	2010	Internazionale
1971	Ajax	1991	Red Star Belgrade	2011	Barcelona
1972	Ajax	1992	Barcelona	2012	Chelsea
1973	Ajax	1993	Marseille (see p83)	2013	Bayern Munich
1974	Bayern Munich	1994	AC Milan	2014	Real Madrid
1975	Bayern Munich	1995	Ajax	2015	Barcelona

▲ *Manchester United's Wayne Rooney in action during the 2009 Champions League final.*

▼ *Robert Lewandowski scores Borussia Dortmund's first goal in their Champions League semi-final first leg-game against Real Madrid. In an extraordinary match, Lewandowski became the first player ever to score four goals in a semi-final. Dortmund won 4-1 in that game, and went on to reach an all-German Champions League final versus Bayern Munich.*

FACTFILE
Lionel Messi and Cristiano Ronaldo ended the 2014–15 season as the Champions League's all-time leading goal scorers, each with 77 goals.

The competition was revamped as the Champions League in 1992. Group stages were introduced, guaranteeing more games and vast sums of television money for the competing clubs. Champions League success is now essential for the financial health of Europe's top teams. A report in 2005 showed that taking part in the tournament can add 10–20 per cent to a club's total income in a season. For a big side, failure to qualify can be a financial disaster.

The number of games in the Champions League soared from 25 in 1992–93 to 157 in 2002–03. From the 2003–04 season, the number of group stages was reduced from two to one, partly due to criticism that the competition was overblown. Yet, for every one of its critics, there are a thousand fans of the Champions League, as it pits more of the world's elite players against each other than any other club competition.

FACTFILE Up to 2004, only Dutchman Clarence Seedorf had won the European Cup with three different clubs – Ajax (1995), Real Madrid (1998) and AC Milan (2003).

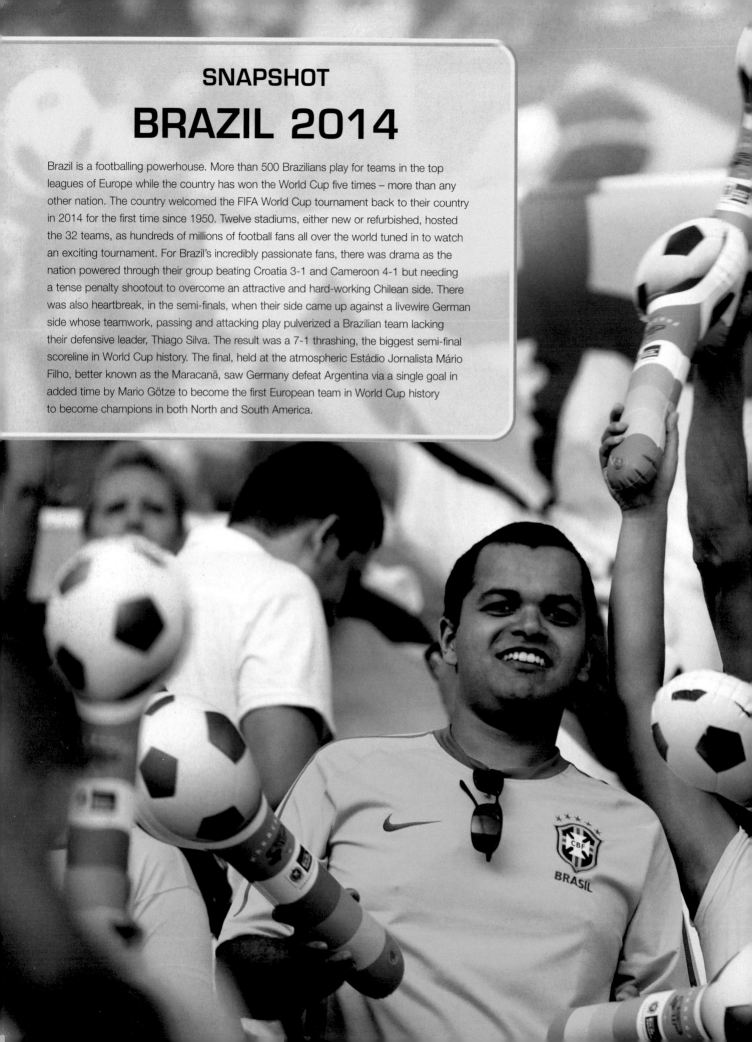

SNAPSHOT
BRAZIL 2014

Brazil is a footballing powerhouse. More than 500 Brazilians play for teams in the top leagues of Europe while the country has won the World Cup five times – more than any other nation. The country welcomed the FIFA World Cup tournament back to their country in 2014 for the first time since 1950. Twelve stadiums, either new or refurbished, hosted the 32 teams, as hundreds of millions of football fans all over the world tuned in to watch an exciting tournament. For Brazil's incredibly passionate fans, there was drama as the nation powered through their group beating Croatia 3-1 and Cameroon 4-1 but needing a tense penalty shootout to overcome an attractive and hard-working Chilean side. There was also heartbreak, in the semi-finals, when their side came up against a livewire German side whose teamwork, passing and attacking play pulverized a Brazilian team lacking their defensive leader, Thiago Silva. The result was a 7-1 thrashing, the biggest semi-final scoreline in World Cup history. The final, held at the atmospheric Estádio Jornalista Mário Filho, better known as the Maracanã, saw Germany defeat Argentina via a single goal in added time by Mario Götze to become the first European team in World Cup history to become champions in both North and South America.

▲ Thomas Müller of Germany celebrates with the trophy after winning the 2014 World Cup final game against Argentina.

Brazilian fans watch the first official international match (a friendly) at the newly refurbished Maracanã Stadium in Rio de Janeiro – a lively 2-2 draw between Brazil and England.

BRITISH FOOTBALL

Britain is thought of as the birthplace of football – in the late 19th century, pioneering league and cup competitions were set up in England and Scotland. Many of them survive to this day.

CHANGING DIVISIONS

The English league kicked off in 1888, with 12 teams playing in a single division. It was expanded to two divisions of 18 clubs in 1898 and to four divisions containing 92 teams in 1950. Despite several changes in structure – including the creation in 1992 of a Premier League for the top 22 clubs (reduced to 20 teams in 1994) and the rebranding of the football league as the Championship, League One and League Two – the figure of 92 clubs linked by promotion and relegation between the divisions remains in place. In 2013, Cardiff City were promoted to the Premier League, joining Swansea City as the two Welsh clubs in the top four English divisions, while one England-based club, Berwick Rangers, plays in the Scottish league (formed in 1891).

Many clubs have moved to new grounds, but only one has moved towns – in 2004, Wimbledon became Milton Keynes Dons.

In protest, Wimbledon supporters set up their own amateur club, AFC Wimbledon, which has begun the long climb up the English league pyramid. Between February 2003 and November 2004, the team went unbeaten in 78 games, a British record. They entered the Football League in 2011.

CUP DREAMS

Despite the growing influence of European competitions, the FA Cup and Scottish Cup retain their appeal for clubs and fans alike. A staggering 758 clubs entered the 2012–13 FA Cup, most starting in the extra-preliminary rounds. It is the dream of every non-league and lower league club to reach the third round and have the chance of giving one of the huge teams a run for their money. The histories of the two cups are littered with notable giantkilling acts – as a non-league side, Yeovil Town (now in the English league) beat league opposition 20 times. Despite the gulf in finance and quality of players, teams from lower divisions do still beat higher-placed opponents. The 2012–13 FA Cup saw giant-killing triumphs such as Luton from the Conference defeating Norwich of the Premier League and Oldham beating Liverpool, while in 2014-15 Bradford City knocked Chelsea out of the competition.

At the start of the season, the winners of the FA Cup and the Premier League meet in the Community Shield (formerly the Charity Shield). The first Charity Shield match, in 1908, was between amateur side Queens Park Rangers (the Southern League champions) and Manchester United (the professional league champions). The 2015 game between Arsenal and Chelsea was the first since 2006 not to feature Manchester United or City.

FOREIGN IMPORTS

In the past 15 years, foreign players from all over the world have come to play in the Scottish and English leagues. Rangers and Chelsea were the first top-flight teams to field sides containing no British players in a league match, while 110 footballers at the 2014 World Cup played their club football in the English Premiership. Foreign managers were far less common until the mid-1990s. Since then, José Mourinho at Chelsea, Arsène Wenger (at Arsenal) and Dick Advocaat (at Rangers) have all enjoyed major success. The reigns of foreign coaches of British national teams, such as Fabio Capello and Berti Vogts, were less smooth, however.

INTERNATIONAL PROSPECTS

At international level, Wales, Scotland and Northern Ireland have struggled in recent years to qualify for tournaments. Qualification for Euro 2016, however, provided great encouragement with England cruising through their group, Scotland competing hard in a group containing Germany and Poland, and Northern Ireland beating Hungary and Greece in Group F. In Group B, Wales topped their group after six games including a victory over Belgium – the second-ranked team in the world.

MAGAZINES AND BOOKS

World Soccer Magazine (IPC Media)
The best magazine available for fans of world football, with coverage of all the major and minor leagues as well as news and features on international competitions.

Soccer Skills and Techniques (Armadillo Books, 2015) Excellent, in-depth guide to the skills of the game with lots of step-by-step photos and diagrams.

The Football Hall of Fame (Robert Galvin and the National Football Museum, Portico, 2011) An interesting look at football legends using artefacts from the National Football Museum, based in Manchester.

Soccer Rules Explained, Revised and Updated (Stanley Lover, Lyons Press, 2005) One of the best books on football's laws.

Inventing the Pyramid: The History of Football Tactics (Jonathan Wilson, Orion, 2008) A comprehensive look at changing football tactics over the decades.

Boots, Balls and Haircuts (Hunter Davies, Cassell Illustrated, 2004) A thorough and entertaining look at the history of football.

The UEFA European Football Yearbook 2014–15 (Mike Hammond, Carlton Books, 2015) A comprehensive guide to everything in European football.

An Encyclopedia of Scottish Football (David Potter & Phil H. Jones, Know The Score Books, 2008) A 400-page guide to all the records in Scottish football.

FACTS AND FIGURES

ENGLISH LEAGUE CHAMPIONS

Clubs from the Midlands and the north dominated the start of the English league, and it was not until 1931 that a southern club, Arsenal, won the title. Doncaster Rovers hold the record for the most wins in a season and the most defeats. Manchester United and Liverpool have won the most league titles. Below are the post-war records.

2015 Chelsea
2014 Manchester City
2013 Manchester United
2012 Manchester City
2011 Manchester United
2010 Chelsea
2009 Manchester United
2008 Manchester United
2007 Manchester United
2006 Chelsea
2005 Chelsea
2004 Arsenal
2003 Manchester United
2002 Arsenal
2001 Manchester United
2000 Manchester United
1999 Manchester United
1998 Arsenal
1997 Manchester United
1996 Manchester United
1995 Blackburn Rovers
1994 Manchester United
1993 Manchester United
1992 Leeds United
1991 Arsenal
1990 Liverpool
1989 Arsenal
1988 Liverpool
1987 Everton
1986 Liverpool
1985 Everton
1984 Liverpool
1983 Liverpool
1982 Liverpool
1981 Aston Villa
1980 Liverpool
1979 Liverpool
1978 Nottingham Forest
1977 Liverpool
1976 Liverpool
1975 Derby County
1974 Leeds United
1973 Liverpool
1972 Derby County
1971 Arsenal
1970 Everton
1969 Leeds United
1968 Manchester City
1967 Manchester United
1966 Liverpool
1965 Manchester United
1964 Liverpool
1963 Everton
1962 Ipswich Town
1961 Tottenham Hotspur
1960 Burnley
1959 Wolverhampton Wanderers
1958 Wolverhampton Wanderers
1957 Manchester United
1956 Manchester United
1955 Chelsea
1954 Wolverhampton Wanderers
1953 Arsenal
1952 Manchester United
1951 Tottenham Hotspur
1950 Portsmouth
1949 Portsmouth
1948 Arsenal
1947 Liverpool

SCOTTISH LEAGUE CHAMPIONS

Rangers and Celtic have dominated the Scottish league. In its first year, 1891, Rangers shared the title with Dumbarton; Celtic claimed their first title in 1893. In 1998–99, the top division was rebadged the Scottish Premier League (SPL).

2015 Celtic
2014 Celtic
2013 Celtic
2012 Celtic
2011 Rangers
2010 Rangers
2009 Rangers
2008 Celtic
2007 Celtic
2006 Celtic
2005 Rangers
2004 Celtic
2003 Rangers
2002 Celtic
2001 Celtic
2000 Rangers
1999 Rangers
1998 Celtic
1997 Rangers
1996 Rangers
1995 Rangers
1994 Rangers
1993 Rangers
1992 Rangers
1991 Rangers
1990 Rangers
1989 Rangers
1988 Celtic
1987 Rangers
1986 Celtic
1985 Aberdeen
1984 Aberdeen
1983 Dundee United
1982 Celtic
1981 Celtic
1980 Aberdeen
1979 Celtic
1978 Rangers
1977 Celtic
1976 Rangers
1975 Rangers
1974 Celtic
1973 Celtic
1972 Celtic
1971 Celtic
1970 Celtic
1969 Celtic
1968 Celtic
1967 Celtic
1966 Celtic
1965 Kilmarnock
1964 Rangers
1963 Rangers
1962 Dundee
1961 Rangers
1960 Heart of Midlothian
1959 Rangers
1958 Heart of Midlothian
1957 Rangers
1956 Rangers
1955 Aberdeen
1954 Celtic
1953 Rangers
1952 Hibernian
1951 Hibernian
1950 Rangers
1949 Rangers
1948 Hibernian
1947 Rangers

FA CUP

The FA Cup is the world's longest-running knockout competition. Manchester United are the most successful side, while Preston North End hold the record for the biggest win in an FA Cup game, pummelling Hyde United 26-0 in 1887–88. Below are the post-war winners and runners-up of the FA Cup. An asterisk denotes that extra time was played.

2015 Arsenal 4 Aston Villa 0
2014 Arsenal 3 Hull City 2*
2013 Wigan 1 Manchester City 0
2012 Chelsea 2 Liverpool 1
2011 Manchester City 1 Stoke City 0
2010 Chelsea 1 Portsmouth 0
2009 Chelsea 2 Everton 1
2008 Portsmouth 1 Cardiff City 0
2007 Chelsea 1 Manchester United 0*
2006 Liverpool 3 West Ham United 3 (3-1 penalties)
2005 Arsenal 0 Manchester United 0* (5-4 penalties)
2004 Manchester United 3 Millwall 0
2003 Arsenal 1 Southampton 0
2002 Arsenal 2 Chelsea 0
2001 Liverpool 2 Arsenal 1
2000 Chelsea 1 Aston Villa 0
1999 Manchester United 2 Newcastle United 0
1998 Arsenal 2 Newcastle United 0
1997 Chelsea 2 Middlesbrough 0
1996 Manchester United 1 Liverpool 0
1995 Everton 1 Manchester United 0
1994 Manchester United 4 Chelsea 0
1993 Arsenal 2 Sheffield Wednesday 1 (replay after 1-1)
1992 Liverpool 2 Sunderland 0
1991 Tottenham Hotspur 2 Nottingham Forest 1*
1990 Manchester United 1 Crystal Palace 0 (replay after 3-3)
1989 Liverpool 3 Everton 2*
1988 Wimbledon 1 Liverpool 0
1987 Coventry City 3 Tottenham Hotspur 2*
1986 Liverpool 3 Everton 1
1985 Manchester United 1 Everton 0*
1984 Everton 2 Watford 0
1983 Manchester United 4 Brighton and Hove Albion 0 (replay after 2-2)
1982 Tottenham Hotspur 1 QPR 0 (replay after 1-1)
1981 Tottenham Hotspur 3 Manchester City 2 (replay after 1-1)
1980 West Ham United 1 Arsenal 0
1979 Arsenal 3 Manchester United 2
1978 Ipswich Town 1 Arsenal 0
1977 Manchester United 2 Liverpool 1
1976 Southampton 1 Manchester United 0
1975 West Ham United 2 Fulham 0

1974 Liverpool 3
Newcastle United 0
1973 Sunderland 1
Leeds United 0
1972 Leeds United 1 Arsenal 0
1971 Arsenal 2 Liverpool 1
1970 Chelsea 2 Leeds United 1
(replay after 2-2)
1969 Manchester City 1 Leicester
City 0
1968 West Bromwich Albion 1
Everton 0*
1967 Tottenham Hotspur 2
Chelsea 1
1966 Everton 3
Sheffield Wednesday 2
1965 Liverpool 2 Leeds United 1*
1964 West Ham United 3
Preston North End 2
1963 Manchester United 3
Leicester City 1
1962 Tottenham Hotspur 3
Burnley 1
1961 Tottenham Hotspur 2
Leicester City 0
1960 Wolverhampton
Wanderers 3
Blackburn Rovers 0
1959 Nottingham Forest 2
Luton Town 1
1958 Bolton Wanderers 2
Manchester United 0
1957 Aston Villa 2
Manchester United 1
1956 Manchester City 3
Birmingham City 1
1955 Newcastle United 3
Manchester City 1
1954 West Bromwich Albion 3
Preston North End 2
1953 Blackpool 4
Bolton Wanderers 3
1952 Newcastle United 1
Arsenal 0
1951 Newcastle United 2
Blackpool 0
1950 Arsenal 2 Liverpool 0
1949 Wolverhampton
Wanderers 3
Leicester City 1
1948 Manchester United 4
Blackpool 2
1947 Charlton Athletic 1
Burnley 0*
1946 Derby County 4
Charlton Athletic 1*

SCOTTISH CUP
The Scottish Cup began in 1873 and for half a century was won by a wide range of teams. Arbroath have never won the cup, but in 1885 they thrashed Bon Accord 36-0, the biggest win in British football.

2015 Inverness Caledonian Thistle
2014 St Johnstone
2013 Celtic
2012 Heart of Midlothian
2011 Celtic
2010 Dundee United
2009 Rangers
2008 Celtic
2007 Celtic
2006 Hearts
2005 Celtic
2004 Celtic
2003 Rangers
2002 Rangers
2001 Celtic
2000 Rangers
1999 Rangers
1998 Heart of Midlothian
1997 Kilmarnock
1996 Rangers
1995 Celtic
1994 Dundee United
1993 Rangers
1992 Rangers
1991 Motherwell
1990 Aberdeen
1989 Celtic
1988 Celtic
1987 St Mirren
1986 Aberdeen
1985 Celtic
1984 Aberdeen
1983 Aberdeen
1982 Aberdeen
1981 Rangers
1980 Celtic
1979 Rangers
1978 Rangers
1977 Celtic
1976 Rangers
1975 Celtic
1974 Celtic
1973 Rangers
1972 Celtic
1971 Celtic
1970 Aberdeen
1969 Celtic
1968 Dunfermline Athletic
1967 Celtic
1966 Rangers
1965 Celtic
1964 Rangers
1963 Rangers
1962 Rangers
1961 Dunfermline Athletic
1960 Rangers
1959 St Mirren
1958 Clyde
1957 Falkirk
1956 Heart of Midlothian
1955 Clyde
1954 Celtic
1953 Rangers

1952 Motherwell
1951 Celtic
1950 Rangers
1949 Rangers
1948 Rangers
1947 Aberdeen

THE LEAGUE CUP
The League Cup began in 1960 and is open only to the 92 English league clubs. Since 2003, it has been known as the Carling Cup. The competition now awards a UEFA Cup place to the winners and is a major prize for clubs not chasing a Champions League spot.

Number of wins
8 – Liverpool
5 – Aston Villa, Chelsea
4 – Manchester United, Nottingham Forest, Tottenham Hotspur
3 – Leicester City, Manchester City
2 – Arsenal, Birmingham City, Norwich City, Wolverhampton Wanderers

ON THE CONTINENT
For over four decades, British teams have had plenty of success in Europe. Below is a list of the clubs that have made the final of a major European cup competition.

2013 Chelsea, Europa League, winners
2012 Chelsea, Champions League, winners
2011 Manchester United, Champions League, runners-up
2010 Fulham, Europa League, runners-up
2009 Manchester United, Champions League, runners-up
2008 Manchester United, Champions League, winners
2008 Chelsea, Champions League, runners-up
2008 Glasgow Rangers, UEFA Cup, runners-up
2007 Liverpool, Champions League, runners-up
2006 Arsenal, Champions League, runners-up
2006 Middlesborough, UEFA Cup, runners-up
2005 Liverpool, Champions

League, winners
2003 Celtic, UEFA Cup, runners-up
2001 Liverpool, UEFA Cup, winners
2000 Arsenal, UEFA Cup, runners-up
1999 Manchester United, Champions League, winners
1995 Arsenal, Cup-Winners' Cup, runners-up
1994 Arsenal, Cup-Winners' Cup, winners
1991 Manchester United, Cup-Winners' Cup, winners
1987 Dundee United, UEFA Cup, runners-up
1985 Everton, Cup-Winners' Cup, winners
1985 Liverpool, European Cup, runners-up
1984 Liverpool, European Cup, winners
1984 Tottenham Hotspur, UEFA Cup, winners
1983 Aberdeen, Cup-Winners' Cup, winners
1982 Aston Villa, European Cup, winners
1981 Liverpool, European Cup, winners
1981 Ipswich Town, UEFA Cup, winners
1980 Nottingham Forest, European Cup, winners
1980 Arsenal, Cup-Winners' Cup, runners-up
1979 Nottingham Forest, European Cup, winners
1978 Liverpool, European Cup, winners
1977 Liverpool, European Cup, winners
1976 Liverpool, UEFA Cup, winners
1976 West Ham United, Cup-Winners' Cup, runners-up
1975 Leeds United, European Cup, runners-up
1974 Tottenham Hotspur, UEFA Cup, runners-up
1973 Liverpool, UEFA Cup, winners
1973 Leeds United, Cup-Winners' Cup, runners-up
1972 Tottenham Hotspur, UEFA Cup, winners
1972 Rangers, Cup-Winners' Cup, winners
1972 Wolv. Wanderers, UEFA Cup, runners-up
1971 Leeds United, UEFA Cup,

winners
1971 Chelsea, Cup-Winners' Cup, winners
1970 Manchester City, Cup-Winners' Cup, winners
1970 Arsenal, Inter-Cities Fairs Cup, winners
1970 Celtic, European Cup, runners-up
1969 Newcastle United, Inter-Cities Fairs Cup, winners
1968 Manchester United, European Cup, winners
1968 Leeds United, Inter-Cities Fairs Cup, winners
1967 Celtic, European Cup, winners
1967 Rangers, Cup-Winners' Cup, runners-up
1967 Leeds United, Inter-Cities Fairs Cup, runners-up
1966 Liverpool, Cup-Winners' Cup, runners-up
1965 West Ham United, Cup-Winners' Cup, winners
1963 Tottenham Hotspur, Cup-Winners' Cup, winners
1961 Rangers, Cup-Winners' Cup, runners-up
1961 Birmingham City, Inter-Cities Fairs Cup, runners-up
1960 Birmingham City, Inter-Cities Fairs Cup, runners-up

APPEARANCE RECORDS
Most league appearances
1005 – Peter Shilton (1966–97)

Most league appearances at one club
770 – John Trollope, Swindon Town (1960–80)

Most appearances in consecutive games
401 – Harold Bell, Tranmere Rovers (1946–55)

Most international caps
England
125 Peter Shilton (1970–90)
115 David Beckham (1996–)
114 Steven Gerrard (2000–14)

Scotland
102 Kenny Dalglish (1972–87)
91 Jim Leighton (1983–99)
77 Alex McLeish (1980–93)

Wales
92 Neville Southall (1982–98)
85 Gary Speed (1990–2004)
78 Craig Bellamy (1998–2013)

Northern Ireland
119 Pat Jennings (1964–86)
96 Aaron Hughes (1998–)
95 David Healy (2000–)
91 Mal Donaghy (1980–94)

Youngest international caps
England – Theo Walcott (17 years, 75 days)
Scotland – Denis Law (18 years, 235 days)
Wales – Lewin Nyatanga (17 years, 195 days)
Northern Ireland – Norman Whiteside (17 years, 41 days)

GOALS
Most goals in a career
550 – Jimmy McGrory (Celtic, Clydebank and Scotland)
464 – Arthur Rowley (West Bromwich Albion, Fulham, Leicester City, Shrewsbury Town)

Most Premiership goals
250 – Alan Shearer (1992–2005)

Most goals in a season
60 – Dixie Dean, Everton (1927–28)

Most goals in a game
13 – John Petrie for Arbroath v Bon Accord, 1885

LEADING INTERNATIONAL GOALSCORERS
England
49 Bobby Charlton (1958–70)
48 Wayne Rooney (2003–)
48 Gary Lineker (1984–92)
44 Jimmy Greaves (1959–67)

Scotland
30 Kenny Dalglish (1972–87)
30 Denis Law (1959–74)
23 Hugh Gallacher (1924–35)

Wales
28 Ian Rush (1980–96)
23 Ivor Allchurch (1951–66)
23 Trevor Ford (1947–57)

Northern Ireland
36 David Healy (2000–)
14 Kyle Lafferty (2006–)
13 Colin Clarke (1986–93)
12 Gerry Armstrong (1977–86)

HIT THE NET

www.thefa.com
The webpages of the English Football Association, with information on the England national team, clubs and league tables, plus a section on the FA Cup.

www.premierleague.com
The official website of the English Premier League.

www.football-league.co.uk
Home of the English Football League on the net, with club profiles and the latest news and results.

www.scottishfa.co.uk
The website of the Scottish Football Association, with links to its museum of football, as well as match reports and results at all levels of the game.

www.football-history.net/who-is-who.htm
Biographies of dozens of footballers of the past, arranged in alphabetical order.

www.faw.org.uk
The website of the Welsh FA, with details on competitions in Wales, as well as details on its international squads.

www.irishfa.com
The homepage of Northern Ireland's FA, with news and details of their international men's, women's and youth teams.

www.thepfa.com
The website of the Professional Footballers Association (PFA), with features on the top players of the past and present, the latest football news and interviews with players and managers.

www.statto.com/football/stats/england/premier-league
Final standings of every single Premier League and Division 1 season from 1888–89 to the present day.

www.kickitout.org
Learn more about today's initiatives to stop racism occurring in football.

www.shekicks.net
The home on the web of 'She Kicks' magazine, devoted to news and features concerning women's football.

www.footballeconomy.com
A fascinating website looking at the economics of football, with attendance figures and finances of the leading clubs.

www.clivegifford.co.uk
The author's website, which features regularly updated football tips and links to other football web pages.

GLOSSARY

Advantage rule A rule that allows the referee to let play continue after a foul if it is to the advantage of the team that has been fouled against.

AFC The Asian Football Confederation, responsible for running football in Asia.

Agent A person who represents footballers and negotiates contracts and transfer moves.

Anchor A midfielder positioned just in front of, and who protects, the defence. An anchor player may allow other midfielders to push further forwards.

Assist A pass that releases a player to score a goal. An assist can be a pass on the ground, a flick or a cross from which a headed goal is scored.

Away goals rule A rule used in some cup competitions. If the scores are equal over two legs, the team that has scored more goals away from home wins.

Backpass rule A law stating that a deliberate pass backwards by a player to his or her goalkeeper cannot be handled by the keeper.

CAF The *Confédération Africaine de Football*, which runs football in Africa.

Cap Recognition given to a player for each appearance in an international game for his or her country.

Catenaccio A defensive tactical system in which a sweeper plays behind a solid defence.

Caution Another word for a yellow card (a warning from the referee to a player for a foul or infringement). A player who receives two yellow cards in a match is automatically shown a red card and sent off.

Central defender The defender who plays in the middle of the last line of defence.

Chip A pass lofted into the air from a player to a team-mate or as a shot on goal.

CONCACAF The Confederation of North, Central American and Caribbean Association Football, which runs football in North and Central America.

CONMEBOL The *Confederación Sudamericana de Fútbol*, which runs football in South America.

Counter attack A quick attack by a team after it regains possession of the ball.

Cross To send the ball from a wide position towards the centre of the pitch, often into the opposition penalty area.

Cushioning Using a part of the body to slow down a ball in order to bring it under control.

Derby A match between two rival sides, often located in the same town or city.

Direct free kick A kick awarded to a team because of a serious foul committed by an opponent. A goal may be scored directly from the kick.

Dissent When a player uses words or actions to disagree with the referee's decision.

Distribution The way the ball is released by a goalkeeper or is moved around the pitch by a team.

Dribbling Moving the ball under close control with a series of short kicks or taps.

Drop ball A way of restarting play in which the referee releases the ball for a player from each team to compete over once it has touched the ground.

Extra time A way of deciding a drawn match. It involves two periods of additional play, usually lasting 15 minutes each.

FA (Football Association) The national football federation of England.

Feinting Using fake moves of the head, shoulders and legs to deceive an opponent and put him or her off balance.

FIFA The *Fédération Internationale de Football Association*, the international governing body of soccer.

Formation The way in which a team lines up on the pitch in terms of the numbers of defenders, midfielders and forwards.

Foul An action committed intentionally by a defender to stop an opponent who has a clear run on goal.

Fourth official An additional match official responsible for displaying added-on time, checking substitutions and aiding the referee and his or her two assistants.

Futsal A type of five-a-side football, supported and promoted by FIFA.

Golden Boot An award given to the player who scores the most goals at a World Cup. It is also an annual award given to the top goalscorer in European club football.

Golden goal A system used to decide a drawn knockout game in extra time. The first goal scored wins the game.

Handball The illegal use of the hand or arm by a player.

Hat-trick Three goals scored by a player in a single match.

Hooligan An unruly and violent fan.

Indirect free kick A kick awarded to a team because of a minor foul committed by an opponent. A goal cannot be scored from the kick unless the ball is first touched by a player other than the kicker.

Instep The part of a player's foot where his or her bootlaces lie.

Interception When a player gains possession of the ball by latching onto a pass made by the opposition.

Jockeying A defensive technique of delaying an attacker who has the ball.

Laws of the game The 17 main rules of football, established and updated by FIFA.

Libero *See* sweeper.

Man-to-man marking A system of marking in which a defender stays close to and goalside of a single opposition player.

Marking Guarding a player to prevent him or her from advancing the ball towards the goal, making an easy pass or receiving the ball from a team-mate.

MLS Major League Soccer, the American professional male league.

Narrowing the angle A technique in which a goalkeeper moves towards an attacker who has the ball in order to cut down the amount of goal the attacker can aim a shot at.

Obstruction When a player, instead of trying to win the ball, uses his or her body to prevent an opponent from playing it.

OFC The Oceania Football Confederation, which runs football in Oceania.

Offside A player is offside if he or she is closer to the other team's goal than both the ball and the second-to-last opponent at the moment that the ball is played forwards.

Offside trap A defensive tactic used to trick opposition attackers by leaving them offside. Defenders who play the offside trap usually move upfield together, in a straight line, when the ball is played towards their goal.

Overlap To run outside and beyond a team-mate down the side of the pitch in order to create space and a possible passing opportunity.

Overload When an attacking team has more players in the opposition's half or penalty area than the defending side. An overload often leads to a scoring chance.

Penalty shootout A method of deciding a drawn match by a series of penalties, all taken at one end of the pitch.

Playmaker A skilful midfielder or deep-lying attacker who co-ordinates the attacking movement of a team.

Play-off A match, pair or series of matches used to decide a final placing. In the World Cup, the two losing semi-finalists contest a single play-off game for third place. In many leagues, play-off matches are used to decide relegation and promotion issues.

Referee's assistant An official who assists the referee during the game by signalling for fouls, infringements and offsides.

Reserve team A team made up of players who are not in the first team at a club or national side.

Scout A person employed by a football club who attends games and training sessions to look for up-and-coming players.

Set piece A planned play or move that a team uses when a game is restarted with a free kick, penalty kick, corner kick, goal kick, throw-in or kick-off.

Shielding A technique used by the player with the ball to protect it from a defender who is closely marking them. The player in possession keeps his or her body between the ball and the defender.

Silver goal A system, used at Euro 2004, to decide a drawn knockout game. If a goal is scored in the first 15 minutes of extra time, it wins the game. If no goal is scored, a second period of extra time is played.

Simulation Pretending to be fouled or feigning injury in order to fool the referee. A player found guilty of simulation by the referee receives a yellow card.

Stoppage time Time added to the end of any period of a game to make up for time lost during a major halt in play – to treat an injured player, for example. Also known as added time or injury time.

Substitution Changing the team line-up on the pitch by replacing one player with another from the substitutes' bench.

Sweeper A defender who can play closest to his or her goal, behind the rest of the defenders, or in a more attacking role with responsibility for bringing the ball forwards.

Tactics Methods of play used in an attempt to outwit and beat an opposition team.

Target man A tall striker, usually the player furthest upfield, at whom team-mates aim their forward passes.

Through ball or pass A pass to a team-mate that puts him or her beyond the opposition's defence and through on goal.

Total football A style of football in which players switch positions all over the pitch. It was made famous by the Dutch national side and Dutch clubs such as Ajax.

UEFA The Union of European Football Associations, which organizes football in Europe.

Volley Any ball kicked by a player when it is off the ground.

Wall pass A quick, short pair of passes between two players that sends the ball past a defender. Also known as a one-two pass.

Wing-back A defender on the sides of the pitch who, when the opportunity occurs, makes wide runs forwards in attack.

WUSA The world's first professional football league for women, based in the USA.

Zonal marking A defensive system in which defenders mark opponents who enter their area of the pitch.

INDEX

Note: references to main entries are in **bold**.

ACKNOWLEDGEMENTS

The publisher would like to thank the following for permission to reproduce their material.
Top = t, bottom = b, centre = c, left = l, right = r
Front cover: l Alamy/Action Plus Sports; c Getty/Laurence Griffiths The FA Collection; r Getty/Jean Catuffe; back cover: Alamy/epa european pressphoto agency bv; Inside images supplied by PA/Empics with the exception of: pages 4-5 The FA via Getty; 6bl PA/DPA; 6-7c Getty/ Shaun Botteril; 7br Image Source; 7tr PA/AP/Hassan Ammar; 8tr Getty/Oli Scarff; 8l Getty/ AFP; 9t Getty/ J.A. Hampton; 11br Getty/ Reinhold Thiele; 11tl Getty/The Asahi Shimbun; 12c Getty/ Clive Mason; 13bl Getty/LatinContent; 14-15 PA/PA Archive; 16tr Corbis/Julien Hekimian/ Sygma; 16cl PA/ABACA Pess; 16cr Getty/Christof Koepsel; 17bl PA/AP/Andrew Brownbill; 17br Getty/R Yeatts; 18tr Shutterstock/efecreata mediagroup; 19br Getty/AFP/Patrick Lin; 20c Getty/Michael Reagan; 20bl PA/Anders Wiklund/TT News Agency; 21cl Getty/Patrick Hertzog/ AFP; 21bl Getty/Stu Forster; 22tr PA/Paulo Duarte; 22bl Getty/Javier Soriano; 23tl Getty/Paul Ellis; 23cr Getty/Stuart Franklin; 23b Shutterstock/LazloSzirtesi; 24cl Getty/Glynn Kirk/AFP; 24cr Getty/AFP/Stan Honda; 24br Getty/Mike Hewitt; 25cl Getty/Phil Cole; 25cr PA/Christophe Ena/AP; 26cl Getty/Valery Hachie/AFP; 27bl Getty/Khaled Desouki/AFP; 27br Shutterstock/Maxisport; 28c Getty/ John Peters; 28br Getty/Adnreas Rentz; 29t Corbis/Reuters/Kai Pfaffenbach; 29c Shutterstock/Photo Works; 29b Getty/AFP/Patrick Hertzog; 30bl Getty/Matthew Peters; 30br Corbis/Reuters; 30-31 Getty/ AFP/Stringer; 31tr PA/AP/Antonio Calanni; 31br Getty/Alexander Hassenstein; 32-33 PA/DPA/Deutsche Press Agentur; 34bl Shutterstock/efecreata media group; 35t PA/PA Archive; 36bl PA/PA Archive; 36c Alamy/imageBROKER; 38tr PA/Witters; 41tl Shutterstock/Photo Works; 42cr Shutterstock/ Natursports; 42b Corbis/Eddie Keogh/ Reuters; 43cr PA/Topham Picturepoint; 44c Shutterstock/Jonathan Larsen; 46br Getty/Stephen Dunn; 48t Shutterstock/Natursports; 49cr Getty/Ben Radford; 49b PA/DPA; 51b PA/Topham Picturepoint; 53t PA/ Digital Sports Archive; 53br Getty/ Junko Kimura; 54c Getty/Rolls Pess/Popperfoto; 54tr Getty/Lars Baron/Bongarts; 56-57 Getty/Bob Thomas Sports Photography; 57tr PA/Daniel Moltz; 58b PA/DPA; 59tr Getty/Emmanuel Dunand/AFP; 59cl Getty/Christophe Simon; 60t Shutterstock/Maxisport; 60cr Getty/Claudio Volla/Grazia Nero; 61tl Shutterstock/Photo Works; 62tr Shutterstock/Photo Works; 63cl Corbis/Reuters/Jose Manuel; 63br Getty/AFP/Franck Fife; 64cl Getty/Gonzalo Arroyo Moreno; 64br Shutterstock/Maxisport; 65tr Getty/ Javier Soriano; 65br Getty/ Mike Lawrie; 66cr Getty/Ben Radford; 67bl Corbis/Reuters/Ian Hodgson; 68-69 PA/PA Archive; 71b Getty/Kevin C Cox; 72tl Getty/Ben Radford/Allsport; 72b Getty/AFP/Roberto Schmidt; 73tr Getty/

VI-Images; 73b PA/DPA; 74tr Corbis/Srdjan Suki/epa; 74bl Shutterstock/Maxisport; 75b Getty/AFP/ Boris Horvat; 77 Getty/AFP; 78t Corbis/Christian Liewig; 79tl Corbis/Reuters; 79b Shutterstock/Jaggat Rashidi; 80tr Corbis/ Reuters/Petr Josek; 80bl PA/Barnaby's Picture Library; 81tr Getty/Helio Suenaga/ STR; 81bl PA/Topham Picturepoint; 82tr Getty Sports/Laurence Griffiths; 82bl Corbis/Reuters/Andres Stapff; 83tr Getty/AFP/Chi Jae-Ku; 84tl Corbis/Reuters/Bruno Dominges; 84br PA/Sean Dempsey; 85tl Corbis/Reuters/Bruno Dominges; 86cl Getty/Alexander Hassenstein; 87bl Getty/Victor Decolongon; 88tl Getty/AFP/Fethi Belaid; 88bl Getty/AFP/ Daniel Sosa; 90bl PA/AFP/Roberto Candia; 91tr Getty/AFP/Sergei Supinsky; 91c PA/Topham Picturepoint; 91br Getty/Angel Martinez; 92-93 Corbis/Sygma/Jacques Langevin; 94c PA/Tony Quinn/International Sports Images; 94bl Getty/ AFP/Oliver Lang; 94-95 Getty/Alfonso Cervantes; 95tr Getty/Tom Shaw; 95br Getty/Chris Lobina; 96bl Shutterstock/katatonia82; 96cr Getty/Christof Koepsel; 96br Getty/Gonzalo Arroyo Moreno/ Stringer; 97tl PA/Marko Lukunic/Pixsell; 97tr PA/Nick Potts; 97br Getty/Alexander Hassenstein - FIFA; 98b Getty/Ross Kinnaird; 99br Getty/Christophe Simon; 100cl PA/Andrew Parsons; 101tl PA/Sean Dempsey; 101tr Getty/Lutz Bongarts; 101b Getty/Mike Hewitt; 102tr Getty/AFP/Goh Chai Hin; 103tr Getty/Laurence Griffiths; 103b PA/DPA; 104c PA/Studio Buzzi; 104br Getty/S.A.S.I.; 105tl Getty/ Laurence Griffiths; 105c Getty/Pascal Rondeau; 105br Getty/AFP; 106-107 Getty/Shaun Botteril; 108cl Getty/Pierre-Philippe Marcou; 108br PA/Buzzi Press; 109t PA/DPA; 109b Getty/AFP; 110 PA/ DPA; 112b PA/Wilfried Witters; 113c PA/DPA; 113cl Corbis/Bettmann; 113br PA/DPA; 114 Getty/AFP; 114b Getty/Simon Bruty 115tr Getty/Jimin Lai; 115br Getty/AFP; 116tc Getty/Bob Thomas Sports Photography; 116bl Shutterstock/Jefferson Bernardes; 117t Getty/Guang Niu; 117br FIFA via Getty Images; 118br Getty/Phil Cole; 119b Shutterstock/YiAN Kourt; 120b Getty/Michael Regan; 122bl Getty/Heuler Andrey; 123l PA/Anesh Dbeiky/Sports Inc; 123br PA/Christian Liewig; 124tc Corbis/Reuters; 124bl Corbis/Reuters/Andrew Wong; 125tr Getty/stringer; 125bl Getty/Jeff Gross; 125br PA/Mario Castillo; 126tr Getty/AFP/Robert Vos; 126bl PA/Zuma Press; 126br Getty/ AFP/Jiji Press; 127tl Getty/Robert Cianflone; 127br Corbis/Reuters/Marcos Brindicci; 128tr Getty/New Press; 128cr PA/DPA; 128b Getty/Stuart Franklin; 129tl Getty/Adrian Dennis; 129b Corbis/Reuters; 130bl Getty/Hassan Ammar/AFP; 130-131 PA/Andre Penner; 131tr Getty/Jose Jorden/Stringer; 131c Getty/Jamie McDonald;132tr Corbis/Reuters/Gleb Garanich; 132cl PA/Topham Picturepoint; 133tr Getty/Bob Thomas Sports Photography; 133b Getty/Angel Martinez; 134-135 Getty/AFP; 135 Shutterstock/A.Ricardo.